JESTING IN EARNEST

JESTING IN EARNEST

Percival Everett and Menippean Satire

Derek C. Maus

Published by the University of South Carolina Press
Columbia, South Carolina 29208

www.sc.edu/uscpress

Manufactured in the United States of America

28 27 26 25 24 23 22 21 20 19
10 9 8 7 6 5 4 3 2 1

Library of Congress Cataloging-in-Publication
Data can be found athttp://catalog.loc.gov/.

ISBN 978-1-61117-962-0 (hardback)
ISBN 978-1-61117-963-7 (ebook)

Contents

Introduction

When writing about Percival Everett, it has become customary to begin with a caveat that the conspicuous variety within his body of work will inherently frustrate any attempts at definitive classification. For example, Joe Weixlmann opened his introduction to *Conversations with Percival Everett* (2013) by noting that Everett "remains as much the maverick as ever, producing risk-taking work that is so wide-ranging in tone, form, and subject matter that it is often described with such terms as 'characteristically uncharacteristic,' 'uncategorizable,' and 'all over the map'" (xii). Similarly, Keith B. Mitchell and Robin G. Vander were barely three pages into the introduction of *Perspectives on Percival Everett* (2013) before musing that "perhaps what problematizes Percival Everett's writing for readers and critics, even more than his formal narrative innovation, is his refusal as an African American writer to be categorized at all" ("Changing" xi–xii). Despite this refusal on Everett's part, numerous critics have nevertheless attempted to situate his work under such umbrellas as African American literature, experimental writing, or postmodernism, while just as many have limited themselves to intentionally vague, if also defensible, claims such as "all of [his works] have in common the author's preoccupation with language and representation" (Déon 1). Still another contingent flatly insisted that "so thoroughly do his books complicate identity and undermine logic—in terms of both content *and* form—that they elude critical categories" (Miller). Although at first glance it might seem that this last option is the one closest to his own point of view, Everett has addressed it with his typically mischievous derision, noting that "'uncategorizable' is a category. Which I resent" (Stewart, "Uncategorizable" 303).

Everett undoubtedly enjoys playing the role of curmudgeonly trickster—or tricksterish curmudgeon—during interviews; nevertheless, the peculiar and acute nature of his antagonism toward what he dismisses as "labels, schmabels" ("An Interview") actually offers the would-be critic equal measures of metaphorical stick and carrot. After all, Everett rejects categorization even as he disavows either the desire or the ability to control his readers' reactions to his work: "all meaning in any work is something I stay out of completely. That's the reader's job" (DeMarco-Barrett and Stone 152). He extends to readers the freedom to interpret his books as they will, provided that they do not presuppose their understanding of a given text: "If anybody takes anything they read, history or fiction, as some gospel, then . . . who cares? The point is, take it and then play with it" (Shavers, "Percival" 49). Everett insists that "all thinking is good. . . . It sure beats an absence of thought" (Reynolds 180); and he sees labels as ready-made excuses that impede the reader's need to think rigorously about the worlds and ideas presented in his books. Given that many of his protagonists struggle with and/or suffer from mind-sets that are constrained by preconceived notions, taking Everett up on his conditional offer of interpretive freedom becomes a useful starting point for drawing conclusions about what the recurrent tendencies within his otherwise dauntingly variegated body of work might mean.

Over the course of more than three decades, Everett has published twenty novels—from *Suder* (1983) to *So Much Blue* (2017)—along with four collections of short stories, four volumes of poetry, an illustrated children's book, and dozens of uncollected stories, poems, and essays. His general scorn for being pigeonholed makes sense, given that this prodigious literary output is marked throughout by a diversity of form and subject matter that few other writers can match. The Venn diagram of the twenty-nine—thirty if one includes his work as an illustrator—books he has published as of late 2017 is sprawling and complex, with few if any intersections common to the whole. Even where there are clusters of books within his oeuvre whose similarities to one another might suggest some meaningful categorical relationship, such similarities tend to be overwhelmed by the volume and nature of the corresponding differences.

For example, his novels *Walk Me to the Distance* (1985), *God's Country* (1994), *Watershed* (1996), *Grand Canyon, Inc.* (2001), *American Desert* (2004), *Wounded* (2005), and *Assumption* (2011)—as well as dozens of his short stories—are all set in the high desert plateaus and mountain ranges of the American West. Despite the similarity of their geographic settings, Everett insists that there is little overlap in terms of plot or characterization among these books that would justify categorizing any of them except *God's Country* as "Western fiction" in the manner that Daryl Jones, Loren D. Estleman, or Stephen McVeigh have used that terminology: "When I write about the contemporary West, those get called westerns, and I don't know why. They're not westerns. They're set in the contemporary West. That's where they happened to be. . . . The western, to me, is a very precise genre. Precisely defined. Being placed in the West—I mean, is a movie that's set in Los Angeles in 1997 a western? The only thing that makes *Assumption* a western is that it's set in the West. There's none of the stuff of westerns in it. I don't use the term. I'm always curious about terms" (Dischinger 260).

Walk Me to the Distance is set in a fictional town in Wyoming with the unlikely, and unlovely, name Slut's Hole. Its protagonist is David Larson, a Vietnam War veteran originally from Georgia who is looking for a fresh start and a new place to call home. *God's Country* is a self-conscious, race-conscious, and bitingly satirical parody of the language, mentality, and conventions of the classic Western popularized by Zane Grey's novels and John Ford's films. *Watershed* tells the story of a hydrologist named Robert Hawks who comes to northern Colorado for the solitude of a fishing trip but instead becomes embroiled in a violent conflict between a local Native American tribe and the FBI that is reminiscent of the Wounded Knee incident of 1973. *Grand Canyon, Inc.* again unleashes Everett's overtly satirical tenor but focuses this time on a sociopathic millionaire named Winchell Nathaniel "Rhino" Tanner, whose sole talent is being a "remarkably good rifle shot" (41) and who wants to transform the Grand Canyon into a massive amusement park. *American Desert* too works in the satirical realm, though it does so in a more abstractly metaphysical and philosophical sense than either *Grand Canyon, Inc.* or *God's Country* does. The novel ponders the meaning of life and death through the story of Theodore Street, a professor of English at the University of Southern California (like Everett), who dies in a car accident while on the way to commit suicide but who also miraculously rises from the dead at his own funeral for reasons that are unclear to everyone, most of all to Street himself. *Wounded* returns to the laconic yet severe rural Wyoming depicted in *Walk Me to the Distance.* Its protagonist John Hunt is a widower drawn to the isolation and relative anonymity of the area for many of the same reasons that David Larson is. The tension of the novel, however, arises from the brutal murder of a gay college student nearby and the subsequent arrival of another young gay man named David, who also happens to be the estranged son of one of Hunt's college friends. *Assumption* is an unexpectedly parodic triptych of offbeat detective-fiction stories set in the mountains of New Mexico and featuring a largely unremarkable deputy sheriff named Ogden Walker, who would rather be fly-fishing than investigating the spree of violent crimes that suddenly seems to be plaguing his hometown.

The tone of these seven works set in the West runs the gamut from stark psychological realism (*Walk Me to the Distance, Watershed,* and *Wounded*) to lampoonish absurdity (*God's Country, Grand Canyon, Inc.*). Although they all engage to some extent with the culture and history of the United States in general and the American West in particular, the manner in which they do so is sometimes satirically abstracted (*God's Country, Grand Canyon, Inc., American Desert*), sometimes marked by an emotionally distant character escaping or avoiding that culture/history (*Walk Me to the Distance, Assumption*), and sometimes inextricably tied to particular events and issues from the world outside the novel (*Watershed, Wounded*). There are overlaps among the characterizations of his protagonists as well: Larson, Hawks, Street, Hunt, and Walker all share an aloofness that verges on but never fully becomes misanthropy; Hawks and Walker both withdraw from the world through fly-fishing but are pulled into conflicts that do not necessarily concern them directly because of their fundamentally ethical sensibilities; Tanner, Street, and Curt Marder, the antihero of *God's Country,* are all self-centered to the point of being wholly unsympathetic for most of their respective stories; Larson, Marder, Street, and Walker all have children—sometimes blood relations, sometimes not—in their lives who present them with obligations they are not always willing or prepared to meet; and race plays a significant role—even if only as a subject to be avoided—in the lives of Hunt, Hawks, Walker, Marder, and Bubba, the black tracker whose help Marder enlists in *God's Country.* In short, a wealth of individual tropes, themes, plot devices, and genre conventions recur within Everett's writing often enough to be called tendencies; however, these rarely agglomerate in ways that become interpretive patterns through which substantial portions of his body of work might be diagnosed.

Everett fervently refutes the validity of any formulaic presumptions about the meanings of his writing, whether they arise from his identity, his past works, academic schools of thought, or conventions related to literary genre: "If anybody thinks they're actually going to delineate the necessary and sufficient conditions for any literary work of art, then they're greatly mistaken and would probably be better served picking up some other line of work, like computer maintenance" (Shavers, "Percival" 48). The narrator of his unconventionally metafictional novel *Percival Everett by Virgil Russell* (2013) gives voice to thoughts that align well with Everett's own views on "the nature of meaning. It is a force that hazards to subjugate other forces, other meanings, other languages. We understand that all too well and yet, and yet—well, it is like the infirmity, the defect at the base of a dam. It will hold and it will hold and then it will give up, the dam will give up. As will we all" (74). At the same time, Everett embraces and even welcomes the idiosyncrasies of his readers' interpretations, as long as they originate in a jovial and genuine thought process: "Play with ideas and have some fun with them and admit that that's what you're doing. . . . That's probably the most important question to me in the world. What can you do with thinking?" (Shavers, "Percival" 48). Weixlmann has summarized Everett's intentions toward his readers: "[He] most definitely does not set out to proselytize in his writing. Rather, he seeks to engage readers sufficiently in his stories that they will spend time thinking about what they've read when they finish one of his texts. In contrast to Ishmael Reed's formulation 'writin' is fightin',' Everett's very different literary formulation—at least with respect to those he terms 'serious' readers—might be expressed this way: writing + reading = thinking. And he sees this thinking, in turn, serving as a prelude to readers' producing 'meaning' and 'truth' —or what more conventionally is termed insight" (*Conversations* xix). In essence, he aims to be literally thought-provoking and has little use for overly reductive reactions—even when they are sympathetic—as he asserted in an interview conducted not long after the publication of *Erasure* (2001): "There's been a lot of people getting onboard and agreeing with me, and there's nothing more boring than that" (Ehrenreich 26).

When faced with readers who are still hell-bent on classifying his work, Everett generally expresses a combination of bemused puzzlement and deference concerning an author's role in the process of interpretation: "I don't put myself in a camp. I want to write what works for the story at hand. I serve the story, basically. I don't think that as the author I'm terribly important, and I don't want to be. I want to disappear. If anybody's thinking about me when they're reading my work I've failed as a writer. The work is supposed to stand by itself" (Shavers, "Percival" 48). Everett's desire to "disappear" from the reader's consciousness recalls Roland Barthes's influential essay "The Death of the Author," the thesis of which is summed up in its final line: "the birth of the reader must be at the cost of the death of the Author" (148). Barthes's assertion that to "give a text an Author is to impose a limit on that text, to furnish it with a final signified, to close the writing" (147) explains why the metaphorical death of the author appeals so strongly to Everett; he is profoundly opposed to limitations, finalities, and closures of meaning, particularly those that arise from an interpretive process in which the "*explanation* of a work is . . . sought in the man or woman who produced it, as if it were always in the end, through the more or less transparent allegory of the fiction, the voice of a single person, the *author* 'confiding' in us" (143). Everett does not "confide" in his reader or engage in overt didacticism because he ultimately believes that "the work is smarter than I am. Art is smarter than us . . . I have no desire to offer a political message in a novel. An artist cannot hide from her or his political beliefs; they will be in the work. But to presume that I am smart enough to preach a position runs counter to my artistic sense" (Goyal).

Barthes crops up frequently in Everett's fiction: he appears as "a *commedia dell'arte* caricature" (Berben-Masi, "Jailhouse" 54) of his real-life self in *Glyph* (1999), and a parody of his lengthy essay *S/Z* features prominently in *Erasure;* but perhaps the most telling use of his ideas appears in *Percival Everett by Virgil*

Russell. The form and structure of the latter novel are far too complicated to summarize at this point (see chapters 1 and 4 for additional commentary); it suffices for the moment to observe that it is a highly fragmentary work whose main narrative consists of what appears to be a kind of conversation between a father and a son, albeit one in which both characters at times inhabit the first-person perspectives of both author and narrator. For example, early on we read what seems to be the father telling his son, "This is the story you would be writing if you were a fiction writer" (6), but seven pages later the first-person voice of the son asks, "Is this supposed to be my story? The story I'm supposed to write or would write if I were a writer?" (13). By the middle of the book, the narrative voice articulates what by that stage may be the reader's own exasperation: "Just who the fuck is telling this story? . . . Is it an old man or the old man's son?" Prefacing his remarks with the quintessentially Everettian caveat that he is not "by nature disposed to behaving deferentially to any reader," the narrator insists that he "will clear up the matter forthwith, directly, tout de suite" and then unhelpfully—if also accurately—reveals that "*I* am telling the story" (107).

Barthes becomes directly relevant to Everett's play with authorial-narrative perspective when the son states, "Dad, you realize that I'm dead," to which the father replies, "Yes, son, I do. But I wasn't aware you knew it" (14). This exchange is repeated almost verbatim, albeit with the roles reversed, on the novel's final page (227), thereby suggesting that both of the nominal "authors" within the text are somehow "dead," a state which the narrator earlier extols: "The author takes such shit. Probably better to be dead" (39). Everett repeatedly lures the reader toward an interpretation based on presumptive knowledge about the novel's details and then figuratively enacts the death of each of its multiple possible internal authors in order to make such interpretations impossible. Barthes's theory is therefore valuable to Everett not because it creates meanings of its own but rather because it causes the defective "dam" of author-centered explanations to "give up" (74).

Everett's allusion to one of the most famous authorial duos in Western literature helps to cloud the narrative perspective further. The one-page chapter entitled "So Wide a River of Speech" begins with an overt parody of the opening stanzas of the first canto of Dante Alighieri's *Inferno,* in which the despairing Dante encounters the Latin poet Virgil, who will eventually lead him through Hell and Purgatory: "Deep, well past halfway, into the journey of my so-called life, I found myself in darkness, without you and you and you and you, a whole list of you." The "son" eventually interrupts the parody, and the ensuing exchange ends with a narratively important question that remains unanswered:

> and I yelled to him in that barren place to help me and he said that he was a poet and
>
> Dad.
>
> Yes?
>
> Okay, okay.
>
> You will be my Virgil?

Everett's technique throughout the book insures that whoever turns out to be the guiding "Virgil" of this text will not lead the corresponding "Dante"—whether figured as the reader or the text's coauthor—out of the "darkness, rough and stern" in which the narrator finds himself. As Sylvie Bauer has observed, "'Percival Everett' is immediately included in the circle of 'Virgil,' 'Dante,' or 'Bertrand Russell,' whose real referents can only haunt the fictitious personae [«Percival Everett» est d'emblée inclus dans le cercle de «Virgile», «Dante» ou «Bertrand Russell» dont les référents réels ne peuvent que hanter les personae fictifs]," a simultaneously associative and dissociative process that results in "the effacement of an author who has become a composite creation of his text, itself announced from the outset as a living memory of important parts of Western culture [*l'effacement d'un auteur devenu création composite de son texte lui-même annoncé d'emblée comme mémoire vive de pans importants de la culture occidentale*]." The "effacement" to which Bauer referred results in a situation in which the novel's actual author—Everett himself—is rendered figuratively "dead" but in which other "narrative voices seem to return from the land of the dead, thus putting language in relation to its own limit in order better to confront the chaos by flying over it [*dans lequel les voix narratives semblent revenir du pays des morts, mettant ainsi le langage en rapport avec sa propre limite pour mieux affronter le chaos en le survolant*]" ("A good place" 2–3). In essence, the author's death revives the voices and the language of the text itself, precisely the effect that Everett repeatedly has asserted he desires as an artist.

As his repurposing of the person and the ideas of Barthes illustrates, Everett's attitude toward literary theory exemplifies the mindfully iconoclastic perspective that he brings to his subject matter and to the interrelated acts of creating and reacting to art: "I like theory, I actually do. But it's bullshit. It's ridiculous but it's wonderful. I like thinking about it. I love that somebody has thought it, and I get excited about it. I get excited about Lacan. But it's all supposed to be fun. And that's how I teach it" (Allen, "Interview" 108). For Everett, theory is interesting or valuable not because of its ostensible capacity to explicate a text but rather for the possibilities it presents as the raw material for further creativity: "Anytime anybody goes through that much trouble to come up with something nonsensical you have to have fun with it. It's hilarious stuff. It's not important that it means anything that takes us somewhere, because it's not going to. But the fact that anybody wants to think it is, that's fascinating" (Shavers, "Percival" 48). He has elaborated on this elsewhere in noting that he believes satirical mockery to be part of meaningful and respectful discourse, rather than contemptuous dismissal: "One of the most ironic things about my satire is that I'm fairly earnest about it. There's a lot of irony in the fact that I take the things I'm talking about seriously. I actually like literary theory, for example, so to write my novel *Glyph,* I had to believe I understood enough of it to write about it, and to make fun of it. I found that I had to respect it. It doesn't mean I agree with it. I just think that it's funny" (Bolonik 98). From a writer who performs his due diligence in trying to understand the topics about which he writes—he claims, tongue only partly in cheek, "I only write books because it allows me to study" (Medlin and Gore 157)—Everett's books compel a similar degree of "seriousness" from their readers, even when their style is comic or absurdist.

The occasionally self-deprecating and jocular resistance to categorization that Everett has demonstrated in interviews has become an increasingly more intrinsic aspect of his writing over time, with his novels more frequently featuring plots and characters that metafictionally explore various answers to what Everett calls "the most important question . . . in the world." He not only uses his writing to show what can be done *with* thinking but often also shows—explicitly or implicitly—the consequences of a life *without* thinking, especially in the context of the interrelated acts of reading and writing. Although he describes his writing process more often than not using words such as "play" and "fun," he also has insisted, "I would love people to talk about my work with Sterne and Twain. Cervantes." He produces books that resemble Cervantes's *Don Quixote,* Twain's *The Adventures of Huckleberry Finn,* and Sterne's *The Life and Opinions of Tristram Shandy*—the latter of which Everett has singled out as "probably the best novel ever written" because it "takes every form of literary discourse of its time and exploits it" (Shavers, "Percival" 48)—in using comic forms to achieve serious ends. Everett has explained why he values such an approach in two complementary ways: "If you can get someone's attention and confidence by having them laugh, you can pretty much do with them what you will" (Toal 164); and "If you can get someone laughing, then you can make them feel like shit a lot more easily" (Shavers, "Percival" 48). A hybrid of these two impulses pervades nearly everything Everett has published.

There are countless obstacles that make encapsulating Everett's writing a difficult task; nevertheless, the remainder of *Jesting in Earnest* strives to achieve a pair of parallel goals in the hope of offering some meaningful insights into Everett's work while also heeding his admonitions against putting either him or his work into overly tidy boxes. This book lays out the case for an interpretive framework—and perhaps, pace *Percival*, a "label, shmabel"—that creates opportunities for insight into his work without concurrently precluding or subjugating others. It is viable to interpret Everett's authorial output between 1983 and 2017 as a thirty-volume megawork of the literary mode known as Menippean satire. Essentially the contention here is that Everett has always approached the creation of literary art from the vantage point of a Menippean satirist, even if the individual works he has created vary substantially in the degree to which they fit the already somewhat nebulous definition of Menippean satire. The intention is not to suggest that Menippean satire is the sole or even the best key with which to unlock meaning in any one of Everett's works, but it is an analytical strategy that offers interpretive insights across his entire career while also willingly accepting and even explaining his deliberate ambiguity.

In light of Everett's stated regard for such Menippean satirists as Cervantes, Sterne, Twain, Robert Coover, Ralph Ellison, Thomas Pynchon, and Samuel Butler (Stewart, "Uncategorizable" 306–7; Kincaid "Interview" 378; Shavers, "Percival" 48), it makes sense to take up a task originally suggested as a footnoted aside in an article by Michel Feith, one of the foremost Everett scholars: "There would be much to say about the formal connection between several of Everett's more 'philosophical' novels and Menippean satire" ("Hire-a-Glyph" 318). A handful of other Everett scholars—Françoise Sammarcelli, Marguerite Déon, and Sebastian Fett—have briefly engaged with Menippean satire in discussing his work, but no one has yet used it as the focal point for interpretation. Such an approach provides pathways into Everett's work without conversely pinning it in place, giving guidance to the reader without foreclosing his or her ability—or, as Everett would insist, responsibility—to think further about a particular work's meaning. Everett's candid and complete reassignment of the meaning-making process to his reader is both obligating and liberating, and the remainder of *Jesting in Earnest* accepts the former enthusiastically while gratefully acknowledging the latter.

Given that no extensive biography of Everett currently exists and that he remains—partly by choice—far from a household name among contemporary authors, chapter 1 is a partial attempt to provide some real-life scaffolding for his literary output. However, my aim is decidedly *not* to establish any one-to-one correlations between Everett's life and his writing; some critics have gone down that road in the past, only to have Everett deliberately confound their efforts with a series of misleadingly self-referential characters—including three named Percival Everett—in his recent fiction, a subject addressed directly in chapters 3 and 4. The purpose of this biographical overview is mostly to give experienced Everett scholars and those new to him and his work a bird's-eye view of his lengthy and complicated career in order to contextualize more clearly my eventual critical hopscotching amid his sprawling output. A secondary intent, though, is to provide some initial observations regarding the origins and development of Everett's resistance to categorization that can serve as part of the rhetorical foundation for my subsequent hermeneutic.

It is my contention that Everett's biography provides little, if any, *direct* insight into his characters' thoughts and motivations; moreover, it seems abundantly clear that even if a critic were somehow to discern a parallel between Everett's life and the biography of one of his fictional characters, Everett has no intention of commenting on or otherwise validating such an observation, thereby drastically limiting its potential value. What an overview of Everett's life does offer, though, is possibilities of *indirect* insights into some aspects of how and why he constructs the narratives through which his characters' stories are told. For example, Everett's graduate-level study of ordinary language philosophy shows up throughout much of his writing in various ways, both subtle (*The Water Cure*) and overt (*Glyph*). It seems defensible to assert that Everett's life experiences have occasionally proved useful to him as a form of research—intentional as well as serendipitous—that he transforms into fiction; he even allowed as much when he told Justin Taylor that "the research is ongoing. Take *Wounded,* for example. First, I'd been researching it my entire adult life, working with horses—research that doesn't always find its way into the work—then suddenly I was going into caves everywhere. I was going into undeveloped caves, developed caves, any hole I could find, until a friend said, You're working on a novel. I didn't realize it" ("Art" 67). Such a framing is, however, still a far cry from contending that his fiction is autobiographical, and I explicitly deny making any such claims from the outset.

Following a brief historical overview of Menippean satire and its development, chapter 2 presents a taxonomy of the mode's contemporary usage that is derived from several of its most prominent champions. Each of this study's final three chapters then surveys works from Everett's oeuvre that collectively employ motifs, character types, or techniques that shed some light on the protean, yet pervasive, Menippean tendencies of his writerly craft. Chapter 3 looks at the five novels of Everett's that most explicitly correspond to the critical definition of Menippean satire: *God's Country; Glyph; Grand Canyon, Inc.; Erasure;* and *A History of the African-American People (Proposed) by Strom Thurmond, as Told to Percival Everett and James Kincaid*. Chapter 4 turns to a second five-book cluster—*Cutting Lisa, American Desert, Suder, I Am Not Sidney Poitier,* and *The Water Cure*—whose Menippean qualities are less overt than those of the first cluster, but whose intentional destabilization of reality and language still fulfills the primary functions of the Menippean satirical mode. Chapter 5 engages something of a critical experiment by using Menippean satire as an alternative method of critically binding together four of Everett's books—*Walk Me to the Distance, Watershed, Wounded,* and *Assumption*—that, as noted above, seem more immediately associable by their common setting in the American West.

This selection of texts spans nearly the full length of Everett's career as a writer and includes his most popular works as well as some of his more obscure ones. It is intended as a sampling of the whole, not a ranked list; one should not infer from the emphasis on these fourteen works that Everett's remaining sixteen books are necessarily of lesser significance or lesser quality. In the interest of coherence and brevity, it is simply not feasible to give equal attention in this volume to all of Everett's publications. I also do not intend my emphasis on his fiction as a slight to his talents as a poet, though I would argue that his published poetry thus far has generally extended themes and even specific concepts that are initially—and, for my purposes, more effectively—raised in his fiction.

Wherever relevant, an attempt has been made to suggest connections to his texts that were not selected for extended discussion. Fortunately, the rapidly expanding body of scholarly work on Everett helps to fill in some of the gaps created by the somewhat arbitrary yet wholly necessary selective focus here. The extensive bibliography at the end of this book and the indispensable online bibliography (https://percivaleverettsociety.com/bibliography/) created and fastidiously updated by Joe Weixlmann of Saint Louis University provide additional resources to any Everett scholar looking for still more critical material.

CHAPTER 1

An Overview of Everett's Life and Career

Everett has consistently been reticent to divulge details of his personal life, a practice that aligns with a comment he made to Ben Ehrenreich in a 2002 interview: "my mission has always been to disappear" (26). Though this comment was intended as a Barthesian response to a question concerning his role as an author in influencing the interpretation of his works, it is equally applicable to the extent that he avoids the limelight generally: "Though the literary market is demonstrably more interested in celebrity than in language, he [Everett] stubbornly keeps his head down, and does so without any of the paranoid staginess of better-known reclusive writers. He rarely agrees to be interviewed. He has always refused to do publicity tours for his books, though he made an exception for [*Erasure*], only because, he says, 'I need a new roof on my house in Canada'" (Ehrenreich 25).

Everett is far from reclusive, having worked in numerous academic settings over the course of three decades, but he generally shares little about himself beyond the basics. Taylor prefaced his 2017 interview by noting that Everett "asked that we keep our focus on his work and make as little reference as possible to his life off the page" (42), a request that speaks volumes to Everett's lack of desire for any kind of authorial celebrity. My wish here is not to violate Everett's desire for privacy but merely to compile already available information into a single narrative that might serve as a reference; accordingly, some of the following information is comparatively sparse, gleaned a particle at a time from scattered interviews and biographical essays as well as from more inherently limited sources, such as the blurbs on dust jackets of his books. Furthermore, since much of Everett's work beyond *Erasure* is likely to be unfamiliar to readers—not even dedicated Everett scholars have read all of his books—a brief summary of each publication along with a representative sample of the critical reactions to it are provided in order to paint a picture of his life and career that is both comprehensive and comprehensible, if also necessarily somewhat sporadic.

To Be (or Not to Be) from South Carolina

Percival Leonard Everett II was born to Percival Leonard Everett and Dorothy Stinson Everett on December 22, 1956, at Fort Gordon, Georgia, where his father was stationed as a sergeant in the United States Army. Not long after the younger Percival's birth, his family moved to Columbia, South Carolina, and his father took up dentistry, continuing a family tradition—his grandfather, paternal uncles, and younger sister were or are also physicians (Taylor, "Art" 56–57)—from which the future author excused himself: "I had to break the chain" (Markazi 16). In addition to noting the history of doctors in his family, Everett traces his ancestry back in other ways that "dispel some of the stereotypes of the South. I have a 'white' great grandfather, a Jew who lived in Texas where he married a former slave. He sent my grandfather to medical school in Tennessee, which he left to eventually become a practitioner in South Carolina" (Mills and Lanco 230). His family lived "on a hill off Harden Street" near the University of South Carolina in the center of Columbia. He has described his memories of growing up in Columbia as "very pleasant" and remembers "books being around the house and accessible" during his childhood. He likewise recalls "sneak[ing] over to McKissick [Library] on the university campus and into the stacks, . . . [which] were so musty and the books so strange and wonderful I could read forever" (Starr, "I Get Bored" 19). His early literary experiences developed his taste for both breaking rules and solitude: "I remember quite well, early on, reading something I thought I shouldn't be reading, Maugham's *Of Human Bondage,* which I got from my father's shelf. I think I was nine. It was fun because I didn't think I was supposed to read it. As I look back, I think that it's reading, probably even more than writing, that I find important. Reading is subversive because you necessarily do it by yourself" (Taylor, "Art" 69). The hook for reading and inquiry was evidently set quite profoundly during Everett's childhood.

Despite these kind words for Columbia, Everett has also stated elsewhere that he has "a troubled relationship with the South and with the United States in general" (Mills and Lanco 230). He graduated in 1973 from A. C. Flora High School—coincidentally also the alma mater of the controversial political strategist Lee Atwater—at the age of sixteen and quickly departed for Florida, never again to live in South Carolina. After being invited in the late 1980s to address the South Carolina legislature as the recipient of the Governor's Award in the Arts, he was outspokenly disdainful of South Carolina's continued display of the Confederate battle flag on the State House grounds. In a 2001 essay entitled "Why I'm from Texas," Everett renounced his South Carolinian origins while recalling his aborted speech before the lawmakers of the Palmetto State:

> I don't discuss South Carolina and the confederate flag anymore because I'm sick of it. Since telling the South Carolina State Legislature in 1989 that I couldn't continue my address because of the presence of such a conspicuous sign of exclusion, I have not really considered South Carolina. I was invited to Charleston's Spoleto Festival by my dear friend Josephine Humphreys to participate in a writers' protest over the Confederate flag, but I could no longer generate enough concern. There were two things at work. First, the flag probably ought to be there—in the same way that a big sign saying "Land Mines!" ought to be set at the edge of a field containing land mines. If it is so hard for the government of the state to decide to remove the stupid thing, then there must be a reason and that reason can't be good. Second, who gives a rat's ass[?] It's a waste of energy to fight over it. It's an ugly flag with an ugly history becoming the emblem of a state with more than its share of ugly people. (62)

Although he has expressed his fondness for the topography of the state and for "a few people there," there is no mistaking his vitriol toward those South Carolinians who insisted that the Confederate battle flag stay aloft at the State House until it was finally removed under protest in the summer of 2015: "the image of those neanderthal, pathetically under-educated, confederate-clad, so-called descendants of pathetically under-educated cannon fodder of the middle 19th century sticks in my head like a John Waters version of the Dukes of Hazzard" (63). Everett demonstrated that this view does not encompass all South Carolinians by accepting his selection into the South Carolina Academy of Authors Literary Hall of Fame in 2011.

Comparatively little of Everett's fiction is set in South Carolina or in the South generally; nevertheless, three moments from Everett's career in which he does use southern settings illustrate the ways in which his downplaying of southern and/or South Carolinian identity goes beyond his claim not to "write out of any loyalty to a place" (Dischinger 260). Everett finds it a "vacuous marker to say that someone is a Southern writer" because the "implication is that their concerns as a writer and a person are going to be different than a person somewhere else" (261). He does not, however, merely reject the "southern" label; he also actively transmogrifies what those who would affix it to a writer are intending to signify by doing so.

Everett has stated that his "entire relationship with the South has been formed by [his] family background" (Mills and Lanco 230), and his second novel, *Walk Me to the Distance,* is an early instance in which Everett questions the extent to which such ties actually bind an individual. Roughly two-thirds of the way through the novel, there is a brief section in which the protagonist,

David Larson, leaves his newly adopted home in rural Wyoming for a visit to his native Savannah, Georgia, which is separated from South Carolina only by the unimposing Savannah River. David has not been back to Savannah since returning from the Vietnam War, during which his parents were killed in a car accident, and before leaving Wyoming he can articulate his reasons for wanting to go back only in formulaic terms: "He needed some distance from the ranch. Especially with winter coming. And he did feel, or thought he felt, some need to connect again with family" (139). While back in Savannah he has several brief and stiff conversations with his sister Jill and her husband, both of whom have gone from being antiwar activists to advocates helping Vietnam War veterans "adjust to the system" (38). He also encounters a high-school friend named Stan Grover, who is missing an eye and now working as a security guard in a labyrinthine and "disorienting" (148) shopping mall. Furthermore he inadvertently engages in a series of increasingly awkward interactions with three women: a divorcée named Elaine, with whom his sister attempts to set him up; Stan's alcoholic wife Beth, who reveals that Stan is missing his eye because he mutilated himself to avoid being drafted; and a woman named Carol, who picks him up in a bar and who lives with her Parkinson's-afflicted grandfather.

After these "quickly passing, uncomfortable days in Savannah" he hastens back to his new life in Wyoming, and the narrator remarks that his brief sojourn in Georgia had "left David with a haunting sense that something significant had presented itself to him" (163). That "something significant" seems apophatically to be the understanding that *nothing* significant is left for David in the city where he grew up. The novel's opening has already rejected another possible influence related to geography, noting that David returned from Vietnam "as unremarkable as he had been when he left" (3). The narrative thus suggests that neither Savannah nor Vietnam—synecdochical analogues, respectively, for the compulsory aspects of familial and national identity—has formed David in the ways that both the human and natural environments of Slut's Hole, Wyoming, potentially can. By the end of the novel, David decides that even though it is not true that "he was there [in Wyoming] because he wanted to be," it is also true that "he couldn't be anyplace else" (207).

On numerous occasions Everett has noted his belief that "truth has nothing to do with reality or facts" (Champion 166). In "Why I'm from Texas," Everett employs this philosophy as he bypasses South Carolina entirely, eschewing factual biography in favor of emotionally truthful biography: "I'm from Texas. My grandfather was from Texas, from outside Dallas. Great-grandparents flipped a coin to determine whether my grandfather or his brother would head east to attend Meharry Medical College in Nashville, Tennessee. My grandfather won the toss, I guess. And after working his way through school playing trombone in a circus band, he married my grandmother who was from South Carolina and that's where they lived. That's where my father grew up. That's where my mother grew up. And that's where I grew up. But I'm from Texas" (63). Although one should always beware of drawing parallels between Everett and his characters, this passage illustrates that David at least resembles his creator in recognizing his emotional detachment from the places in his past.

More than a decade later Everett published a short story entitled "The Appropriation of Cultures" (1997), which was later included in his collection *damned if i do* (2004). The story's protagonist, Daniel Barkley, shares even more biographical details with Everett than David Larson does, but he departs from both Everett and David in having moved back "home" after being away for a while. In Daniel's case, home is Columbia, South Carolina, to which he returns after receiving the "degree in American Studies from Brown University that he had earned, but that had not yet earned anything for him" (Everett, *damned* 91). Daniel lives a relatively idle life in Columbia at first, casually maintaining himself by spending a monetary inheritance while simultaneously becoming aware of his desire to claim a different and unusual cultural inheritance. One night while Daniel is sitting in with a local jazz band, "some white boys from a fraternity . . . began to shout 'Play "Dixie" for us! Play "Dixie" for us!'" (91). Rather than being either offended or threatened by this ignorant request for "the song he had grown up hating, the song the whites had always pulled out to remind themselves and those other people just where they were" (92), Daniel performs the song in a way that reclaims it as part of his own heritage, not just that of the powerfully racialized elite that the fraternity boys represent: "He sang it, feeling the lyrics, deciding that the lyrics were his, deciding that the song was his. . . . The irony of his playing the song straight and from the heart was made more ironic by the fact that as he played it, it came straight and from his heart, as he was claiming Southern soil, or at least recognizing his blood in it. His was the land of cotton and, hell no, it was not forgotten" (92–93). Encouraged by his success at transforming "Dixie," he returns home and reads about the Confederate infantry attack during the Battle of Gettysburg known as "Pickett's Charge," dreaming afterward about confronting rebel soldiers en route to the battle and demanding that they "give back my flag" (93).

This dream spurs him to action in his waking life, and he proceeds to answer a classified ad for a pickup truck decorated with a decal of the Confederate battle flag in the rear window. Daniel's interest in the truck baffles the white woman selling it, especially when he claims that he feels exceptionally fortunate "to find a truck with the black-power flag already on it" (100). Later, when a pair of angry rednecks with a "rebel front plate" on their car demand to know why he is driving a truck with the flag decal on it, he coolly explains that he is "flying it proudly. . . . Just like you, brothers" (101). When a carload of young black teenagers pulls up just as the two white men begin pushing Daniel, the rednecks drive off and Daniel exhorts the teenagers to continue the symbolic expansion/undermining of the nostalgic mythology of the South that both "Dixie" and the Confederate battle flag represent: "Get a flag and fly it proudly" (101). Although the text does not indicate the teenagers' response, the final paragraph of the story suggests the ultimate outcome of Daniel's efforts at appropriating the previously exclusionary symbols of southern heritage:

> Soon, there were several, then many cars and trucks in Columbia, South Carolina, sporting Confederate flags and being driven by black people. Black businessmen and ministers wore rebel-flag buttons on their lapels and clips on their ties. The marching band of South Carolina State College, a predominantly black land-grant institution in Orangeburg, paraded with the flag during homecoming. Black people all over the state flew the Confederate flag. The symbol began to disappear from the fronts of big rigs and the back windows of jacked-up four-wheelers. And after the emblem was used to dress the yards and mark picnic sites of black family reunions the following Fourth of July, the piece of cloth was quietly dismissed from its station with the U.S. and State flags atop the State Capitol. There was no ceremony, no notice. One day, it was not there. (102–3)

Eighteen years before the actual removal of the Confederate battle flag from the S.C. State House, Everett imagined a means of turning the "ugly flag with an ugly history" ("Why I'm from Texas" 62) into merely "a piece of cloth" by the simple act of asserting a different, idiosyncratic truth about its meaning. As Everett stated in an interview conducted not long before Gov. Nikki Haley finally decided to remove the flag from the State House, "It's pretty obvious that if you appropriate something, you can change it" (Dischinger 262). William Ramsey has noted that the change Everett envisioned does not simply invert racial power "in the spirit of black cultural nationalism"; it achieves an alteration "through *mutation* rather than a rationalistic clash of abstract ideas" (129). It is, as Anthony Stewart asserted, an "opportunity to see differently an artifact so steeped in a very specific reading" ("About" 190). The incredulity of the white people in the story when faced with Daniel's act of (re)appropriation illustrates Everett's broader concern with any act of "specific reading" that prescribes meaning. Daniel's act is simultaneously subversive and creative, mirroring Everett's own stated preference.

Everett continued this mutational approach to southern history and identity by confronting the mythology surrounding one of South Carolina's most controversial and most beloved sons in *A History of the African-American*

People (Proposed) by Strom Thurmond, as Told to Percival Everett and James Kincaid (2004). This wondrously strange book is discussed at length in chapter 3, but the basic premise is that Everett and his University of Southern California colleague, and actual coauthor, James R. Kincaid are approached via letter by a man named Barton Wilkes, apparently an overzealous, and possibly insane, junior aide to Sen. Strom Thurmond. Wilkes wants the two of them to ghostwrite a book on African American history that will be attributed publicly to the then-nonagenarian politician in an effort to articulate the "true and unmistakable understanding (ripe to the core)" of "the colored people (aka Afro-Americans, negroes, people of color, and blacks)" (7) that Thurmond has ostensibly acquired during his decades of stalwart public support for legal segregation and other racist policies. Kincaid wrote about the book's intentions in 2005: "Strom was so brilliantly successful because he operated with so little awareness of any world but his own. He was a laughing stock and a power; a dangerous segregationist and a softie. . . . Strom, we decided, was an ideological marvel and we would treat him as such"; doing so entailed "mak[ing] the novel turn from satire into something more serious" ("Collaborating" 370). Everett noted, "I realized . . . that I didn't dislike him as much as I thought I did. Not that I would ever champion him at all. He's a racist asshole, but he became a little more human for me, and he became interesting to me. . . . Thurmond isn't important enough for me to vilify him so greatly. He's interesting to me historically and culturally, but he's just kind of a sad man, in many ways, who did have a very full and strangely important American life" (Stewart, "Uncategorizable" 309, 311). This comment hearkens back to Everett's previously noted comment about needing to "respect" the things he writes about despite not agreeing with them—as is clearly the case with Thurmond. Even in the case of a target as ripe for satirical savaging as Thurmond would seem to be, Lavelle Porter has insisted that Everett still prefers to dismantle his legacy and mutate the resultant fragments rather than simply lampoon him: "Thurmond is already a cartoon character on his own, and yet Everett manages to spin a madcap story out of this ludicrous, deadly life, all the while showing America its ugly true self sans all the patriotic bluster about exceptionalism, integrity and honor" (L. Porter).

An Everett in Motion Tends to Stay in Motion

These three moments from Everett's career not only illustrate his relationship to his personal past in South Carolina but also shed some light on his tendency to keep moving, literally and figuratively, throughout his adult life. His lack of interest in his prospective audiences' expectations or desires—"I write to make art. . . . I don't think about the audience" (Bengali 113)—suggests his comfort with thinking and writing in the moment, and Everett's connections to ideas, to places, and to people are neither absolute nor eternal, regardless of their intensity. Where some might be inclined to see instability or restlessness in Everett's frequent physical relocations; his extreme variations in style, genre, and medium as an artist; or perhaps even in the fact that he has been married four times, it is more productive to see this penchant for vagabondage as the natural by-product of a personality that freely admits to being "pretty bored with myself" (Anderson 52) and constantly needing to discover "stuff that's smart, stuff that challenges me and makes me think differently, that introduces me to things I didn't know before" (Shavers, "Percival" 48). Moreover, when Everett encounters such new "stuff," he devotes himself to it intently:

> I have a novel, *Watershed,* which is about a hydrologist. I didn't know anything about hydrology. So I read twenty-five or twenty-six texts on geomorphology and hydrology and went out with a hydrologist in Wyoming to do some stream studies before I wrote a word. I wanted to be able to write and sound like a hydrologist without sounding like someone who had read twenty-six books on geomorphology and hydrology. That required me to know enough to stop speaking about hydrology and start thinking about it. When I finally started working on the novel, I actually drew topographical maps of an imagined watershed in northern Colorado and wrote hydrologic reports about that watershed. I was imagining myself doing the research that the character from my novel was doing. One or two of the hydrologic reports actually became a part of the novel. (Medlin and Gore 157–58)

Whether or not such a personality makes him a difficult individual is for those closest to him to decide, but his interviewers, students, and collaborators echo one another in noting that his innate "sense of alienation" and "blessedly independent" mind-set (Ehrenreich 28) do not prevent him from being "quite gregarious and generous with his time" (Shavers, "Percival" 47). There is no doubt, however, that his attitude toward the world around him helps explain his prodigious artistic output, especially in light of how he manages the demands placed on his time by his many and varied interests. Ben Ehrenreich cataloged Everett's days in a 2002 interview:

> Everett keeps busy. He sleeps about four hours a night, but only, he says, because his wife has been encouraging him to sleep more. Left to himself it would just be two or three. He spends a lot of time painting, colorful abstract work reminiscent of Kandinsky or Klee. He reads a lot, "not so much fiction as everything," he says. . . . He writes a lot too, but says he's

> trying to figure out a way to write less. He does woodworking, and did a lot of the construction on the ranch [outside Los Angeles] himself. In Canada, during the summer months, he fly-fishes. He's learning to slice wine bottles in half. He maintains an insect collection. Of course, he teaches, both writing and literature, last year chairing USC's English department. (27)

Ehrenreich's astute observation that his "work consistently betrays a deep and abiding mistrust for all human collectivities" (27) hints at Everett's preference for the solitude of a writing desk, a fishing stream, or a mule-training corral. However, the fondness with which Everett speaks about his decades-long career as a classroom teacher—"I like to sit with these bright young people and talk about their work. I learn a lot from them. I'm privileged" (Mills, Julien, and Tissut 222)—and the fact that his colleagues in multiple academic departments have trusted him with the often-contentious task of serving as department chair mitigate the impression that his penchant for solitude is some kind of character flaw. Kincaid claimed that Everett is "very much a loner, despite being such a warm person" (Bengali 115), but Everett is no misanthrope, despite expressing the sentiment that "people are worse than anybody" (*Wounded* 166; Ehrenreich 27) repeatedly in his interviews and his fiction. He clearly understands the extent to which writing, especially in the manner and volume he practices it, is an isolating and possibly even damaging endeavor: "Starting a novel is like entering a bad marriage. No matter what I do, it's going to end badly, to be full of emotional ups and downs. It's going to alienate me and I'm going to be alienated from anyone I know, family, friends—and it's going to *last* a lot longer [than] I want it to" (Mills, Julien, and Tissut 224).

Everett's wandering began in earnest immediately after he graduated from high school, when he moved on to study at the University of Miami, from which he earned a bachelor's degree in 1977 with a major in philosophy and a minor in biochemistry. He has specified that the presence of the logician Howard Pospesel on the faculty was among the reasons for choosing to attend Miami (Taylor, "Art" 57). He paid his tuition in part via two, among a multitude, of his curious avocations, playing guitar in various jazz clubs around Miami as well as teaching high school. Everett noted that although he "remained a Southerner there, considering that Florida is as far South as you can go in the United States," he also felt significant—and welcome—cultural distinctions between Miami and Columbia: "It was there I got a foreign accent, in college where everyone around me was actually speaking Spanish. The character of Miami was not at all like South Carolina where the Civil War started and where I had a high school teacher who taught us the Civil War was a war of aggression" (Mills and Lanco 230).

The next period of his life involved a pair of gradual transformations, both from a would-be philosopher into a writer of fiction and from an ostensible southerner to the westerner he self-identifies as to this day: "I am a Westerner. I don't think about the South. I don't want to return and live in the South. I want to see the sun set on the ocean" (Mills and Lanco 231). In a 2013 interview he recalled driving through the West immediately after graduating from Miami and having a reaction similar to that of David Larson at the end of *Walk Me to the Distance:* "He passed through Utah's Canyonlands, and then carried on into Wyoming where he beheld the Wind River Range. 'I said, "All right, this is it; this is where I belong,"' Everett recalls. 'I fell in love with the landscape. I fell in love with Wyoming'" (Mernit). Everett's first extended experience of living in the West took place in the college town of Eugene, Oregon, where he continued his study of philosophy, doing coursework for a doctorate at the University of Oregon under the guidance of the noted ordinary language philosopher Frank Ebersole from 1978 to 1980. His extracurricular connection to the region was deepened by the fact that he "worked on sheep and cattle ranches all the while" (Ehrenreich 26). Everett has continued this intertwining of academic and agricultural life since then and resists defining himself by one more than the other, often celebrating the perceived contradictions: "I'm a card-carrying member of the ACLU, and I go to the ballet, and I train mules and I write fiction for a living. . . . It means absolutely nothing. People live in the worlds they live in, and they're interested in the things that interest them" (Shavers, "Percival" 49). Moreover, he has indicated that his work as an animal trainer is indispensable to his writing: "Animals teach me patience. . . . What working with the animals allows me is the opportunity to trust myself. As I realize they trust me, then I can trust myself. I know that I'll get the work done" (Mills, Julien, and Tissut 226).

Although Everett abandoned academic philosophy two years into his graduate studies at Oregon, he still found inspiration of a different kind in the concepts to which he had been exposed: "I was interested in logic as an undergraduate. I seem to have a talent for mathematical logic. I started reading Wittgenstein and became interested in language. I continued to study ordinary language philosophy, and it turns out a lot of ordinary language philosophy was the construction of scenes in which people talked about or around philosophical questions. I became disenchanted with philosophy. Wittgenstein said, 'Philosophy is a sick endeavor,' and I realized that the patient, at least for me, was terminal. . . . So I started writing fiction as a better way to approach philosophical ideas" (Starr, "I Get Bored" 20). Everett has maintained this interest in and engagement with philosophy throughout his career of writing and teaching literature. Sylvie Bauer has contended that "if he claims to have made the choice of literature, it is nevertheless the voices of philosophers that permeate his work, both openly and more discreetly, and intersect with it [*S'il affirme avoir fait le choix de la littérature, il n'en reste pas moins que les voix des philosophes traversent son œuvre, ouvertement et plus discrètement et s'entrecroisent avec elle*]" ("A good place" 10). He stated in a 2005 interview that "basically, all of my books come out of a desire to explore something about language and how language works, even though I do write stories that deal with other things, maybe" (Mills, Julien, and Tissut 218). He likewise told Taylor that his writing is innately rooted in philosophical inquiry: "I start with something that bugs me, some philosophical problem, and then I look for a way to explore it" ("Art" 49). He expanded on the lingering influence of his formal training in ordinary language philosophy by noting, "I come back again and again to the work of J. L. Austin, who not only intrigues me but entertains me and calls into question what I think about language" (53).

His fiction sometimes foregrounds formal philosophy even more explicitly. For example, *Glyph* (1999) is not only stuffed to the point of bursting with the vocabularies of poststructuralist theory, semiotics, and continental philosophy, but it also turns such notable philosophers as Socrates, G. E. Moore, Maurice Merleau-Ponty, and Ludwig Wittgenstein into literary characters within parodies of Platonic dialogues. In a less comical vein, large sections of his grim novel *The Water Cure* (2007) consist of fragmentary observations drawn from philosophy of language, ranging from the classical to the contemporary. In a similar vein, Everett has indicated that the "working title for *Percival Everett by Virgil Russell* was 'Frege's Puzzle.' The novel is in three sections—'Phosphorus,' 'Hesperus,' and 'Venus,' in other words, the evening star, the morning star, and the planet Venus. These are all the same thing, but are different *things*. That was Frege's puzzle—how is it that we have these referents for different things that are the same thing? It's one way of approaching a problem of identity, and that's often what drives me and a lot of my work—the notion of logic and identity" (Taylor, "Art" 49).

Everett told Anthony Stewart in 2007 that he continues to use Wittgenstein in his literary theory courses at USC, albeit in ways that demonstrate his commitment to writing fiction rather than practicing academic philosophy: "I'm not teaching this to give them theories as much as I am to demystify the reasons we have them. And to teach them to make fun of it, and I do mean to make fun of it. To ask the question that Wittgenstein would have us ask of any philosophical premise or treatise or statement, which is 'What do you mean by that?'" ("Uncategorizable" 304). Although Everett has never stated the connection himself, the formal philosophical roots of his interest in writing fiction align him perfectly with the original conception of Menippean satire as a literary counterargument to flawed philosophies (see chapter 2).

Everett returned to the East Coast in the fall of 1980 to study creative writing at Brown University in Providence, Rhode Island, albeit under somewhat unusual circumstances: "I was never a student in the workshop at Brown. I guess I tend to be a little bit cranky, and . . . I said I didn't want to go to any classes. And Brown, then, was kind of interesting. They said okay. And so I just wrote and lived in Providence basically" (Allen, "Interview" 107). While there, he developed a relationship with Robert Coover, to whom Everett dedicated an unconventional short story entitled "Between Here and There" (2012), which consists mainly of a mathematical formula followed by a three-page list of gerunds. Everett repurposed this story—without the dedication—a year later in *Percival Everett by Virgil Russell*. Coover's work resembles Everett's in many ways, not the least important of which is that both are "interested in hyper-reality" (Reynolds 179). Coover is also like Everett in his erudition, his love of formal experimentation, his diversity of subject matter, and his refusal to conform to the expectations of the literary marketplace. His 1977 novel *The Public Burning*, about the trial of Julius and Ethel Rosenberg, was a best seller but was also widely condemned by the literary establishment for its vulgarity, in particular a scene in which Uncle Sam, the iconic American self-representation, gleefully sodomizes Richard Nixon on a golf course to consecrate the latter's selection as an acceptable future president. Coover was in residence, though not yet teaching, at Brown in 1981, but Everett has recalled that he "liked him" (Allen, "Interview" 107). Everett also struck up an odd friendship with R. V. Cassill, another member of the writing faculty at Brown. Everett recalled "play[ing] chess every night" with Cassill and "lik[ing him] as a person" despite "not [being] a fan of [his] work" (Allen, "Interview" 107). While at Brown, Everett produced what would become his first published work, a two-page short story titled "Rose Nose" that was published in the *Aspen Journal for the Arts* in 1982.

The manuscript for his first novel, *Suder*, was originally submitted as his master's thesis under the title "Suter." The novelist Barry Beckham, a longtime member of the graduate creative writing faculty at Brown, is listed as the director of Everett's thesis, though Everett had not spoken about their collaboration in any published interview as of late 2017. One may reasonably infer some degree of influence from Everett's choice of subject matter and tone, given that Beckham's satirical novel *Runner Mack* (1972) deals with the trials and tribulations of an African American baseball player who is "hoping in vain that he will one day play professional baseball and achieve the American Dream for which the game purportedly stands" (Rutter, "Barry" 74). Beckham has stated that "the main part of our relationship was friendly" and that Everett "may have been" influenced by his novel but "didn't want to tell him that" (90n2). In the same interview he also expressed sentiments about authorship that could just as easily have come from Everett: "the role of the writer in general is not to solve the problem. I don't think that is our responsibility or objective. More importantly, we bring up the issues and leave it [*sic*] there for the reader" (76). In her analyses of both books, Emily Rutter made a case for reading *Suder* in the context of *Runner Mack,* whether or not there was any direct or intentional influence on Everett: "Beckham originated a tradition of black baseball fiction, extended by Everett's *Suder,* that critiques dominant American myths without replacing them with an alternative mythos or pantheon of heroes" (77).

Everett has indicated that Cassill's assistance was invaluable in getting the adapted manuscript of his thesis published as a book: "It was Verlin [Cassill], who was not my professor, who took my first novel and sent it to his agent without telling me and I received a call from her. And she asked if she could represent me, and that was the start of my career. It was very generous of him" (Allen, "Interview" 107). *Suder* was ultimately published by Viking Press in 1983, when Everett was only twenty-six years old.

Five Novels, Four Residences

The exact details of Everett's next three years are somewhat hard to pinpoint, but he continued to move around the country while he established his literary credentials. The dust jacket for the first edition of *Suder* indicates that "Mr. Everett is currently living on Cape Cod, where he is writing a new novel," and one can reasonably assume that this "new novel" was *Walk Me to the Distance,* which was published by Houghton Mifflin's Ticknor and Fields imprint in 1985. Although none of Everett's interviews or biographical essays corroborates either detail, the dust jacket for this second novel claims that Everett was living in the West again and married at the time of its publication: "Mr. Everett and his wife, Julie, live in Portland, Oregon, where he is writing a new novel [likely *Cutting Lisa,* which is set on the Oregon coast]." The curriculum vitae accompanying Everett's faculty profile on the USC Web page indicates that he received the D. H. Lawrence Fellowship from the University of New Mexico in 1984. This award provided a paid month of residence at a ranch near Taos, New Mexico, that formerly belonged to the esteemed British novelist for whom the fellowship is named. As they did for Lawrence, both Taos in particular and New Mexico generally seem to have left a lasting impression on Everett, as he set several subsequent works—for example, *American Desert, The Water Cure, Assumption*—there. In the fall of 1985 Everett moved to Lexington, Kentucky, where he served as a visiting assistant professor of English at the University of Kentucky for a year before taking a continuing position there that would eventually also include becoming director of the graduate creative writing program. Ticknor and Fields published his third novel, *Cutting Lisa,* in 1986.

Despite the major differences in their settings and in the basic outlines of their plots, both *Suder* and *Walk Me to the Distance* feature protagonists who seem to be questing after something. Nearly two decades after *Suder*'s publication, Everett spoke to Bauer about his general affinity for such narratives: "One of my fascinations is with the western figure. But it doesn't start there but with Cervantes, all those novels of chivalry. *The Bible:* nothing but quest stories. Some fail, some don't. . . . In my novels, it depends on what you mean by failure" ("Percival Everett" 9). In Everett's first novel, Craig Suder is suffering from a profound slump in performance, both in his professional life as a third baseman for the Seattle Mariners and in his personal life as a husband and father. His difficulties stem in part from haunting childhood memories of his mother's descent into insanity, and he worries that his troubles are a sign of similar problems manifesting in him. He leaves home for a cabin in the mountains and acquires an unlikely pair of companions—a precocious nine-year-old runaway named Jincy and a circus elephant he names Renoir—for his attempts at getting his head straight. The story alternates among comic tableaux, flashbacks to Craig's childhood, episodes of profound psychological disturbance, and meditations on the power of art—most specifically Charlie Parker's song "Ornithology"—to transcend human limitations.

Walk Me to the Distance focuses on David Larson, who finds himself in Slut's Hole, Wyoming—ostensibly given its crude name by cowboys because "everybody comes here and then they leave" (5)—for the sole reason that he has perforated his radiator while shooting at jackrabbits during his aimless drive through the western mountains and prairies. Facing a two-week wait for a new radiator, he strikes up a friendship with an old woman named Chloe Sixbury, who runs a ranch outside town and cares for her mentally disabled adult son Patrick. David eventually moves in with Sixbury and takes a job as the caretaker of an interstate highway rest area an hour's drive away. This job initially requires him only to dump noxious chemicals in the toilet occasionally and serve as nonsexual company for a prostitute working among the truckers who pass through. However, when a seven-year-old Vietnamese girl is abandoned at the rest area, David ends up taking her home and becoming her surrogate father, as much by default as by intention. He names the girl Butch, and a strange, decidedly nonnuclear family begins taking shape at Sixbury's ranch, though not before a pair of violent incidents involving Patrick.

Cutting Lisa is yet another striking thematic departure, telling the story—from his own rather stodgy first-person perspective—of a widowed obstetrician named John Livesey, who leaves his home in the northern Virginia suburbs of Washington, D.C., to visit his son Elgin and daughter-in-law Lisa in coastal Oregon. Not long after he arrives, the young couple discover that Lisa is pregnant, spinning the narrative off into unexpected directions as Livesey recalls a harrowing, and foreshadowing, episode from his career as an obstetrician and as he deduces unpleasant facts about the role that infidelity played in the conception of Lisa's baby. By the end of the story, Livesey feels entitled to dispense his personal notion of justice in response to Lisa's betrayal of his son. With his characteristic blend of self-assurance and ambiguity he claims that "sometimes, sometimes you just have to do something" (121) and ends up doing what the book's title foreshadows, cutting into Lisa's womb without her consent to terminate the pregnancy. The novel is dedicated—albeit only by first name—to the visual artist Shere Coleman, who is explicitly mentioned as being Everett's wife in the biographical blurb on the back cover of Everett's fourth book, *The Weather and Women Treat Me Fair,* a collection of stories published with little fanfare by the independent August House press in 1987.

Each of Everett's first three novels garnered generally positive reviews. *Suder* was hailed by his fellow novelist Carolyn See as a "mad work of comic genius, combining symbols and myths from ancients and moderns, juxtaposing heartbreak with farce to make up a narrative that has never been told before" (8); and *Walk Me to the Distance* led Steven Weisenburger to state presciently that Everett "gives every indication of becoming a productive, first-rate writer" ("Out West" 490). *Cutting Lisa*'s reviews were more varied, in no small measure because its ending involves a man self-righteously justifying a forcible abortion that he plans to perform on his daughter-in-law. Nonetheless these three books are perhaps equally significant within Everett's body of work for the mere fact that each of them was released by relatively major publishers. With the exception of *God's Country,* initially published by Faber and Faber; *Erasure,* first published in hardcover by University Press of New England but republished soon thereafter in paperback by Hyperion; and *American Desert,* published by Hyperion, all of Everett's subsequent books have been published by small, independent presses.

As unconventional as Everett's first three novels were, he was also moving in thematic and stylistic directions that conflicted still more severely with the limitations that he saw as by-products of both the unhealthy intellectual environment of the United States and the market-driven mind-set of mainstream publishing: "The problem that economic censorship presents is a hushing of ideas and indeed the censorship itself is merely a symptom of the insidious political disease which infects our culture" ("Signing to the Blind" 9). Not surprisingly, Everett chose to move his work to venues in which his ideas would not be "hush[ed]," a decision that in itself becomes part of a Menippean critique of the metastasis of this cultural "disease." The negative effects of this choice on his potential sales and renown have presumably been offset many times over in Everett's view by his books finding their way into the hands of the kinds of conscientious readers he desires.

In 1989 Everett moved north to South Bend, Indiana, where he began a two-year stint as professor of English at the University of Notre Dame. Although he has never commented on it directly, this must have been a somewhat uncomfortable situation, given that institution's conspicuously Catholic identity and Everett's complete disconnect from religion: "My grandfather was an atheist, my father is—was—an agnostic and I am what I call an 'apath.' I simply don't care" (Mills, Julien, and Tissut 224). During his time at Notre Dame, he published two novels that moved him still further away from the comparatively realistic style and contemporary settings of his first four books.

As his only long-form foray into science fiction, *Zulus* remains distinct within Everett's motley output to this day. As Darryl Dickson-Carr noted, it has more in common with the linguistically complex and formally challenging science fiction of Samuel R. Delany—best known for his epic 1975 novel *Dhalgren*—than with the works of such mainstream SF writers as Isaac Asimov or Arthur C. Clarke (103). The novel is set in the fairly distant aftermath of a nuclear war, and the plot is interspersed with short poetic fragments corresponding to the letter denoting each alphabetically sequenced chapter. It tells the story of Alice Achitophel, a massively obese woman who also has the distinction of being perhaps the only fertile female remaining in her society, a fact that becomes immeasurably more significant after she is raped in the opening pages of the book and instantly becomes convinced that she is pregnant. She lives in a quasi-normal urban landscape that evokes the dystopian underground community of Topeka depicted in Harlan Ellison's postapocalyptic masterpiece *A Boy and His Dog* (1969). The literally and figuratively sterile remnant of American society is kept docile with government cheese and crackers, horrendously vapid television, and an intrusive bureaucracy, within which Alice works as a minor cogwheel in a massive clockwork. As the novel progresses, Alice falls in with a group of rebels who offer her not only the rarity of fresh fruit but also protection for her unborn child and a means of escape from the oppressive world she inhabits. Alice undergoes a literal and figurative transformation among the rebels, who end up caring more for the potential of her baby than for the reality of her, and the novel ends with the newly thin but disillusioned Alice and her lover/collaborator Kevin Peters seemingly about to release a gas that will kill off what remains of human life on earth. Everett's fellow novelist Clarence Major reviewed the book for the *Washington Post,* praising Everett's "gifts as a lyrical writer" and the novel's "display of [his] interest in language and its relation to the activity of the imagination" (4). Again, Everett's choice of publisher—Permanent Press, a small press based in the Long

Island seaside community of Sag Harbor—limited the novel's potential audience, but even so it received the New American Writing Award for 1990 from the influential California literary magazine/press Sun & Moon.

For Her Dark Skin (1990) regresses Everett's temporal focus from the dystopian future to the mythic past. Everett again mutates an existing narrative to serve his own artistic goals, retelling the Greek story of Jason and Medea. He has declared that the idea for the novel arose "out of my long-standing dissatisfaction with the slant of the existing story—that the excuse for [Medea] killing her children was that this woman had gone mad. That seemed too simple. . . . She is a hero in my estimation" (Mills, Julien, and Tissut 219). Published by Owl Creek, a now-defunct small press in Seattle, the novel received far less notice upon release than his previous books. Nevertheless subsequent readers have praised its wit and inventiveness: "With its use of modern slang and humorous literariness, Everett's novel, for the most part, emerges as an aesthetically charming retelling of the Medea myth that is, boldly, not totally reliant upon Euripides'[s] version of it" (Flota 90). *For Her Dark Skin* also serves as a real-life analogue for one of the books authored by "Monk" Ellison, the protagonist/narrator of Everett's subsequent novel, *Erasure* (2001). Ellison finds a copy of his novel *The Persians* shelved in the "African American Studies" section of a chain bookstore and expresses his frustration with this categorization: "Someone interested in African American Studies would have little interest in my books and would be confused by their presence in this section. Someone looking for an obscure reworking of a Greek tragedy would not consider looking in that section any more than in the gardening section. The result in either case, no sale" (28).

Also in 1990 a made-for-television movie called *Follow Your Heart* was produced by the NBC network, ostensibly as an adaptation of *Walk Me to the Distance*. Everett was not directly involved in writing the screenplay or in the production of the film, but he still described the entire process as a "terrible experience" (Mills, Julien, and Tissut 227). The story of *Walk Me to the Distance* was altered superficially to make David into a veteran returning from military duty in Panama, rather than Vietnam, and he comes to Wyoming from New York rather than Savannah. The story's overall tone is considerably softened, even if it somewhat surprisingly retains many of the book's more memorably grotesque elements. Anne-Marie Pacquet-Deyris cataloged and analyzed all the "drastic cuts and 'alterations'" (168) that make "the book's specific sense of *place* virtually disappear . . . in the film" (161); given that the producers rather curiously chose to alter the two places from David's past that Everett explicitly makes insignificant, the diminution of Wyoming's symbolic role in the story is particularly baffling. Although the reviewer for the *New York Times* praised it for being "among this year's better television movies" (O'Connor), Everett has little regard for the end product: "Even if you read my novel and then watch that film, you will not recognize it." He has succinctly stated his lack of interest in further film and television adaptations by referring to Hollywood as "a bad neighborhood [that] I don't feel like going in" (Mills, Julien, and Tissut 227). His attitude toward *Follow Your Heart* echoes and amplifies the misadventures—including turning down Sidney Poitier as a director, trying to cast Eddie Murphy or Richard Pryor in the lead, and trying to convince Everett to rewrite the screenplay to make the lead character white—concerning a proposed adaptation of *Suder* that he describes in his 1991 essay "Signing to the Blind."

A Relatively Young Man Goes West

After two years at Notre Dame, Everett departed the Midwest in 1991 to return to Wyoming, having accepted the William Robertson Coe Chair in American Studies at the University of Wyoming in Laramie. Judith Lewis Mernit noted the peculiar circumstances under which Everett accepted the position:

> He did so on one unusual condition: that he could live among the Arapahoe and Shoshone on the Wind River Reservation. To this day, he doesn't know why. "I had no connection with the reservation, and I had no prior interest in Plains Indians," he says. "I just wanted to be there. . . . The university had a pilot who had a plane, a Cessna like the one in [the 1950s television series] *Sky King* . . . and every Thursday they'd fly me in to teach my class and then fly me back to the reservation." He stayed for a year and a half, slept on sofas, made friends. Before he left, he helped a Cheyenne elder document two ceremonies, the Arrow Worship and Sun Dance, for future generations. "He was the last man alive who knew them." (Mernit)

Although his residence in Wyoming occurred in the midst of one of the slowest periods of his career in terms of publication, he stored aspects of his experiences among the Shoshone and Arapahoe as raw material for later works. The Wind River Reservation likely provided some conceptual building blocks for the fictional Plata Indian Reservation on which most of *Watershed* is set, and several of Everett's other works since that time have prominently featured Native American characters, most notably Daniel White Buffalo in *Wounded* and Warren Fragua in *Assumption*. His lasting affinity for the place is apparent in his observation that "a lot of the senses of humor I experienced on the reservation were not so different from my own, and that was part of what made me comfortable" (Taylor, "Art" 66).

The only book he published during the time he lived in Wyoming, a children's counting book entitled *The One That Got Away* (1992), shows signs of having been influenced by his surroundings too, albeit in a fashion rather less fraught with political and cultural significance. The book was summarized in a review:

> Three cowboys (one female) and a furry black dog catch "one" on their "first day out." The one, a chunky geometric numeral, fights back with its spindly arms and legs and bares its teeth in a fierce grimace, but is duly corralled to be photographed and admired. Then, in a comic variant of Picasso's *Guernica,* a whole herd of ones (different sizes and colors but recognizably of the same species) are rounded up to join the first. In the night, the tall fuchsia one escapes; while his captors are out looking for him, the rest undergo an unexpected but logical transformation [from being eight separate "ones" to being one unified "eight"]. ("The One")

Featuring illustrations by Dirk Zimmer, the book was generally reviewed positively, although those reviewers who were familiar with Everett's previous novels were apparently helpless to avoid noting that he was a most unlikely entrant into the field of children's literature.

In autumn 1992 Everett moved to California, the state in which he has maintained his primary residence ever since. He accepted a position as professor of creative writing at the University of California at Riverside, the campus of which lies roughly forty miles inland from downtown Los Angeles. He would return to the University of Kentucky for a semester as a visiting professor of English and Honors in the fall of 1993 but otherwise remained in Riverside until 1998, serving as department chair for his final four years there. While at Riverside, Everett was married again, this time to his UC-Riverside colleague Francesca "Chessie" Rochberg, a decorated Assyriologist and historian of science who won a MacArthur Foundation grant at the tender age of thirty in order to support her study of astrology and astronomy in ancient Babylon. Possessing a capacious intellect that could match Everett's, Rochberg evidently made a strong impression on him: "When she told me what she did, I proposed" (Monaghan 73). Everett dedicated several of his books to her during their marriage, which ended in 2005.

In 1994 Faber and Faber published *God's Country,* Everett's first novel in nearly four years. *God's Country* garnered strong reviews and a considerably larger readership, partly because of its publishers' expanded reach but also because the book is, at least on the surface, more accessible than much of Everett's prior work. The novel parodies the familiar form of the Western, giving readers something moderately conventional to latch onto as the novel begins, although that set of conventions quickly falls away as the story develops—exemplified by the appearance of a cross-dressing George Armstrong Custer later in the book. The narrator, Curt Marder, is a comically absurd ancestor of *Cutting*

Lisa's John Livesey, inasmuch as it is his stubborn insistence on hewing to his hidebound worldview that not only estranges Bubba, the tracker whose skills Marder needs in order to find his kidnapped wife, but also constantly leads him deeper into trouble throughout the book. David Bowman's glowing review in the *New York Times* insisted that the book achieves its excellence only after Everett leaves the formulaic expectations of the Western behind: "[*God's Country*] starts sour, then abruptly turns into Cowpoke Absurdism, ending with an acute hallucination of blood, hate and magic. It's worth the wait. The novel sears" (43).

Everett's editor at Faber and Faber was Fiona McCrae. Not long after *God's Country* was published, McCrae left for Minneapolis to become the director of Graywolf Press, to which Everett likewise migrated. Everett has frequently expressed his preference for working with small presses such as Graywolf and has specifically lauded McCrae for being his ideal "serious" reader:

> I have the great fortune of having Fiona McCrae at Graywolf as my editor. She is my editor. That's how I think of her. And I like being at Graywolf . . . . It's an independent publisher, a non-profit publisher. Ironically, they're under more pressure to turn a profit than for-profit publishers, but I've never had a talk with them about marketing. . . . I want to talk about books. And that's what we talk about. When she reads my work, it's great that she gets it. I love that. But she wants to make it the best book she can make it, and so edits it seriously. . . . She's done far more than anyone in any large house has ever done as far as understanding the work and trying to understand the work. So, that means a lot to me. (Stewart, "Uncategorizable" 318).

Graywolf has published or republished thirteen of Everett's novels and short story collections, by far the most of any press with which he has worked.

Also in 1994 Everett became the fiction editor of the influential African American arts and culture journal *Callaloo,* to which he had been contributing stories and essays as far back as 1986. As of late 2017 he remained a regular contributor and a member of its editorial board. Additionally, *Callaloo* in 2005 published a special issue that was dedicated to Everett and guest-edited by his friend, colleague, and collaborator James Kincaid.

A brief lull followed the appearance of *God's Country,* but Everett made up for that by publishing four books in less than two years. The story collection *Big Picture* and the novel *Watershed* were both published by Graywolf in 1996, and the novels *The Body of Martin Aguilera* (Owl Creek) and *Frenzy* (Graywolf) appeared in 1997. *Big Picture* anthologizes three previously published stories alongside six new works, and the collection as a whole reinforced many of the existing critical views, both positive and negative, concerning

Everett's writing. *Kirkus Review* stated that he "returns to familiar themes with his usual subtlety and eccentric comic flourishes" ("Big Picture" 244), while Maggie Garb's review in the *New York Times* added that he "uses a laconic style that sometimes seems to work against his characters' eccentricities, but at others it feels perfectly apt, giving them a strangely appealing complexity" (30). The book won the PEN/Oakland-Josephine Miles Award for Excellence in Literature in 1997 and was also selected as a finalist for that year's Paterson Fiction Prize, which is awarded by the Poetry Center in Passaic, New Jersey.

Watershed arose partly out of Everett's experience living on the Wind River Reservation in Wyoming but also out of the extensive research in hydrology that he conducted in order to depict his protagonist, Robert Hawks, believably. Attempting to disentangle himself from a messy relationship with an unstable girlfriend, Hawks departs Denver for the solitude of his fishing cabin in the mountains north of the city on the reservation of the fictional Plata tribe. While there, he becomes entangled in an intrigue involving some of the local Plata as well as FBI agents, two of whom are discovered dead in the woods not long after Hawks has arrived at his cabin. Moreover, Hawks discovers a mountain creek on the reservation that has been mysteriously diverted and tries to piece together how this might be related to the recent violence. In his blurb on the dust jacket praising Everett and the book, fellow novelist Madison Smartt Bell offered an assessment that has become a commonplace on the covers of Everett's books since: "If Percival Everett isn't already a household name, it's because more people are interested in politics than truth. Maybe *Watershed,* with its fine combination of humor, satire, and well-founded outrage, will do the trick."

Like *Watershed, The Body of Martin Aguilera* involves an unsolved murder, in this case that of the character mentioned in the book's title. Lewis Mason, a retired professor from Vermont, travels with his daughter to visit Aguilera, his longtime friend, at the latter's house in the rugged backcountry of New Mexico. Upon arrival, they find his body and set in motion an investigation that involves the beleaguered local sheriff, Manny Mondragon, and a suspicious veterinary surgeon named Cyril Peabody, who is implicated in a chemical weapons storage scheme that appears somehow to be related to Aguilera's demise. The novel received almost no attention from reviewers when it was published, again most likely because of its limited release and publicity. Anthony Stewart, one of the foremost scholars and champions of Everett's work, even quipped to the author in a 2007 interview that he had "yet to find a copy" of the book ("Uncategorizable" 319). It has been mentioned in a handful of scholarly articles that survey Everett's Western fiction, but it remains perhaps the least consequential of his works to date, if for no other reason than its relative scarcity.

Frenzy returns somewhat to the cultural context of *For Her Dark Skin* in reworking a story from Greek mythology. Everett focuses in this novel on the deity Dionysos and the combination of physical and emotional ecstasies—the titular "frenzy"—that he inspires in his worshipers. The story is told from the perspective of the deity's human associate, Vlepo, who records and interprets Dionysos's actions, words, and being without being affected by them as other mortals are: "I was there to watch his dance, just as I was there to watch all else. I was there in the midst of the frenzied Bakkhanal, watching and noting. Such a row needs an unfrenzied observer. I was there to exercise proper remonstrance and askance-looking. I was there to tell the participants what it was they enjoyed or did. My usual place was at the side of the god . . . as his aide, his chronicle, his mortal bookmark" (3). Both the positive and the negative reviews of the novel accentuated its unconventional approach to storytelling. Irving Malin's review of the book claimed that it was "surely mad" but also that "it makes other novels seem lifeless." George Garrett called it an "altogether indescribable accounting" of the Greek myth but also urged the reader to "let it happen and it will work for you." In contrast, Maria Simson felt that the "choppiness of the narrative . . . prevents any real tension and saps the book's effectiveness."

Everett's short story "The Appropriation of Cultures" too received recognition in 1997, being named as one of roughly seventy stories published in the previous year to receive the Pushcart Prize. As a result the story was included in the anthology *Pushcart Prize XXII: Best of the Small Presses.*

Farther into the City and Further into the Spotlight

Everett moved his workplace from suburban Riverside to the center of Los Angeles in 1998, accepting a position as professor of English at the University of Southern California, where he has remained on the faculty since. He served as chair of the English department at USC from 1999 to 2002 and was promoted to the rank of distinguished professor of English in 2007. He also directed the doctoral program in literature and creative writing from 2009 to 2012. Despite his scholarly job in the city, Everett initially chose to retain his residence on a ranch more than an hour's drive east of the city near the community of Moreno Valley, and he later added a summer home on Vancouver Island in British Columbia: "when George W. Bush became president I went to Canada and bought a house" (Mills and Lanco 231). In the late 2000s he moved into central Los Angeles, where he lives with his fourth wife, fellow novelist/teacher Danzy Senna, and their two sons, Henry and Miles.

Everett has called *Glyph,* the first novel he published after his move to USC, "perhaps my favorite, only because it was the easiest for me to write as it is closest to my own voice. I didn't have a lot to do to change the rhythm of the thinking" (Mills, Julien, and Tissut 225). For an author given to provocative and offbeat statements, this one is especially noteworthy, inasmuch as the "voice" and the "thinking" of the novel are—superficially, at least—those of an infant named Ralph who opens the novel by remarking that "by the age of ten months I not only comprehended all that [my parents] were saying but that I was as well marking time with a running commentary on the value and sense of their babbling" (6). His parents become aware of Ralph's remarkable intellectual talents while he is still only a year old. His father, an academic specializing in poststructural theory and mockingly nicknamed "Inflato" by his unimpressed son, initially doubts the reality of the boy's talents, but Ralph's mother, an artist by trade, cultivates them immediately: "She gave me magazines and novels and philosophy books and history texts and volumes of poetry. I consumed them all, trying at once to escape myself and stay as close to my own thought as possible, feeling more pure and freer with each turned page" (9). By the time he is four years old, Ralph's IQ is measured at 475 and he becomes the object of obsessive and criminal curiosity by a host of characters, including his academically ambitious psychiatrist, an unhinged couple who want to turn him into an asset for military intelligence, a security guard in search of a child to raise as his own, a corrupt priest, and a set of bumbling television journalists.

The novel's structure is an elaborate parody of contemporary academic prose incorporating diagrams, copious footnotes, dialogues, and formulas amid Ralph's already digressive and hyperintelligent first-person narrative. George Needham lauded Ralph as "an amazing creation, a narrator who can imagine conversations between Wittgenstein and Nietzsche but who hasn't quite mastered toilet training" and rather charitably claimed that the novel "can be enjoyed by almost anyone" (417). Although he generally praised the novel, David Galef's observation that "if the novel has a shortcoming, it's . . . that you probably had to have been in the academy in the 1970's and '80s to appreciate the infatuation with literary 'big theory'" (20) contradicted Needham's assertions regarding the universality of the novel's potential audience.

Everett's next flurry of book-length publications proved to be his most successful in terms of mainstream attention. This fact remains a source of moderate exasperation to the author, given what he has identified as the stimulus for writing *Erasure,* the book that briefly catapulted him into the broader public consciousness. He published both *Erasure* and *Grand Canyon, Inc.* in 2001, the latter being a relatively brief satire of a mind-set summed up by "Rhino" Tanner's relentless desire to be "a real American, a real success story, a boot strap kind of guy, a man's man, a ladies' man, a hero, a mover, a shaper, a visionary" (105–6). Tanner's means of accomplishing this self-conception is by turning the

Grand Canyon from a natural wonder into a sterile amusement park that will bear his name and celebrate his mastery of life—and, by extension, the living. Published by Versus, a small start-up press in San Francisco, the book received relatively little notice and was furthermore drowned amid the tidal wave of attention that *Erasure* received not long after its publication.

Although Everett has taken great pains to resist overly close associations with *Erasure*'s protagonist "Monk" Ellison—"despite the glaring similarity between that character and myself, he's not me. It's not an autobiographical novel" (Mills, Julien, and Tissut 219)—there can be little doubt that the book arises substantially from Everett's experiences in academia and in publishing. The bulk of *Erasure* consists of a set of parodies and metaparodies of various literary and scholarly discourses with which Everett is intimately familiar from firsthand exposure to, and use of, them. Most prominently among these is a grotesque parody of stereotypically "black" fiction entitled *My Pafology*, the title of which is later changed to simply *Fuck*. The text also includes Monk's curriculum vitae, which overlaps with Everett's in a number of tellingly close, if not exact ways—such as the fact that both received the D. H. Lawrence Fellowship, albeit three years apart. As Everett frequently points out, though, *Erasure* also features a series of nonparodic and nonautobiographical plot elements, such as those involving Monk's Alzheimer's-afflicted mother, his father's infidelity and suicide, the murder of his obstetrician sister by an antiabortion protester, and his brother's simultaneous processes of getting divorced and coming out as gay.

Despite these obvious departures from Everett's own family history, most critics of the novel have seized upon the fact that Monk prominently shares Everett's oft-stated objection to being categorized as an African American writer. Neither the fictional character nor his creator objects to such labeling because of being African American; they object because that designation applies to their person, not their writing, and confusing the two establishes an unwanted limitation to both their artistic and their personal means of expression. In an interview with James Kincaid, Everett described the significance of his blackness to his writing: "I am a black writer the way you are a white professor or that man over there is a fat banker. You might point me out as a black writer when trying to betray me to the KKK or the Bush administration. If I get lost and you're trying to tell the police what I look like, you will say 'He's devastatingly handsome, tall and black.' You might then add, 'Look for him in office supply or bookstores; he's a writer'" (Kincaid, "Interview" 379).

Elsewhere he has troubled this racialized labeling further: "I don't have any problem with identifying myself with any number of groups, races, people, and

I suppose, given [that] my great-grandfather was Jewish, I'm a Jewish novelist" (Allen, "Interview" 104). In the opening pages of *Erasure,* Monk expresses similar sentiments while lamenting audiences' reactions to his novels: "Some people in the society in which I live, described as being black, tell me I am not *black* enough. Some people whom the society calls white tell me the same thing. I have heard this mainly about my novels, from editors who have rejected me and reviewers whom I have apparently confused and, on a couple of occasions, on a basketball court when upon missing a shot I muttered *Egads*" (2). Given that Monk mentions being told that these problems of identification would go away "if I'd forget about writing retellings of Euripides and parodies of French poststructuralists and settle down to write the true, gritty real stories of black life" (2), it is not much of a leap to believe that the seed of this novel comes from Everett's own experience, even though the novelistic tree that grows from it eventually departs drastically from his biography.

The novel garnered overwhelmingly positive reviews, although Everett has complained that it "is getting attention for all the wrong reasons . . . the race stuff" (Ehrenreich 26). Moreover, after its initial publication by the University Press of New England—about which Rone Shavers has noted, "It was hilarious seeing your book among titles about reconstructing womanhood in eighteenth-century New Hampshire" ("Percival" 51)—a number of major publishers approached Everett about reprinting it: "All the other houses ran away from it because they were afraid of some backlash. It turned out there was no backlash. . . . And so then the same people who had been afraid of it lined up to see the paperback run" (Shavers, "Percival" 51). Everett has singled out one publisher in particular for ridicule: "The first in line was [Doubleday] . . . and they wanted it to be the inaugural book of an imprint called Harlem Moon. And my first question to my agent was 'Have they read this book?' And I briefly toyed with the idea that, you know, it would be great to have a press publish a book that immediately invalidated the press itself. . . . But forever my book would have 'Harlem Moon' written on it, and I couldn't do it" (Allen, "Interview" 105). For the paperback edition, he ultimately settled on Hyperion (with another later reprint by Graywolf), which would also publish his novel *American Desert* (2004).

Erasure received the Hurston/Wright Legacy Award, was named one of the year's ten best novels by the American Library Association, and was a finalist for the International IMPAC Dublin Literary Award. Although it was given in recognition of his career's work, he also received the 2003 American Academy of Arts and Letters Award for Fiction in the wake of the buzz surrounding *Erasure.* Everett has pointed out the irony of the literary establishment's readiness to bestow awards upon a novel that mocks the process of the literary establishment bestowing awards, especially when it gives them to demonstrably awful books such as *My Pafology* was intended to be: "Everett was puzzled recently after being given a book award sponsored in part by Borders [the same chain in which Monk finds his novel *The Persians* objectionably shelved]. Sitting at the ceremony, observing the Borders executives all around him, he says, 'I turned to one of the judges and said, "Have they *read* this book?" I seem to be asking that question a lot'" (Ehrenreich 25). Everett summed up his feelings about *Erasure*'s status as his "most successful novel" by telling one interviewer, "I can't tell you how much that pisses me off" (Allen, "Interview" 105).

After *Erasure*, a Deluge of Publications

Everett again took a break from book-length publishing after *Erasure*, but he returned with three books in 2004. As sole author he published the darkly comic metaphysical novel *American Desert* and his third collection of short stories, *damned if i do*, the lead story of which, "The Fix," had previously been included in *The Best American Short Stories* anthology for 2000. With Kincaid as coauthor, he also published the epistolary novel *A History of the African-American People (Proposed) by Strom Thurmond, as Told to Percival Everett and James Kincaid*. The two novels continued a trend toward more explicit and frequently metanarrative satire that began with *Glyph* and has remained prominent in Everett's work ever since. By the time *American Desert* was published, Everett was beginning to be identified as a satirist regularly in reviews and criticism. For example, Alan Cheuse wrote in the *Chicago Tribune* that "Everett has leapt into the front ranks of that small group of first-rate American satirists who keep us laughing at ourselves as we jog along toward oblivion" ("Satirical" 1), and Peter Monaghan referred to him as "a satirist whose frame of mind will not permit him to keep that topic [of race] out of his novels" (72). Not all of his works fit the conventional parameters of satire as well as those from the 1999–2004 period do, but Everett's assertion that "all of my novels are subversive and militant, but none is social protest" (Mills, Julien, and Tissut 223) further opens the door to interpreting his overall authorial project, to the extent that he has one, as an inherently Menippean one.

The reaction to *American Desert* was for the most part approving, as evidenced by its inclusion on lists of 2004's best novels compiled by the New York Public Library and the *San Francisco Chronicle*. Everett's collection of shorter works likewise received extensive praise, with Jim Krusoe writing in the *Washington Post* that *damned if i do* "creates the happy effect of never hearing the same chord progression twice . . . as the stories shift from naturalistic to philosophic to surreal" and celebrating Everett's "free-flowing generosity that engages not only the heart but the mind." The critical reaction to *A History of the African-American People* (hereafter this shorter form of the book's serpentine title is used) was similarly positive, though as is frequently the case with Everett's work, the unconventional form of the book led to a wide range of views about its intentions and whether it accomplished them. Jeffrey Renard Allen read the book not as a satire on Thurmond and his racial politics but rather as a metafictional satire on publishing akin to *Erasure:* "Our nation's publishing industry is the novel's true subject, an American institution . . . [in which] the most gifted African-American intellectuals would willingly ghost-write a black history that champions white supremacy, a master narrative that would put men like Strom Thurmond at the center of the struggle for racial equality" ("Percival" 4).

Writing in the *New York Times,* Sven Birkerts called Everett "one of the wilder of our wild-card satirists" but lamented that "we never get into the deeper absurdity promised by the title. Is this meant to be a sendup of the hypocrisy and inertia surrounding American race relations? It's not clear." Birkerts also noted at the outset of his review that Everett "happens to be African-American," a comment that caused Everett to suspend his stated policy of disregarding reviews and write a letter to the *Times* in response. In this letter Everett chided his reviewer for specifying his race superfluously: "I feel confident in stating that the color of my skin has little to do with that novel. I also feel confident in stating that I am sure that Birkerts in previous reviews has not found it necessary to identify other authors as European-American or white." He continued by calling out "this kind of insidious racism" as a blind spot among "those who in all things else would consider themselves liberal, progressive and intellectual," and he finished with the blunt assertion that it "makes one appreciate the overt brand of bigotry practiced by the likes of the late Strom Thurmond" (Everett, "Color" 4).

Everett's unmistakable frustration with this particular form of labeling helps explain a noteworthy development in his more recent publications. Everett has claimed that he does not "write anything autobiographical. I'm private, and I hate this nonfiction shit that's out in the world" (Shavers, "Percival" 49), and none of his works contradicts the essence of this assertion. Nevertheless, in many of the works he has published since the early 2000s, he has intentionally and consistently tantalized readers with such characters as Monk in *Erasure* and Theodore Street in *American Desert* who share obvious biographical details with Everett, practically daring the reader to (over)identify these characters with their creator. Everett raises the stakes on this dare in three of his later books: *A History of the African-American People; I Am Not Sidney Poitier;* and perhaps most curiously, *Percival Everett by Virgil Russell.* In each of these he inserts a character who shares his name, his profession, and/

or other extensive autobiographical details into a scenario that is unmistakably counterfactual and bordering on the absurd, a technique that has likewise been used by such varied contemporaries as Kathy Acker, Paul Auster, John Barth, J. M. Coeztee, Philip Roth, David Foster Wallace, and Charles Yu.

Everett was already satirizing simplistic correlations—as well as overly simplistic correctives such as Monk's unrecognized satirical novel—between an African American author's racial identity and the meanings of his/her works in *Erasure,* and Birkerts's comments seem only to have reaffirmed and amplified for him the reprehensibility of such a mind-set. Everett's overtly reflexive strategy of naming characters in these three books thoroughly disrupts such reductive associations: "If you remember the name on the front of the book when you get to it, then it has a dual effect. One is a chilling effect, where it will pull you out of the text. The other is antithetical to that. It brings the text into a circle, into perhaps a reality that you haven't imagined" (Dischinger 262). By keeping the reader simultaneously conscious of Percival Everett as the name of the real-life author and as the name of a fictional character, he calls into question the ways that a reader's presumptions about a writer's identity distort or otherwise hinder that reader's ability to interpret the work, a topic that has fascinated him since his study of ordinary language philosophy during his collegiate years. The shift to a somewhat more metafictional mode became predominant when *I Am Not Sidney Poitier* was published in 2009; prior to that, though, Everett published four distinct books at the rate of one a year between 2005 and 2008.

Published in 2005, his novel *Wounded* hearkens back in both geography and tone to *Walk Me to the Distance.* John Hunt is a widower who has become fairly content living in the relative isolation of rural Wyoming with only his seventy-nine-year-old uncle Gus and the mules and horses he trains for a living as company. Hunt has some friends and acquaintances scattered through the countryside around the sleepy town of Highland, none more significant than another rancher named Morgan Reese, whose obvious signs of attraction he has been attempting to ignore for some time as the book opens. Within ten pages of the novel's opening, a young gay man is found murdered nearby. His body is described as being "strung up like an elk with his throat slit" (12), evoking the brutal killing of Matthew Shepard near Laramie in 1998. Highland soon becomes the center of media attention, and Hunt's recently hired ranch hand Wallace is the prime suspect in the killing. Hunt's life becomes increasingly complicated as David, the gay son of a college friend, arrives on the scene. David's initial impetus for coming to Wyoming is a protest rally, but he eventually decides to stay and work on Hunt's ranch. Hunt gives in to Morgan's advances, and the two of them begin a romantic relationship, his first since the death of his wife. Furthermore his beloved and cantankerous uncle is diagnosed with cancer and several of the animals in his care—including a fire-scarred coyote pup, an escape-prone mule, and a wild young horse named Felony—begin demanding considerable attention just as winter is setting in. To top it all off, the cattle of one of his Native American neighbors are being killed by unknown individuals who are leaving behind neo-Nazi messages scrawled in the slaughtered animals' blood. Hunt's blackness becomes an issue against his will at this point, because he finds himself—in a manner reminiscent of Robert Hawks's impromptu comradeship with the Plata in *Watershed*—somewhat reluctantly sympathetic to the plight of the various groups and individuals targeted by the wave of hate crimes. In the end he is forced to abandon his isolation in order to protect those he loves and do something about the perpetrators. As with Sixbury's homestead in *Walk Me to the Distance,* Hunt's ranch becomes the site of unconventional kinships that transcend categories such as race, sexuality, and even species by demanding an unambiguous and conscious demonstration of solidarity in place of a simplistic label.

Although the novel received the PEN Center USA Literary Award for 2006 and its French translation by Anne-Laure Tissut received the Prix Lucioles in 2008, the critical reception was mixed. For example, Tyrone Beason praised Everett in the *Seattle Times* "for even attempting to simultaneously plumb this nation's complexes over race and sexuality" but felt the novel's ending to be "a disappointment, given the social tensions Everett takes on." Jane Yeh of the *Village Voice* was more positive, writing that Everett "creates a complex portrait of a man desperately struggling to maintain reason in the face of chaos [and] lures us into the cozy world of his characters only to pull the rug out from under us at the last, exposing a reality so harsh that it can barely be expressed in words." In an interview with Everett, Kera Bolonik expressed a criticism about the novel's gay characters that was echoed in several other reviews: "all of the gay men in the novel . . . are represented as physically defenseless. They need a burly straight man to come to the rescue." Everett replied that he "only meant it as a function of youth, not of their sexuality" (95), but Christopher Bell discerned a similar lack of compassion in Hunt's characterization: "given the ever-present risk of physical violence that haunts the narrative, one would expect the protagonist and his cast of supporting characters to be more interested in the outcome of this bashing" (46).

The frontier realism of *Wounded* disoriented readers familiar only with the absurdist and comic voices that Everett uses in *Erasure* and *American Desert.* This reaction emphasizes a perceived schism among Everett's works that Zach Vasquez articulated in 2011:

> Percival Everett has been writing novels since 1983, and in the intervening years it seems as if he's split off into two different writers. First there's the Everett . . . who etches out simple—but not simplistic—morality tales involving stoic narrators, who, by book's end, will have to test the limits of their wills when confronted with hard truths and harder remedies. . . . That's one Everett. . . . Stoic, stolid, and lean, though without being mean-spirited. Serious in mood, though not without bits of humor usually made in passing observation. . . . Then there's the other Everett. The one who's fucking hilarious. The one who fucks with structure and narrative . . .[, t]he Everett who toes the line of what's real and not, before he rubs it the hell out. . . . Though still interested in moral decisions, this Everett does not present easily distinguished choices. This second Everett . . . turns his stories over to blusterers, fools, and mad-men (though he'll often center the stories by making the protagonists the last sane ones in an insane world). Everett in this mode is excitedly experimental. (Vasquez)

This dichotomy is more useful as an observation of a somewhat elusive trend rather than as an attempt at strict classification; after all, Everett's next novel, *The Water Cure,* and earlier works such as *For Her Dark Skin* and *Frenzy* do not align particularly well with either of these descriptions—or perhaps they align with both of them to an extent that belies the dichotomy they supposedly represent. Moreover, *Assumption, Percival Everett by Virgil Russell,* and *So Much Blue,* the three novels Everett has published since Vasquez made his observation, almost seem intent on refuting this theory of there being two different Everetts by (con)fusing both tendencies to a greater extent than most of his prior works do. Nevertheless, there is considerable, if also provisional, use in dividing Everett's works along these lines, if for no other reason than to note the frequency with which such a perception recurs, implicitly and explicitly, in his readers' and critics' reactions.

Meta-Everett in Full Effect

Everett's next publication was a departure not in tone or theme but in genre. His first collection of poetry, *re: f (gesture),* was published in 2006, with the second, *Abstraktion and Einfühlung,* following two years later in 2008. Both were published by the independent Red Hen Press in the Black Goat series edited by Chris Abani, a former student of Everett's in USC's doctoral program in creative writing and literature and an award-winning poet in his own right. Everett has been typically modest in discussing his poetry, telling Bauer in 2012 that it "is meant to prove that I can't write poetry, and it's pretty effective. Most people will agree with me" ("Percival Everett" 2). The collection *re: f (gesture)* is in part an anthology that recontextualizes poems that previously appeared as the lyrical and alliterative chapter headnotes from *Zulus* and the poems that the hyperintelligent infant Ralph wrote in *Glyph.* The third section of *re: f (gesture)* is made up of new poems that reflect Everett's signature brand of wordplay and philosophical musing to such an extent that Brigitte Félix suggested they could just as well "have been borrowed from another textual space in the writer's work" ("Of Weeds" 6). The small print run coupled with Everett's lack of reputation as a poet assured that *re: f (gesture)* received relatively little critical attention, but Kelly Norman Ellis praised it in *Black Issues Book Review,* writing that "Everett is at his best in the simple, lovely poems that muse on the frailties of the modern world."

Abstraktion und Einfühlung shares its title (translated into English as *Abstraction and Empathy*) with an early twentieth-century book by the German art historian Wilhelm Worringer that extols the virtues of nonrepresentational art, a concept that crosses boundaries of medium and genre in Everett's work, as he has noted: "I was very much attempting to employ my method of painting in writing these poems. I love non-representational art. I avoid the term abstract, because I find it misleading. I think non-representational paintings are realistic, perhaps more realistic than literal representations. . . . For me non-representational work is an extension of my vision rather than a replication of my perception" (Brown 161). Sarah Wyman further explained the synaesthetic relevance of Everett's various artistic and intellectual practices to the creation of poetry:

> As poet-painter, novelist, and wood-carver, Everett moves skillfully between various modes of creativity and expression. As an artist well-versed in language, paint, and wood, he investigates the relation between linguistic and formal structure and the production of meaning. As a scholar, he studies the play of signification, as words and paint splotches gesture toward meaning, as sounds and felt forms suggest sense to the one who reads, views, or touches. His poems become paintings of sorts, neat squares of eight lines, like his minimalist and highly abstracted paintings that invite our interpretive commentary. (126)

Reviews of the book were predictably scant, but Fred Muratori hailed "Everett's piercing focus on his subject [and] . . . his desire to distill and to clarify the conceptual dimensions simultaneously exemplified and hidden beneath the surfaces of canvases by painters we think we know."

Everett engages in a formal, highly complex, and often bewildering play with words and sounds in these poems, often testing the boundary between sense and nonsense: "What I love about nonsense is that it has to adhere more rigidly to form than sense. Because that's how the trick works. You're tricked into believing that it means something because you recognize the structure. So I only figured out recently that I'm not so much interested in writing sense that sounds like nonsense, what I really want to do is write nonsense that actually does make sense" (Bauer, "Percival Everett" 2). This impulse to delve deeply into the semantic capacities of nonsensicality is also central to *The Water Cure,* helping to make it perhaps Everett's most challenging novel to read. Part of the challenge comes from the book's subject matter—a father driven insane by grief taking revenge on the man who raped and killed his eleven-year-old daughter by repeatedly waterboarding him in the basement of his house—which is remarkably grim, even among the catalog of deaths and deformations in Everett's works. An equal measure of the difficulty, though, stems from the book's extreme play with language and conventional structure, which Everett described in an interview with the French journal *l'Humanité:* "My intention was to write a book in which there is no logical connection visible from one paragraph to another, so that the structure reflects the way in which we receive the world. We receive a set of stimuli, and given that perceptions are indistinct, each person chooses those that are necessary for the construction of the narrative that gives meaning to one's world" ("*The Water Cure*" 182). He once again crossed not only literary genres but also artistic mediums in describing how he saw the book's structure functioning: "Throughout the novel, the reader constructs the story as if looking at a photograph, choosing a particular angle or detail. It is impossible for the designer to introduce a hierarchy and to guide the reader. My plan was to destroy the fourth wall of the theatrical stage and immerse the spectator and the actor in the same moving stream of illusion" (183). *The Water Cure* may be as close as Everett has yet come to achieving a goal he playfully articulated a decade after the novel's publication: "I want to write a novel that even I don't understand" (Taylor, "Art" 52).

Published in 2007, the novel is "the undertaking" (Everett, *Water Cure* 7) of a man named Ishmael Kidder, who writes romance novels under the pseudonym Estelle Gilliam because a "black man wasn't going to sell many romance novels to . . . middle-aged perm-headed nail-decaled bus drivers, beauticians, and trailer parkers" (202–3). It consists of a series of fragments detailing—among other things—his daughter's death and the revenge he takes on it, as well as flashbacks, philosophical dialogues on the nature of language, conversations with Kidder/Gilliam's agent, direct (sometimes hostile) addresses to the reader, illustrations and paintings, and quasi-poetic passages in which Kidder's language begins to devolve visibly toward gibberish, while still fulfilling Everett's desire to "write nonsense that actually does make sense." For example, Kidder describes the police arriving to deliver the bad news about his daughter's death: "Gnarly the nixt mourning, a defective, a wombman, keyme to Carelot's dour and we call thaw this as a bid sighn and din pact twasm as the mwes she deviled was that a jung guirrel matchking Lane's dyscryption had beleaf sound kin a ravene bedsighed a parque by twooth bouys and fir daweg" (214). Even the most garbled of such passages are still comprehensible, though they tax the reader's patience and interpretive faculties immensely. As is the case with a series of simple drawings included within the text that gradually move from being a single mark on a page to being a simple picture of a cat, they also allow Everett to explore the question "How many elements are necessary to recognize an object, and how many can be taken away before the object is no longer recognizable," which Everett has stated is "a metaphor for the text [of the novel] itself" ("*The Water Cure*" 183). By removing or obscuring many of the usual devices of novelistic prose, *The Water Cure* dramatically ups the ante on Everett's insistence that the reader do the work of making meaning out of the narrative.

I Am Not Sidney Poitier is more superficially familiar in its form as an apparent bildungsroman but nevertheless presents the reader with substantial complexities in regard to representation and signification. Not the least of these is the main character, who is "tall and dark and look[s] for all the world like Mr. Sidney Poitier," which he claims his mother could not have anticipated when she named him "Not Sidney Poitier" after a two-year pregnancy that may or may not have been the result of sexual intercourse (3). Much like Craig Suder's mother and Robert Hawks's girlfriend Karen in *Watershed,* Not Sidney's mother "was absolutely, unquestionably, certifiably crazy" (6). She proves wise, though, in being an early investor in a company that would eventually become the massive Turner Broadcasting Corporation. This investment has allowed her to become "filthy, obscenely uncomfortably rich" (6) and to pass that money—as well as her friendship with the company's eccentric founder and CEO, Ted Turner—on to Not Sidney upon dying when her son is only eleven years old. Among the many people Not Sidney meets during the course of his unconventional coming-of-age story is a bumbling, grouchy professor named Percival Everett, who (quite unlike his namesake) teaches at the historically black Morehouse College in Atlanta and is prone to speaking in mystifying aphorisms. Not Sidney becomes a student at Morehouse between misadventures in such fictional southern havens of bigotry as Peckerwood County, Georgia, and Smuteye, Alabama. Turner and Everett both become surrogate fathers of a sort for the young man as he goes through life constantly answering questions from others and from himself about the significance of his unusual name.

Everett has insisted that he "was not interested in Sidney Poitier" as a real-life person but was interested rather in the cultural role that Poitier was assigned: "I was interested in the name. None of the novel has to do with Sidney Poitier. It has to do with the fact that there existed a character who assumed that place . . .[,] a station of acceptability to one member of a group" that allowed mainstream, that is, predominantly white, American culture to "feel good about itself" (Dischinger 262). The disclaimer that appears between the title page and the start of the book echoes Twain's notice at the start of *The Adventures of Huckleberry Finn:* "Persons attempting to find a motive in this narrative will be prosecuted; persons attempting to find a moral in it will be banished; persons attempting to find a plot in it will be shot" (n.pag.). Rather than facetiously threatening legal action or violence, Everett's disclaimer cautions the reader against reading significance into characters' names, especially those with particularly significant names, such as his own: "All characters in this novel are completely fictitious, regardless of similarities to any extant parties and regardless of shared names. In fact, one might go as far as to say that any shared name is ample evidence that any fictitious character in this novel is NOT in any way a depiction of anyone living, dead or imagined by anyone other than the author. This qualification applies, equally, to the character whose name is the same as the author's" (n.pag.).

The critical reactions to the book frequently referred back to *Erasure,* suggesting that the idea that parody and satire were Everett's "normal" modes of authorial discourse had taken root. Laird Hunt praised *I Am Not Sidney Poitier* for its similarity to *Erasure* in being both "frequently, gut-grabbingly hilarious" and "more [a] serious meditation on the exigencies of the self than [a] comic send-up of an America gone wildly off the rails." Other reviewers were less taken with Everett's return to the comic-satiric mode. For example, although Carolyn Briones generally praised how "the novel humorously investigates the fuzzy boundaries between reality and media without cluttering the narrative with complicated ideology," she also contended that it "does not achieve the brilliancy (and complexity) of some of Everett's other works" (553). Gretlund felt that the novel "is liable to irritate quite a lot of today's established black Americans" in implicating them even more directly than *Erasure* did in the continuation of racist presumptions about blackness ("Black" 7).

In terms of public recognition for his work, 2010 was a banner year. *I Am Not Sidney Poitier* garnered for its author a second Hurston/Wright Legacy Award and the Believer Book Award, presented by the editors of *Believer* magazine to reward otherwise underappreciated works of literature. Marco Rossari's translation of *Wounded* into Italian won the Gregor von Rezzori Prize for best work of foreign fiction from the Santa Maddalena Foundation in Florence,

Italy. Everett also received the Charles Angoff Award from the *Literary Review,* which selected his story "Confluence" as the most outstanding contribution to the journal that year. In addition he received the Dos Passos Prize in Literature from Longwood University in Virginia, joining an illustrious list of American writers who have been singled out for "an intense and original exploration of specifically American themes, an experimental quality, and a wide range of literary forms" ("Writer"). His one new publication for the year was a collaboration with Chris Abani entitled *There Are No Names for Red,* for which Abani wrote poems and Everett contributed several paintings that were reproduced within the book.

Everett returned to both poetry and the West in his next two publications. *Swimming Swimmers Swimming* (2011) is his third collection of verse, about which Walton Muyumba wrote that "the strongest [poems] artfully demonstrate Everett's fascination with American English's refractive qualities—a trait Everett has inherited from Gertrude Stein." He went on to suggest that the poems are a useful tool for interpreting Everett's *Assumption,* a triad of intertwined novellas that was published at nearly the same time: "These new poems backlight the novel's ideas, helping detail Everett's narrative and linguistic aesthetic and offering some direction for understanding his choices" (Muyumba). *Assumption* works in a manner similar to *God's Country* or *My Pafology*—the novel-within-a-novel in *Erasure*—in its conspicuous play with a literary form. However, Everett's method is much less comic and/or exaggerated in *Assumption* than in those previous works: "this novel isn't really a parody. . . . I am toying with the assumptions we have when we enter into that kind of story. You assume that your protagonist is a certain way, and you take some things for granted that maybe in real life you wouldn't. And you also have some assumptions about the writer and the space that you're entering" ("Author Percival" 188). Deputy Ogden Walker and the remainder of the police force of Plata, New Mexico, are not perceptive, streetwise sleuths like the protagonists of the detective fictions written by James Ellroy and Walter Mosley; nor are they technologically savvy crime fighters like those featured on televised police procedurals such as *CSI.* They are not ridiculed for their inadequacies in dealing with the series of murders, frauds, and general criminality that descends on their previously sleepy town. They are all limited yet likable individuals, more obsessed with food and fishing than forensics in ways that are chided gently, if at all. The general sense is that they are caught up in a violent world whose motives remain inscrutable beyond some fairly clichéd presumptions on Walker's part: "Three lives for twelve thousand dollars. I mean, I just can't wrap my mind about it. I guess it wasn't about the money . . . . I don't know. Power, maybe" (172). If Walker is, as the voice of his dead father says to him on the book's opening page, "a fool for working as a deputy in that hick-full redneck county" (3), Everett does not suggest that it is a folly for which he should be condemned. *Assumption* undermines two of the most reassuring aspects of conventional detective fiction, specifically the linked ideas that truth is discoverable and that justice will follow from such a discovery. Each of the three novellas ends not only with a surprise but also without the logical resolution that the genre demands.

Despite being designed to confound readerly expectations, the book was widely praised. Roger Boylan wrote in the *New York Times* that "Everett casts his line, as it were, pretty far, and some of the things he reels in, along with a few red herrings, are weighty indeed: racism, anomie, disillusionment, the meaning (or lack thereof) of one man's life—the American nightmare, in brief, at the end of the line." Not everyone was as taken with it, though, including some longtime devotees. For example, Rone Shavers claimed that the book "falls flat, like most other books written these days, . . . [because] it assumes a simple story, told well, is enough," and Shavers ultimately believed that it would be "judged as one of his lesser, and less important, works" ("*Assumption* and *Erasure*").

The years 2012 and 2013 helped support Everett's contentions that "I make my money in France and Italy" (Reynolds 179) and that "I get recognized on the street in Paris," a situation he calls "the oddest thing" (Mernit). Unlike such predecessors as Ernest Hemingway or James Baldwin, Everett has never expatriated himself to Paris, but there is no doubt that his work has received, until recently, considerably greater critical attention from such French scholars as Sylvie Bauer, Jacqueline Berben-Masi, Michel Feith, Claude Julien, Claire Maniez, and Anne-Laure Tissut—his primary French translator—than it has in North America; for example, the first two collections of critical essays about Everett's work were published in France in 2007, whereas comparable North American volumes were not published until 2013. He has fostered a considerable audience for his works—mostly the novels published since *Glyph*—in French, Italian, German, Spanish, Greek, and Russian translations. Adding to the two previous prizes that translations of his work had won, Tissut's French translation of *I Am Not Sidney Poitier* received the Lucien Barrière Literary Award at the Deauville American Film Festival in 2012. Everett served as a visiting faculty member at Paris-Sorbonne University (Université Paris-Sorbonne, Paris IV) during the 2012–13 academic year and participated in a number of conferences about and celebrations of his work around France during that year as well. Everett has stated that the series of Western-themed short fiction that was published in 2015 as *Half an Inch of Water* began while "I was living in Paris, and for some reason I started writing ranch stories" (Rath).

Upon returning from France, Everett published his nineteenth novel, which fuses the overt play with names found in *I Am Not Sidney Poitier,* the narrative fragmentation found in *The Water Cure,* and the frustration of expectations found in *Assumption* into a single novel that features most of the major developments of his career to this point. *Percival Everett by Virgil Russell* is perhaps the quintessential Percival Everett novel, not because of its quality or even its subject matter but because of how it gleefully thwarts the notion that this book will reveal something more about its creator; after all, the novel's title suggests not only that the book is about Percival Everett but also that it is by someone else, neither of which turns out to be accurate, at least not literally. Despite a narrative filled with elaborate details about a son and his father, the novel never reveals which of them is Percival Everett, instead leaving open the possibility that it could be neither, either, or both of them. Nor does it provide an explanation of who the titular Virgil Russell might be, beyond an allusion to the Latin poet/Dantean guide and the British analytic philosopher, both of whom are mentioned on numerous occasions in the novel.

Everett had the philosophical concept of Frege's Puzzle squarely in mind while writing *Percival Everett by Virgil Russell,* and he embeds one formulation of that concept into the novel early on: "according to the truth A = A is not the same thing as A is A" (8). In pointing out both that two things can have the same name and not be the same, and that two things can be the same thing yet be identified by different names, Everett elaborately plays with the reader's assumptions about storytelling and literary representations. His narrators, narratives, and characters oscillate in and out of phase throughout the book, with the conversation between the father and son frequently being supplanted by snippets of stories that are likewise narrated in the first person. Some of these are fragments of quintessential Everett "horse stuff" (56), such as the story of a man named Murphy who becomes involved with a pair of drug-dealing brothers while simultaneously kindling a flirtatious relationship with a veterinarian who is treating his Appaloosa named Trotsky for a gunshot wound. Others are provocative literary parodies, such as Nat Turner's efforts "to tell William Styron's story, *The Confessions of Bill Styron* by Nat Turner" (16), the name of which not only alludes to the intentionally convoluted title of *Percival Everett by Virgil Russell* but is also first referenced by the father-son narrator as possibly being a dream that Murphy from the aforementioned story might have had. As if that were not enough allusion and reflexivity, Nat Turner also literalizes the Barthesian impulse at one point, noting that "he understood that he had to murder the authorial presence and to do that he'd have to find the author and kill him" (78). In the second part of the novel, Everett confounds his readers still further by seemingly abandoning most of these established narrative threads without resolution in favor of a sustained story that focuses on the abused residents of a nursing home, one of whom appears to be the father from the novel's first part.

Everett jams his narrative full of seemingly significant pieces—and there are far more than can possibly be summarized here—and then undercuts efforts to reassemble them conclusively: "All the details. Everything in the details. Details, details, details. Of rooms, meals, walks, and gardens. Details telling us who we are, where we are, and why. Telling us everything. Telling us nothing. Because we live inside our heads. So much bullshit? In the middle of the middle of middle America. So much bullshit? In the details" (42). Recognizable characters' names suddenly change without altering their significance to the story in which they appear, and the narrative voice intrudes on many of these occasions to muse about the irrelevance of nominal identity: "I'm not so much confused now by the person as I am by the names. It's clear that I have no descriptive material to connect to their respective names and so I have no idea as to which is who and who is what. I used to think they were identical, but disabused of that I believed that they were both simply fat, but it turns out that one, my patient, Douglas or Donald, is quite a bit fatter than his brother, Donald or Douglas. . . . Is his name a defining attribute of the man who is my patient? Does it matter whether he is Donald or Douglas? Would having one of these names or the other alter who he might be?" (92–93). Everett has described the book as being a game of "pin the tail on the narrator; you don't know who's telling the story," making the title's seeming attribution of names and roles into even more of an unfulfilled tease (Cruden). The fact that the book is dedicated to Percival Leonard Everett—the author's father and namesake, who died three years before the book's publication—only deepens the confusion about identity in this "impossible-to-describe-or-summarize ouroboros about parents, death, and aging" (Taylor, "Art" 42) and what any of it might mean. Everett's narrator drops a possible hint when he verbosely alludes to one of his creator's favored notions: "This is what I want all of this to do, to be. I want it to sound like nonsense, have the rhythm of nonsense, the cadence of nonsense, the music, the harmony, the animato, the euphoniousness, the melodiousness, the contrapunctality, lyrphorousness, the marcato, the fidicinality, the vigor, the isotonicity, lyriformity, of nonsense" (56).

Not surprisingly, reviews of the novel were fairly polarized. Lydia Millet, another contemporary writer with a propensity for conspicuous oddity, glowingly reviewed it for the *Los Angeles Times* in a manner that captured its essential strangeness as well:

> When I read Percival Everett's new book . . . I found that I liked not only the book but also Percival Everett. He wasn't there at all, that interesting professor and novelist, that attractive, often humorous, middle-aged black literary stylist who lives and writes in Southern California, experimenting with the structure and conventions of fiction. I liked him anyway. . . . You never know who's telling what in "Percival Everett," . . . but to me there was much that was pleasurable about that fluidity, that openness, there was something that allowed me to get in there, intruding myself pleasantly and even productively into Percival Everett, or, in any case, the fictional impostor pretending to be him. ("Meet Percival Everett")

Despite being a longtime admirer of Everett's work, Alan Cheuse was unenthusiastic in his review of the book for National Public Radio. Believing Everett to be "seduced by the idea of metafiction" and "under the thrall of this longstanding (yet apparently still voguish) tendency," Cheuse contended that the book is marred by the fact that "real, fascinating, important dramas lie buried beneath distracting passages of self-referential rhetoric" and, as a result, "seems forced and pedantic" ("Lost"). The novel was named a finalist for the PEN/Faulkner Award and the *Publishers Weekly* "Best Books" list for 2013. If there were any remaining doubt that Everett means it when he tells interviewers that he does not consider, much less cater to, the wants and needs of his audience, *Percival Everett by Virgil Russell* put it to rest.

Each of Everett's next two book-length publications returns to a shorter form of literary expression. He published his fourth collection of poetry, *Trout's Lie* (2015), the working title of which, according to Everett's curriculum vitae, was "Against Sense." The book's description on the Red Hen Press Web site suggests that Everett is using these poems to play—much as he does in *The Water Cure* and *Abstraktion und Einfühlung*—with the notion of nonsensical language: "[He] explores the semantic relationship between sense and so-called nonsense—and questions whether either is actually possible." He also published *Half an Inch of Water* (2015), which collects the stories that he wrote while living in Paris. Kelsey Ronan called the stories "magical realism for the American West" and praised the manner in which the stories first tantalize with and then deviate from literary conventions: "All the expected features of the landscape are here. . . . In these small Western towns, waitresses don't have to ask for your order at the town's one diner. Their inhabitants are laconic, pragmatic people firmly rooted in place. Everett forces them to confront the incredible, the inexplicable, and the surreal, forever changing their sense of the familiar." Tobias Carroll similarly noted this tension as a strength of the collection: "While stories of plainspoken men and women living in stark, sparsely populated towns are familiar, Everett finds new ways to enliven the setting and the characters."

He published his thirtieth book in 2017, a novel entitled *So Much Blue,* which once again features a protagonist who shares a significant biographical trait with Everett—Kevin Pace is, like his creator, a painter of nonrepresentational art, as well as an artist comfortable in stating his disregard for the critical opinion of his audience—but whose story veers sharply away from autobiographical correspondence soon thereafter. He received a fellowship from the John Simon Guggenheim Memorial Foundation in 2015 to help complete the research for this novel.

Everett also won a National Endowment for the Arts (NEA) creative writing fellowship in 2014, enabling him to travel to Algeria and the Mediterranean island of Corsica to do research for "a screenplay he is writing . . . about the celebrated French Navy submarine, the *Casabianca,* which joined the Free French Forces during World War II and participated in the liberation of Corsica" (S. Bell). In additional to being his first foray into screenwriting, or at least the first publicized one, this project represents yet another departure in geographical and, to a lesser extent, temporal setting from Everett's past work, suggesting strongly that his drive to find new subjects and new forms of artistic expression is far from exhausted.

CHAPTER 2

Everett and Menippean Satire

Menippean satire is generally the least familiar of the three subcategories of classical satire—the others being Horatian and Juvenalian—though it has had something of a resurgence in its critical currency since the late twentieth century. Although the term has been used more frequently to describe individual literary works rather than to encapsulate the output of particular authors—notable exceptions being M. Keith Booker's treatment of Flann O'Brien and Theodore Kharpertian's study of Thomas Pynchon (both discussed in greater detail below)—it is a valuable tool for explicating the authorial mind-set that underlies most, if not all, of Everett's fiction. Although the term "mind-set," like its close cousin "mentality," can certainly be an ambiguous weasel word used to avoid attributing specific intentions to an author, the critic who tackles Everett's work is fortunate to have the substantial corpus of Everett's commentaries on the craft of writing upon which to draw in delineating more precisely what is meant by this term. Everett has made his lack of interest in explaining the meanings of his works exceedingly clear: "I never speak to what my work might mean. If I could, I would write pamphlets instead of novels. And if I offered what the work means, I would be wrong" (Goyal). Nevertheless he has on occasion proved willing to discuss the thought processes that guided the composition of individual works. Such remarks help to substantiate what otherwise would remain mostly inferential speculations about how and why he writes what he does. The pursuit of compelling answers to those two intertwined questions is at least as pertinent to explicating his fiction in the context of Menippean satire as supporting hypotheses regarding the interpretation of individual works.

Although the previous chapter includes a significant number of details from Everett's personal life, these are not presented in an effort to understand Percival Everett *the individual*. Rather, the evidence offered in the chapter can provide a meaningful portrait of Percival Everett *the writer,* a figure who is necessarily dependent on the existence of the real-life Percival Everett and yet is also a wholly distinct entity—see the disclaimer at the start of *I Am Not Sidney Poitier*. Whereas Everett's desired goal is for his flesh-and-blood self to be rendered irrelevant to the interpretation of his texts, he constructs and manipulates fictionalized versions of various aspects of himself in order to serve a wide range of literary purposes, none of which, he would argue, is mimetically autobiographical. He has proved more than willing to mine his life's experiences for literary material, but his authorial processes refine those metaphorical ores to such an extent that even, or especially, a character named Percival Everett should never be confused with his real-life analogue. An attempt is thus made in chapter 1 to clarify Everett's "mind-set" as a combination of the philosophical, political, and/or aesthetic premises that undergird both Everett's attitude regarding his role as a writer and the discernible methods of literary expression he has deemed most suitable to that role at various stages of his career. The argument can be made that these premises and methods correspond with the definition of Menippean satire in a sizable majority of Everett's novels.

The Importance of Earnest Jesting

Menippean satire is a mode of seriocomic satirical expression that dates back to and is named after the ancient Greek writer Menippus of Gadara, who is believed to have lived in the third century B.C.E. Despite there being no physical copies of any of the works attributed to Menippus, this literary mode bears his name because of the characteristics ascribed to those works while they—and their author's reputation—still did exist. For example, the second-century C.E. Greek satirist Lucian wrote a work entitled *Menippus, or the Descent into Hades,* in which a fictionalized version of Menippus travels to the underworld to engage in a highly satirical philosophical debate with the mythic seer Teiresias. Athenaus of Naucratis mentioned Menippus among the Cynic philosophers in his third-century C.E. work *Deipnosophistae* (translated into English as *The Learned Banqueters*), and Athenaus's contemporary Diogenes Laërtius included Menippus among the notable "Ionians" in his *Lives and Opinions of Eminent Philosophers,* naming and describing numerous works reputedly penned by him. Thomas Willard has written that Menippus "was known in antiquity as the earnest jester . . . because his satires lampooned ideas of rival schools. (He thus followed the advice of Gorgias, as reported by Aristotle: 'kill your opponents' earnestness with jesting and their jesting with earnestness') . . . . Menippus was said to have combined verse and prose, and Lucian drew equally on . . . comedy and satire as well as verse and prose . . . [to create] a hybrid form that came to be known as Menippean satire" (778–79). In its classical form, Menippean satire was thus distinguished by its variety of literary forms and by directing its satirical attacks specifically at the ideas of other philosophers, rather than at instances of typical human "folly" or on the moral failings of particular individuals, as was generally the case in the renowned satires of Aristophanes, Horace, or Juvenal.

David Musgrave described how the term developed over the centuries between late antiquity and the Enlightenment, when it enjoyed a resurgence in the literatures of central and northern Europe: "Ancient Menippean satire tended to be a satire of [particular] philosophers . . . which gradually became a satire of philosophy in the middle ages and, later, a satire of religion and other powerful ideologies" (viii). Dustin Griffin expanded on this development by noting that "the Menippean family has several branches" that emerged after the classical period: "a tradition of fantastic narrative, from Lucian to *Gulliver's Travels* and beyond; a parallel tradition of wild and parodic display of learning, from Erasmus through Robert Burton to *A Tale of a Tub;* and a tradition of dialogue and symposium from Plato and Lucian to [Bernard Le Bovier de] Fontenelle and [William] Blake" (33). W. Scott Blanchard further explained how Menippean satire was perceived during the late Renaissance and the Enlightenment: "Menippean satire is a genre for and about scholars; it is an immensely learned form that is at the same time paradoxically anti-intellectual. If its master of ceremonies is the humanist as wise fool, its audience is a learned community whose members need to be reminded . . . of the depravity of their overreaching intellects, of the limits of human understanding" (14). Blanchard also noted that Menippean satire is less inclined than the varieties descended from the Roman writers Juvenal and Horace to become a medium of moral instruction or correction: "[It] refuses to allow an ideal type to emerge from its chaotic sprawl, whereas Roman satire achieves its effect by contrasting the debased world of the present to models of human behavior that are acceptable" (18–19).

Even in these initial and intermediate contexts, one sees parallels emerging between the structures and intentions of this class of texts and Everett's "earnestly jesting" methods as a writer, whether in terms of the multiplicity of genres and forms that make their way into his texts or the ways in which his works implicitly and explicitly reveal the "depravity" underlying various forms of accepted wisdom. While far from "anti-intellectual," Everett is especially Menippean in his unwillingness to insist that his view of the world is the correct one—"I don't approach fiction, or, more generally, writing with the notion that I know what's true and right. I raise questions" (Mills, Julien, and Tissut 221)—or that expressing his criticisms is going to change the world for the better: "I don't operate under any illusions about the world—it's a bad place. . . . Always has been always will be. Human beings aren't particularly admirable . . . . Still, I'll talk about the things that I think are vacuous and the things I think are evil, knowing that certainly not because of my pointing them out will they change" (Monaghan 73). Everett's comments echo Dustin Griffin's claim that satire's "ultimate provocation—what Swift calls vexing the world—is to make readers look in the mirror and see that they are not and can never be what they claim to be. Satire cannot mend them; it can only hope to make them *see*" (62). Howard Weinbrot has attributed a similarly unpromising brand of persistence to Menippean satires specifically: "[These texts'] dominant thrust is to resist or protest events in a dangerous world, however much the protests may fail. . . . Menippean satire lives in a precarious universe of broken or fragile national, cultural, religious, political, or generally intellectual values" (7).

Everett's Menippean qualities come into sharpest focus, though, when one considers the work of Northrop Frye, one of the two scholars—Mikhail Bakhtin being the other—most responsible for defining Menippean satire for the twentieth century and beyond. Wholly familiar with but also departing notably from Menippean satire's long pedigree, Frye has contributed a major innovation that becomes extremely relevant to applying the concept to Everett's work. Frye differs from scholars such as Willard and Blanchard, both of whom considered Menippean satire as a genre of literature—that is, an identifiable form of writing with a particular set of conventions and expectations. A genre-based definition was appropriate for the classical version of Menippean satire, but it proves inadequate in the face of the intentional confusion and deformation of genres that developed in the wake of such innovative novels as Miguel de Cervantes's *Don Quixote* (1605), Jonathan Swift's *Gulliver's Travels* (1726), or Laurence Sterne's *The Lives and Opinions of Tristram Shandy, Gentleman* (1759). Frye instead discussed contemporary Menippean satire as a mode that can appear in and affect the meaning of a work from just about any genre, a perspective that Weinbrot has summarized: "It often attaches itself to other kinds of works within other dominant genres, and peers in as occasion requires. It is perhaps less a clearly defined genre than a set of variable but compatible devices whose traits support an authorial theme" (4). If one accepts this assertion, then Everett's claims about the interrelated nature of all his books expand the possibility of interpreting his entire catalog, not just individual works therein, as Menippean satire: "I see all [my] works as fitting together, as an overall project. I'm writing one big novel. . . . These books are in a dialogue with each other. It's a conversation that I'm having with myself, and the work is having with itself, and I'm having with the work. It's my way of understanding the world" (Stewart, "Uncategorizable" 295–96).

Although taking any passage from *Percival Everett by Virgil Russell* directly at face value is perhaps to stumble into a trap of the author's making, that novel's multitudinous narrator makes a comment that both echoes Everett's real-life sentiments from the previous quote and positions art generally as a

Menippean project of pushing back against "powerful ideologies." The narrator appears to be speaking in the voice of the "father" when he states, "Thus, if I or you, son, can be relied upon, we are at this moment in time in a most grave condition, besieged and beset by that ceaseless host of negative thinkers and would-be controllers and, yes, disbelievers, threatening to undress us publicly." The father then appears to quote his son's amplification of this dire situation:

> The world, says you, as it proceeds, is under an operation of devastation and misapplication and abuse, which, whether by creeping and insidious and assiduous corrosion, or open, hastier combustion, as things might be, will efficaciously enough destroy completely past forms and replace them with, well, whatever. . . .
>
> Forms of what?
>
> I don't know. Society? Art?

Although the precise meaning of these observations remains somewhat opaque, Everett allows for both literal (read: political) and figurative (read: aesthetic) interpretations. Whether it is "society" or "art" that is under duress, the scenario being described is one in which "the world" is under threat from "negative thinkers" and "corrosion." The father's voice posits a strategy for resistance that is itself Menippean and justifies considering Everett's body of work as a larger whole: "For the time being, it is thought that when all our artistic and spiritual interests are at once dispossessed, the uncountable shapes to stories must be burned, but the better stories should be pasted together into one huge poem or graffiti for the defense of language only" (58).

If one defines satire predominantly as a genre with a collection of necessary structural/rhetorical elements—or "formal" and "functional" ones, as Kharpertian did in his incomplete move away from genre-based interpretation (33)—then determining what is or what is not satire is essentially reduced to a checklist or a set of rules. As Frye defined it, though, Menippean satire is a method of literary expression that is innately concerned with violating rigid rules, making it unlikely to be usefully defined by the very type of thing it routinely undermines. Everett's insistence that he does not "believe in genres" diminishes the value of analyzing his satirical impulses from a standpoint that insists on genre-based interpretation. However, his corollary assertion that "stories of stories and literary art transcend any notion of genre" (Cruden) leaves room for and perhaps even invites a modal definition.

The Renaissance scholar Paul Alpers has provided a useful definition of literary modes in his book *What Is Pastoral?* (1997): "Mode is the literary manifestation, in a given work, not of its attitudes in a loose sense, but of its assumptions about man's nature and situation. This definition in turn provides a critical question we implicitly put to any work we interpret: what notions of human strength, possibilities, pleasures, dilemmas, etc. are manifested in the represented realities and in the emphases, devices, organization, effects, etc. of this work?" (50). In *The Anatomy of Criticism* (1957), Frye described Menippean satire in modal terms, thus perceiving it, as Alpers has suggested, more as a philosophical relationship between the author and his/her text than as a series of explicit formal structures and conventions: "Menippean satire deals less with people as such than with mental attitudes. Pedants, bigots, cranks, parvenus, virtuosi, enthusiasts, rapacious and professional men of all kinds, are handled in terms of their occupational approach to life as distinct from their social behaviors. . . . The novelist sees evil and folly as social diseases, but the Menippean satirist sees them as diseases of the intellect, as a kind of maddened pedantry. . . . [Menippean satire] is not primarily concerned with the exploits of heroes, but relies on the free play of the intellectual fancy and the kind of humorous observation that produces caricature" (309–10). Frye's comments about the "free play of the intellectual fancy" coincide closely with Everett's insistence that "it's important to watch how ideas work and how they can be manipulated" as well as his preference for "stuff that challenges me and makes me think differently, that introduces me to things I didn't know before" (Shavers, "Percival" 48). Furthermore, Frye's remark that Menippean satire often "produces caricature" squares well with Marguerite Déon's observation that Everett consciously uses clichés in many of his works as he "disrupt[s] stereotypes or fixed ideas . . . [and] teases the reader by interfering with her reassuring reading habits" (1). Déon even explicitly identified Everett's recurrent use of characters who "go from one idea to another without the least coherence and apparently without the least care for their listeners" as "a form of Menippean satire, aimed at mocking . . . vacuity going by the name of knowledge" (4).

Frye later stated that the "Menippean satirist, dealing with intellectual themes and attitudes, shows his exuberance in intellectual ways, by piling up an enormous mass of erudition about his theme or in overwhelming his pedantic targets with an avalanche of their own jargon" (311). This is practically a word-for-word description of *Glyph,* applies just as directly to *Erasure* and *A History of the African-American People,* and applies more indirectly—and in less comic ways—to *The Water Cure* and *Percival Everett by Virgil Russell.* For example, *Glyph* contains a seven-page "appendix within the text" entitled "(Ralph's Theory of Fictive Space)" and consisting of seventy-eight hierarchically categorized and theory-heavy aphorisms seemingly intended to answer the question "Are Meanings in the Head?" (194), which is posed by the section-heading immediately preceding this gargantuan list. The list is bookended by a pair of fairly reductive statements: "A) What is is what is and all that is is all there is" (194) and "C) Nothing is a story but a story" (200); but the overwhelming effect of digesting the entire list is precisely that which Frye mentions above.

Similarly, an early passage in *Erasure* features "Monk" Ellison at a conference of the "*Nouveau Roman* Society" reading a paper that is a complex parody/adaptation of ideas taken from Roland Barthes. Two years before its inclusion in *Erasure,* Everett published in *Callaloo* a free-standing version of the piece that Monk reads; in its original context, Everett calls it a "piece of fiction, though it might easily be classified as a parody" ("F/V" 18), whereas within the novel its ontological status is still more ambiguous. Monk dismisses his audience as snobbish pseudointellectuals and claims that they have only a "semblance of credibility in the so-called real world" (*Erasure* 11) because they never leave the closed rhetorical confines of their own company. He is smugly convinced that they understand little of his presentation, but he seemingly ignores the concurrent facts that he barely cares about his own ideas and that the paper is, in many ways, intentionally written to be beyond understanding. Monk similarly intends his novel *My Pafology* to mock through parody what he considers to be pervasive and simplistic assumptions about authentic blackness among mainstream readers and publishers. That intention becomes hazy, though, once the book unexpectedly catapults Monk (pseudonymously) to fame and fortune, and his own thought process gradually becomes subject to Everett's satire as the text progresses, rather than serving as the seeming mouthpiece through which it is transmitted.

Some of Everett's earlier satires too contain such reflexive and intertextual Menippean satirical moments, even if the "jargon" being redirected and repurposed is less obscure than the literary theory parodied in *Glyph* and to a lesser extent in *Erasure.* For example, Curt Marder notes early in *God's Country* that he had "read what I could of the dime novels about the frontier, thinking it my duty as a citizen of it to make sure the truth be told, and generally the little books gave a fair account" (10). Everett later incorporates and repurposes wildly skewed versions of precisely the kinds of tropes and conventions one would expect to find in those same "dime novels." Marder's direct announcement of the manner in which these literary elements serve him as an intellectual foundation allows the reader to understand that their usage by Everett is meant as satirical refutation, rather than simple parodic simulation, of the "fair account" they represent in Marder's willfully ignorant, bigoted worldview. Marder and John Livesey from *Cutting Lisa* are both presented as characters whose "maddened pedantry" justifies their appalling actions. Each character outlines his ethical perspective at length and in detail, while the underlying structures of the narratives satirically undercut their convictions, although *God's Country* does so in a much more comic fashion than *Cutting Lisa* does.

The desire to "disrupt" and "shake up" ideas without substituting a new truth for the disrupted one departs from the better-known Horatian or Juvenalian conception of satire as a means of moral or ethical instruction. Dustin Griffin asserted that Menippean satire involves a pair of simultaneous rhetorics that are intended to destabilize existing notions of truth: "If the rhetoric of inquiry is 'positive,' an exploratory attempt to arrive at truth, the rhetoric of provocation is 'negative,' a critique of false understanding. In each case, the satirist raises questions; in provocation, the question is designed to expose or demolish a foolish certainty" (52). As Frye defined it, Menippean satire requires neither prescription nor solution for the ills it depicts; in any case, Everett would likely insist that "diseases of the intellect," such as those from which Monk Ellison, Curt Marder, and John Livesey suffer, are cured by new and more productive uses of one's intellect, rather than simply by following a different set of imposed rules.

Subversive and Degenerative Satire

Especially in his works published since the late 1990s, Everett's use of Menippean satire exemplifies a related quality that Steven Weisenburger named both "subversive" and "degenerative" in his *Fables of Subversion: Satire and the American Novel, 1930–1980* (1995). Weisenburger argued that the "purpose" of this predominantly postmodern variety of satire "is delegitimizing" and that it accomplishes this purpose by eschewing the usual "normative" role in order to "reflect suspiciously on all ways of making meaning, including its own" (*Fables* 3). Much of Everett's recent fiction includes characters who share his name, such as "some guy named Percival Everett" in *I Am Not Sidney Poitier,* who teaches a course at Morehouse on the "Philosophy of Nonsense" and decorates his office with pictures of Terry McMillan, James Joyce, and "the first Bozo the Clown" (87–88). This technique literalizes the innate "suspicion" that the real-life Everett has directed toward his putative authority to "make meaning" throughout his career: "Making fun of what I think and myself is often a way of creating a distance between my own concerns and petty grievances with the world, or desires in it, with the world I'm trying to create" (Champion 173). An exchange between the "father" and the "son" from *Percival Everett by Virgil Russell* that initially resembles a John Barth–like postmodernist joke takes on a more subversive philosophical intonation when considered in the light of Weisenburger's ideas:

Do you have a point here?
It's just a story.
But it's clearly not true.
And? (35)

That no answer to this question—like so many of the others posed in the novel—is forthcoming should not be surprising, given Everett's thorough refusal to suggest what is "true" to his readers.

The traits that Weisenburger ascribes to degenerative satire are consistent with the skeptical impulse Musgrave has identified in claiming that "it is in the fractured form of Menippean satire that the impossibility of a single world view, or the impossibility of an explain-all dogma is realized" (11). Weisenburger's analysis of the salient traits of "degenerative" satire further echoes Everett's claim not to "believe in any rules when it comes to fiction" (Champion 170) and his desire to go beyond "building straw men simply to knock them over" (Mills, Julien, and Tissut 221): "The common thread [is] the contemporary suspicion of *all* structures, including structures of perceiving, representing, and transforming. Narratives, especially, are among the most problematic of such structures, and satire becomes a mode for interrogating and counterterrorizing them. Yet postmodern satire is stuck with the very simulacra of the knowledge it so distrusts—stories. This is why the satirist often turns metafictionist and parodist, seeking out 'intramural' and self-referring ways of striking at the aesthetic rules hemming us in" (Weisenburger, *Fables* 5). Although Weisenburger did not specify any subversive intentions on Everett's part in his 1985 review of *Walk Me to the Distance,* he hinted at such an approach in his description of how that novel questions the conventional form that he refers to as "the Westwarding Story": "In its essentials that story always removes a man from the fractures of his Eastern biological family for him to discover—drop-forged between great skies and flat Western plains—a new nuclear family founded on honor, duty, and love. . . . This is a novel which wonders, paradoxically, if a [man] can be morally instructed by [such] a dead mythology. And if he can, what is it in the carcass that still nourishes? . . . [I]t's a remarkable question to ask" ("Out West" 489–90).

While responding to an interviewer's question about whether his books represent a correction of history, Everett expressed the reflexive suspicion of didacticism that Weisenburger has attributed to subversive satire generally: "I'm not correcting anything. That would mean I know enough to correct. I'm just a dumb writer" (Shavers, "Percival" 49). Moreover, when asked in a different interview whether he considers "artistic creation [to be] a form of gleeful self-sabotage," he replied in a manner consistent with the aims of both

Menippean and subversive satire: “Certainly if you consider disrupting all that you know about the world a kind of sabotage, yes. And I suppose in some ways that can be. If you're walking through life and you think you understand something, and you purposely take that away, then you feel sort of shaken up—your world view. And for some people that can be a sort of sabotage. For me, I consider that a necessary component of living” (Champion 171). The snake of his authorial intentions eats its own tail to such an extent that Everett even has suggested that he is “making fun of satire as well as satirizing social policies.” His sheepish confession “I shouldn't even say this, but I write about satire. . . . I'm exploiting the form” (Shavers, “Percival” 50) communicates the self-aware perspective that Weisenburger insisted is a prerequisite for subversive satire.

Stimulating his readers' intellect by first dismantling their operative assumptions is Everett's implicit task even when he is not writing satirically; however, the degree to which this intention moves powerfully to the forefront when he does produce satire imparts a distinctly Menippean and subversive/degenerative quality to the “one big novel” of his “overall project.” Although his definition of the word may differ somewhat from Weisenburger's, Everett has stated that “all of my novels are subversive and militant, but none is social protest” (Mills, Julien, and Tissut 223). He also has made it clear that his personal politics are not meant to be imparted to his readers, even in *The Water Cure,* which he has explicitly identified “as a protest novel”—and, lest he seem to contradict himself, Everett wrote *The Water Cure* after he made the previous comment. The modal and Menippean nature of his satire is attested to by his claims that “every work of art is necessarily political. Even if you try not to put politics in the work that's a political statement. Because it addresses one's relationship to the world.” His comments about the emotional underpinnings of his satire indicate its concurrent degenerative nature: “Anger is . . . not the same as outrage. You can experience outrage and see injustice, but as soon as you are swallowed by your anger, you stop thinking” (Bauer, “Percival Everett” 8). William Ramsey asserted that Everett's “personal anger finds mature outlet in the form of artistic sublimation” and, correspondingly, that his “trademark comedy—a grotesque humor, satire, surrealism, irrational character motivation, and the flouting of narrative conventions—is the creative sublimation of his rebellious impulses into a socially productive activity” (131). Rather than producing raging philippics or jeremiads that require readers to accept or to reject their “fixed norms or corrective goals” (Weisenburger, *Fables* 14), Everett wants to use his outrage as a general spur to thoughtful consideration of the realities he puts before his readers.

The manner in which other critics have used Menippean satire to analyze the work of writers similar to Everett serves as a framework for this study. In analyzing the work of the mid-twentieth-century Irish novelist Flann O'Brien—one of the pen names of Brian O'Nolan—M. Keith Booker noted, "Within the dialogic doubleness of Menippean satire, one can read O'Brien's work both as a consistent evocation of the theme of futility and as a parody of such evocations. This doubleness informs all of O'Brien's major works. . . . In particular, all of O'Brien's work is centrally concerned with explorations of the uses and social implications of language. O'Brien's comedy is not silly or gratuitous, but participates in important ways with important social, political, and cultural issues in his contemporary Ireland" (7). Though transposed from mid-century Ireland to (mostly) the contemporary United States, Everett's work parallels O'Brien's in using comedy for serious ends, whether artistic, linguistic, or sociopolitical: "Comedy in Everett's novels is grounded in seriousness and love of intellectual knowledge. In *Erasure,* he addresses issues such as the dumbing down of America, the fracturing of nuclear families, violence, racism, Nazism, and Alzheimer's. And always he plays with words, names, and fates" (Winther 185–86). Stewart has even linked O'Brien and Everett directly, claiming that both write "novels that teach literary-theoretical precepts and literary-theoretical texts that feature characters" ("Setting One's" 223).

Theodore Kharpertian similarly framed the work of Thomas Pynchon—a writer whose work Everett has frequently singled out for praise—in Menippean terms, writing that "Menippean satire is, by its contradictory and paradoxical nature, an open and flexible genre, one particularly congenial to Pynchon's radical brand of fictional experimentation, and if contradiction and paradox do indeed in some sense form the absent center of Pynchon's discourse as well, then the Bakhtinian dialogism of the Menippean form provides a productive field for Pynchon to, in one of his own characters' formulations, 'keep it bouncing'" (21).

Kharpertian's reference to Bakhtin, the other major theorist of contemporary Menippean satire, highlights the interrelated "dialogic" and "carnivalesque" aspects of that mode, which Booker summarized: "Menippean satire contains by its very nature a diverse collection of competing styles and voices . . . that is centrally informed by the energies that Bakhtin refers to as 'carnivalesque.' . . . The first and most fundamental characteristic of the carnival (and therefore of Menippean satire) is its ambivalence—different points of view, different worlds, may be mutually and simultaneously present without any privileging of one over the other, so that the different worlds can comment on each other in a dialogic way" (2). Julia Kristeva further clarified the way in which carnivalesque satire is intended to stimulate responses that transcend simple expectations: "The laughter of the carnival is not simply parodic; it is no more comic than tragic; it is both at once, one might say that it is *serious.* This is the only way that it can avoid becoming either the scene of law or the scene of its parody, in order to become the scene of its *other*" (50). Her words strongly echo Everett's contention that he, like Menippus, is "fairly earnest about" his satire: "there's a lot of irony in the fact that I take the things I'm talking about seriously" (Bolonik 98). Let us move on, then, to see what comes into clearer focus when one applies the critical lens laid out above to Everett's idiosyncratic brand of earnest jesting.

CHAPTER 3

Five Exemplary Menippean Satires

Although the argument in this book is that Everett's overarching authorial project is Menippean, there are individual works within that project that exemplify that satirical mode better than others. Closely examining some of the distinctive techniques with which Everett constructs the five novels featured in this chapter helps to frame the recurrence of those techniques in the other, less overtly Menippean works covered in the next two chapters. The larger intention in proceeding thus is to reveal the Menippean sensibility that underlies Everett's approach to writing, regardless of the degree to which any single book resembles the historical exemplars of that mode.

Carter Kaplan's *Critical Synoptics: Menippean Satire and the Analysis of Intellectual Mythology* offers insight concerning the allure of Menippean satire for Everett as a mode of expression. Everett has declared that "writing fiction is a beautiful, cleansing thing" precisely because the process of creating a novel unravels his beliefs about a subject rather than reinforcing them: "I think I know something about the world when I start a book. I'm pretty quickly disabused of that notion in the middle of it, and by the time I finish a book, I realize that a lot of what I thought I knew was wrong—and that I know very little. . . . I'm well on my way to knowing nothing at all, which is my goal" (Medlin and Gore 159). Everett seems willing, even eager, to reduce his own knowledge to a form of "intellectual mythology" subject to analysis and potential abandonment like any other. Kaplan echoed Everett closely when he claimed that "from the Menippean perspective, there is no formula, or theory that can explain the world or natural phenomena. Such mechanisms are products of folly, an exercise in affection perpetrated by those who impose some rigid subjective perception or *a priori* theory on the world and then bow down to it like an idol." Kaplan went on to claim that "Menippean satire is an artistic and scholarly practice which deflates the illusions that define and animate this perception of *mechanism* in nature" (52–53). This deflation, like Everett's goal of "knowing nothing at all," echoes an assertion made by Donald

Barthelme, another contemporary author with more than a passing interest in Wittgenstein and formal philosophy in general: "The not-knowing is crucial to art, is what permits art to be made. Without the scanning process engendered by not-knowing, without the possibility of having the mind move in unanticipated directions, there would be no invention" (Barthelme 12). Where Everett, Kaplan, and Menippean satire have all departed from Barthelme is when he stated that "writing is a process of dealing with not-knowing, a forcing of what and how," whose "aim . . . is finally to change the world" (12, 24). Whereas Barthelme saw artists being able to "imagine alternative realities, other possibilities" by which to "quarrel with the world, constructively" (24), Everett has stopped well short of suggesting that artistic invention's purpose is to play a part in reconstructing the world outside that invention.

Everett's affinity for Wittgenstein's philosophy as an analytical tool associates him even more strongly with Kaplan's views on Menippean satire, provided one accepts Kaplan's premise that "what Wittgenstein finally introduced as a replacement for philosophy shares astonishing conceptual and methodological similarities with the oldest and most trenchant form of literary/critical analysis: Menippean satire" (Kaplan 26). According to Kaplan, Wittgenstein believed that "the purpose of language is to *express* meaning, and careful analysis is required to prevent language itself from becoming a *source* of meaning" (Kaplan 30), a claim that corresponds with the way Everett rejects authorial control of meaning: "I think any time you step away from a novel or any work, you have to wonder, how is this functioning? How does this mean something in the world? It's a terrifying and beautiful idea that you can put together sounds and have them mean something to somebody, but when you release those sounds you can't control what they're going to mean to that somebody" (Medlin and Gore 154).

Kaplan identified synoptic analysis as the core concept of Wittgenstein's mature philosophy and aligned it with the essential traits of Menippean satire:

> In Wittgenstein's later thought, philosophy is not . . . a science. Philosophy "neither explains or deduces anything" . . . but "leaves everything as it is." . . . Philosophical problems are revealed to be nonsense, but not "beyond sense" or metaphysical—as Wittgenstein had conceived them to be in [his earlier work]. Philosophical theories are latent, concealed nonsense; the task of philosophy is to transform them into visible nonsense. . . . His technique of philosophical clarification is therapeutic in that it involves a rearrangement of familiar and unfamiliar contexts for the use of expressions that will make the grammar of the relevant expressions surveyable. . . . It is just this rearrangement of expressions, concepts, and propositions that

> one finds in Menippean satire. And, again, like Menippean satire, the final goal of synoptic analysis is the exposure of intellectual mythology. (28–29)

As an avowed fan of "nonsense that actually does make sense" (Bauer, "Percival Everett" 2), Everett has created characters who explicitly engage in Wittgensteinian synoptic analysis and/or parody thereof in *Glyph* (Ralph Townsend) and *The Water Cure* (Ishmael Kidder). Moreover he mentions Wittgenstein or has him speak as a character in dialogues in both *Erasure* and *Percival Everett by Virgil Russell*. Yet, as befits a thinker who remains skeptical of his own ideas, Everett does not use Wittgenstein's philosophy as any kind of infallible truth or suggest that it might be a pathway by which one might arrive at such a truth. In fact, it is Wittgenstein's self-contradictions that pique Everett's curiosity most: "Wittgenstein that is attractive to me is the part that comes back and refutes what he thought was the answer to raw philosophical questions. . . . But when you start reading the *Philosophical Investigations* . . . you think about both the limits and the limitlessness of language. He attempts to indict philosophers for failing to speak their own languages. And in so doing, commits the same failure" (Bauer, "Percival Everett" 6). Wittgenstein's philosophy is Everett's point of entry into a Menippean mind-set regarding the act of writing; he consistently directs that mind-set not just at a wide range of external subjects but also reflexively at Wittgenstein and at himself, thereby activating both the Menippean and the degenerative satirical modes.

Christian Schmidt has articulated the seeming paradoxes that such reflexivity creates in *Erasure* and *A History of the African-American People:* "by writing books about . . . the refusal to be classified as a black author, or yet again writing a history of the African American people, these novels make an ambivalent gesture: they ridicule and criticize reigning discourses of blackness and refuse to play along with them. Yet at the same time, they cannot but participate within these very discussions, albeit obliquely" (152–53). Everett acknowledges that he "commits the same failure" as Wittgenstein in needing to use language as his medium as a writer, but he also defers to language's primacy in a way that affirms Weisenburger's degenerative/subversive "suspicion of *all* structures, including structures of perceiving, representing, and transforming" (Weisenburger, *Fables* 5): "Language was certainly not invented, certainly not discovered. It was waiting to be discovered. And we manipulate it, we change it, we do all sorts of things to it, we add words to it, we take words from it but it's still language. Language creates religion, it refutes religion. It refutes itself. But in so doing, reaffirms itself. We cannot exist without it. It's responsible for our existence" (Bauer, "Percival Everett" 7). Having suggested *why* Everett can be read as a Menippean, this discussion turns to specific examples of *how* he can be read thus.

The Forms, Topics, and Devices of Menippean Satire

Weinbrot has characterized Menippean satire via two clusters of common traits, the first of which is formal, the second thematic: "We see copiousness, various mixtures of genres, languages, plots, periods, and places whether super- or subterrestrial. We also see finite and recurring topics: concern with dangerous, harmful, spreading views whether personal or public, whether by the individual human being who needs to learn not to fantasize about harmful heroism or beauty, the governor who needs to learn not to tyrannize, or the nation that needs to learn not to destroy its benevolent heritage" (5–6). *Glyph, Erasure,* and *A History of the African-American People* all feature shards of text from numerous literary and nonliterary genres embedded into their overarching novelistic narratives. In the case of *A History of the African-American People,* this narrative substrate must be inferred, as the book consists entirely of what appear on the surface to be letters, interoffice memos, publishing contracts, notes from business meetings, transcripts of conversations, and handwritten personal notes without any sort of conventional fictional framework binding them together.

Margaret Russett's contention that "the integrity of Everett's project consists in maintaining an unrelenting assault on constricting fictions of identity—be they racial, generic, authorial, or . . . even corporeal—while insisting on their real and unevenly distributed effects" (366) helps explain the presence of Weinbrot's "recurring [Menippean] topics" in these three books as well as in *God's Country* and *Grand Canyon, Inc.* All five novels feature characters whose fantasies of "harmful heroism or beauty" are grounded in "constricting fictions of identity." For example, Curt Marder of *God's Country* believes in his own righteousness throughout the book, even though his sole response to bandits burning down his house, abducting his wife, and killing his dog on the novel's opening page is to ride his horse to the top of a nearby hill and watch. Marder's feeble insistence that "[it's] not like I didn't do anything. I did pull my gun out of its holster and stand my ground" (3) undercuts not only his later claims of moral superiority to Bubba, the black tracker he rather grudgingly hires to recover his wife, but also the "code of the frontier" (27) by which he repeatedly professes to live. Similarly, Rhino Tanner intends to lay "claim to a testament to the American Spirit" in *Grand Canyon, Inc.* by transforming one of the nation's most iconic natural locales into an amusement park called "Tanner's Grand Canyon." However, the book's narrative constantly emphasizes the underlying ignorance—"in the famous words of Jesus, 'Live like there is no tomorrow'"—and/or outright fraudulence in Tanner's claims to represent "the *real* American Dream" (113) as well as the notion that such an authentic American identity exists in the first place. Aspects of Tanner's characterization are remarkably prescient of Donald Trump's self-presentation—particularly his nonstop invocation of the "Make America Great Again" slogan during and after the 2016 presidential campaign. It is not entirely impossible that Everett may have had the Trump of the late 1990s in mind when he wrote the novel, but it seems far more likely that Everett recognizes that the various grotesque rhetorics that Tanner employs are readily available and intimately familiar to a distinctly American brand of oligarchic demagogue that has recurred throughout the nation's history.

Dustin Griffin added the element of playfulness to Weinbrot's formal and thematic classification, contending that Menippean satire engages in a form of rhetorical experimentation "in which the point is not to arrive at a conclusion but to let ideas of high principle and worldly accommodation, community good and individual good, liberty and equality jostle against each other in an open and free-wheeling contest" (87). Everett has frequently articulated his ludic outlook on life and on writing: "Well I like to play. And I find the world and the work amusing" (Champion 168). Menippean satire offers a "serious" outlet for such play, making it especially alluring for a writer who, like Everett, is interested in arousing thinking in his audience rather than in pleasantly distracting them. Monk Ellison's attempts at satirical subversion in *Erasure* ultimately fail largely because his efforts lack such a seriously playful element (as is explained in greater detail below). Similarly, Everett implies the value of play in *Glyph* via the apparent preference for Ralph's inherently childish—inasmuch as it comes from a child, albeit a child with an otherworldly intellect—thought process over those of the novel's adult characters. Feith discussed a physical manifestation of this contrast as stemming from the relative freedom of Ralph's play, compared to the morally constrained attitude of his father: "Due to his very young age, Ralph is not described as a fully sexualized being. Yet he plays with his 'willy' with delight, to his prudish father's dismay. . . . If not amoral, his vision of the body is mostly positive, untainted by guilt or social morality" ("Hire-a-Glyph" 306). Everett seems to suggest that Ralph's play with himself—whether physical or intellectual—is ultimately more useful than his philandering, and thus hypocritically "prudish," father's mental masturbation in the form of poststructuralist literary theory.

Weinbrot expanded his initial classification by adding that Menippean satire "may use or combine any of four cognate devices," each of which is determined by the manner through which the satirical mode enters and/or deforms the text:

> [1] Menippean satire by addition enlarges a main text with new generally smaller texts that further characterize a dangerous world. [2] Menippean

satire by genre sets a work against its own approximate genre . . . and either comments on it or uses it as a backdrop to suggest its own subject's danger to the world. [3] Menippean satire by annotation uses the sub- or side-text further to darken the already dark text. [4] Menippean satire by incursion is a brief guerilla attack that emphasizes the danger in the text and then departs. These devices may work together at various times, though one is more likely to be pronounced than the others." (6–7)

Initially giving the reader what looks like a conventional "yellow-back" Western in *God's Country,* Everett gradually "cultivates doubts about the glorious epic of the West" (Bonnemère 157) by using both the second and fourth of Weinbrot's devices to reveal "how deceptive appearances are. First in the literal sense, when Jake, the young boy who accompanies Curt and Bubba in their quest turns out to be a girl, then with Colonel Custer's unexpected cross-dressing. But it is also to be experienced in the figurative sense: one can not say to what genre Everett's books belong" (Déon 5). As Leland Krauth noted, Everett does not wait long to begin his degenerative satirical process: "The first sentence of the novel evokes the traditional Western; the second subverts it." Marder's self-conception as "the very heart of the Western, the dauntless hero of courage and skill, dwindles in a flash to a stick figure of fear and feckless resolve" (315). Krauth marveled at "how many formulaic elements of the traditional Western Everett packs into" the novel, especially since "each episode exaggerates, inverts, or twists its prototype" (316) to produce a Menippean commentary on Marder's ignorant and yet wholly conventional—in both the literary and sociopolitical senses—views on "what this country's all about" (Everett, *God's* 23).

Grand Canyon, Inc. combines devices 3 and 4 in the form of the explanatory observations made by Simpson "BB" Trane, Tanner's "lifelong sidekick and aide" (12), as well as the (initially third-person, later first-person) narrator of the book. BB's nickname comes from being intentionally shot in the forehead—"at ten feet [and] after hundreds of BB's" (16)—by Tanner when both were still boys, and he has spent much of his life willingly "playing a fat Tonto to Tanner's maniacal Lone Ranger" (12). BB ultimately has little ability to mitigate Tanner's destructive plans; in revealing himself as the book's narrator after twelve chapters, he echoes Dionysos's "mortal bookmark" Vlepo in *Frenzy:* "What I did get to do while Rhino Tanner killed everything in sight was read, read and watch, read and watch and wonder" (84). However, BB's incursions into the narrative serve indirectly as Menippean "annotations" that demythologize Tanner's bombastic proclamations about how things are and how they should be. BB performs this function long before the reader knows who he is or that he is the teller of the tale being read. For example, the opening paragraph of the book lists all of Tanner's exalted and hyperpatriotic claims of having been a "Navy Seal, a former Army Ranger, a member of the Delta Force, an on-call DEA agent, a special agent for the President of the United States, and the best rifle shot on the planet." Immediately thereafter the narrator's voice coolly debunks these frauds: "Of all the things he claimed, only the part about being a good rifle shot was true at all" (3). As Sylvie Bauer has noted, this gesture establishes BB as the satirical counterpoint to Tanner, the voice who will present the "unheroic version" of Tanner's fabricated self-conception even as the rest of American culture venerates him: "A process of deflation is at work . . . as if to insist on the gap between saying and being: the more Tanner says, the less it corresponds to reality" ("Percival Everett's *Grand Canyon Inc.*" 262).

On the surface *Glyph* is heavily dependent on Weinbrot's third device; the entire book is a series of "all-invading digressions" away from the central story line of Ralph's "successive abductions by an array of mad scientists, Army secret service officers, childless Mexican immigrants, and paedophiliac priests" (Feith, "Hire-a-Glyph" 302). Michel Feith observed that this core plot "reads like a pastiche of popular literature and TV series," whereas the digressions from it "amount . . . to an ambiguous deconstruction of the poststructuralist vulgate, mostly represented here by Barthes and the 'Great Unreadables,' Lacan and Derrida." The other three devices from Weinbrot's list are suggested by Feith's claim about the seemingly "hermetic"—that is, reminiscent of the occult texts attributed to the quasi-divine figure of Hermes Trismegistus in ancient Greece and Rome—nature of *Glyph:* "the novel comprises an accessible, 'exoteric' face—the story—and an 'esoteric' one, in which postmodern Academese has replaced mystical allegory. The text can therefore be defined in part as a parodic philosophical novel, revolving around the themes of language and fiction" (Feith, "Hire-a-Glyph" 302). Judith Roof likewise has seen the novel in terms of coexisting—though possibly paradoxical—pairs of textual impulses: "The anatomical poetry, the critical terms of art serving as subtitles, the puns . . . , the linguistic diagrams, the mathematical equations, and the commentary snatched from the broad terrain of Ralphie's reading simultaneously cohere as narrative and as disparate commentary on the possibilities of signification, exploding outward to show the assumptions underlying any investment in coherence, narrative, or meaning" ("Everett's Hypernarrator" 210). Whether viewed as a parody of pseudomystical academic prose (device 2) or as a patchwork (device 1) metanarrative (device 4) intended to "destabilize any possibility of linearity, continuity, predictable cause/effect relationships, and correlations of signification" (Roof, "Everett's Hypernarrator" 203), *Glyph* corresponds to the contention that "the Menippean satirist from Rabelais to

Burton to Swift and Sterne does not simply collect shining bits of obscure learning; he mock-pompously shows them off. Scholarship becomes spectacle" (D. Griffin 74).

Erasure incorporates each of Weinbrot's four devices in a similarly "spectac[ular]" fashion in order to "deconstruct . . . the form of the novel. . . . Everett's presentation of his book as a multi-genre piece of literature illustrates the limitations of current genres to express his narrative" (Eaton 223). *Glyph* remains somewhat ambiguous about whether Ralph's hyperintelligent discussions of critical theory mark him as one of the targets of Everett's satire or as the vehicle thereof. In *Erasure,* though, there is a clear contrast between Everett's awareness of satire's limitations and Monk's lack thereof in attempting to use *My Pafology* to chastise ignorant readers of various kinds. As a result, the text's pomposity is attributable only to—and therefore mockable only in—the latter, not the former. Gillian Johns has written that *Erasure* "as a whole encloses a plurality of discourses that imply metacommentary on its embedded stories, satire and parody, and (mis)readings" (89). For example, the essay "F/V: Placing the Experimental Novel" functions as Weinbrot's second device, "satire by genre," in its initial publication under Everett's name in *Callaloo;* however, this display of mock-erudition takes on the functions of the first and third devices—"satire by addition" and "satire by annotation"—when embedded within *Erasure,* a book whose opening page suggests that it is Monk's "journal," a therefore supposedly "private affair" (1).

It is perhaps significant that Monk immediately follows this claim with an expression of anxiety concerning the fact that his journal will likely be read only after his demise: "As I cannot know the time of my coming death, and since I am not disposed, however unfortunately, to the serious consideration of self-termination, I am afraid that others will see these pages." He tries to demur, claiming that "since however I will be dead, it should not much matter to me who sees what or when," but his attempts at playing it cool are unconvincing, since his next three sentences make it abundantly clear how much he is unlike Everett in believing that the author has an integral part to play in controlling the reaction to his work: "My name is Thelonious Ellison. And I am a writer of fiction. This admission pains me only at the thought of my story being found and read, as I have always been severely put off by any story which had as its main character a writer" (Everett, *Erasure* 1). Having written several such stories, Everett is obviously not "put off" in the same way, but a more salient point is that it would not matter to him if he were, at least not in terms of the reaction it would instill in those who "found and read" the manuscript. Unlike Everett, Monk is intensely aware of having an audience and finds the thought of being a "dead" author loathsome, whether that death is literal or figurative. Monk's manic desire to manipulate the public reaction to his writing is what starts him down the path to the trouble in which he finds himself at the book's end. Like Barthes, Everett sees "serious consideration of self-termination" as a desirable and possibly even necessary condition for an author, so Monk's inconsistency in this opening paragraph is a Chekhovian "pistol" that will go off repeatedly as the book unfolds.

The novel's structure forces the reader to interpret the same set of words simultaneously as the products of different people, leading to a greater multiplicity of overlapping realities in Everett's text than in his protagonist/narrator's version: "If *Erasure*'s approach to satiric critique is complex and layered, *My Pafology* is a prime example of Juvenalian satire" (Fett 180). Johns extended this distinction in claiming that "Everett's satire reaches for more than a critique of such stories on their own terms; it bitingly extends to readers (and, moreover, writers like Monk) who would compartmentalize them and believe themselves above suspicion regarding their invention, display, and consumption" (91). *My Pafology* is, of course, an inextricable part of the "complex and layered" (read: Menippean) satire that Everett wrote in *Erasure,* but Monk does not share his creator's satirical subtlety, leading Johns to remind readers "that it is Monk's (not Everett's) work that wins the prize [within the novel], and Monk's novella comprises only 70 pages of the otherwise 265-page, first-person autotext that Monk presents—and that we read—as his diary" (89). Danielle Fuentes Morgan added that *My Pafology*'s multiple meanings arise from the differing relationships between its authors and audiences: "The absurdity apparent to the audience of *Erasure* is not enough, because it does not resonate with the relatively unsophisticated [fictional] readers of *My Pafology.* Although *My Pafology* written by Thelonious 'Monk' Ellison could be coded as satire, the same text written by Stagg R. Leigh is at best unclear" (Morgan 170). She noted that this lack of clarity—and the willingness to capitalize on its ostensibly unintended consequences—is ultimately what makes Monk a part of Everett's satirical scope: "Although readers are guilty for so eagerly devouring Stagg's tale, Monk is even more culpable for writing a supposed satire containing no satirical markers" (167).

Johns's and Morgan's readings contradict (rightly, in my view) the impression with which Houston Baker and numerous other readers have been left, which is that Everett intends Monk to be perceived as possessing "redoubtable talents as a satirist" that make him "a lampooner of the first order" (Baker 136). He is certainly the latter, as *My Pafology* is a nearly letter-perfect parody of the various real (*Native Son*) and fictional (*We's Lives in Da Ghetto*) intertexts that both Everett and Monk intend to mock. Only Everett, though, is successful in conveying his satire to his audience, a point that Baker missed entirely when he insisted that Monk "is intended to be a sympathetic character" (136) or claimed that "Percival Everett and his engaging protagonist" act in lockstep as "they drive us back through a genealogy and critical history of influence and reception" (145). Baker ultimately found *Erasure* "deeply problematic" (145) and spent the bulk of his essay on Everett in *I Don't Hate the South* (2007) taking the novel to task for what he saw as its shortcomings as a work of African American fiction. Perhaps in direct response to this uncharitable assessment, Everett included a thinly veiled version of Baker in *Percival Everett by Virgil Russell*. In that novel a "hack academic" named "Housetown Pastrychef or Dallas Roaster, something like that" is mocked in passing for his theory that "race was not only a valid category but a necessary one," a position with which Everett assuredly does not agree. When the academic, now called "Austin Cooker," and the narrator's friend "nearly [come] to blows," the latter dismisses him with stinging irony: "This nigger believes in race as a valid category." The narrator claims—perhaps facetiously—not to comprehend this insult fully, but he adds a subversively Menippean aphorism that punctuates Everett's satire: "language's function is not to inform but to provoke" (34).

The multiple layers of textual reality that develop throughout *Erasure* confuse all notions of identity and concurrent authority to the extent that even its narrator seems in danger of losing the ability to tell them apart: "Thelonious and Monk and Stagg Leigh made the trip to New York together, on the same flight, and, sadly, in the same seat. I considered that this charade might well turn out of hand and that I would slip into an actual condition of dual personalities" (237–38). Despite Monk's reassurance that he is only "acting, simple and plain" (238), the novel's conclusion—in which Monk unconsciously reenacts the closing scene of *My Pafology* while quoting its final line nearly verbatim—conflates Monk once again with Stagg Leigh. It also further blurs the lines separating those two personalities from each other and from Monk's protagonist, Van Go Jenkins, himself a grotesque parody of Bigger Thomas from Richard Wright's *Native Son* (1940). Morgan noted that this confusion is attributable to Monk's acquiescence to and assimilation by the forces he intended to deride in writing *My Pafology:* "Everett is satirizing both mainstream American culture and the African American literary communities that allow these negative performances to stand in for blackness" (165). Lacking Everett's understanding that "anger is for suckers" (Bauer, "Percival Everett" 8), Monk allows his "very personal anger [to] overwhelm . . . his text, and consequently he lacks the critical stance necessary for a full evaluation of race in American society" (Morgan 165). In the absence of a multifaceted and self-critical Menippean thought process, Monk is doomed to fail: "His novella becomes impotent as he furthers the Stagg R. Leigh charade. . . . Monk is far too cavalier about any ramifications of his portrayal. If his racialized frustrations stem from mainstream willingness to accept the basest stereotypes of blackness, Monk is only embracing them rather than agitating against them" (165).

The authorial doppelgängers quickly multiply out of Monk's control in *Erasure,* but Everett adds even more layers of textual and extratextual confusion in *A History of the African-American People.* In this novel he has created a character who not only resembles him abstractly but also shares his job, his colleagues, and his name. The intentional bewilderment of the reader begins with the full title of *A History of the African-American People (Proposed) by Strom Thurmond, as Told to Percival Everett and James Kincaid,* which is as notable for its verbosity as for the bizarre and unlikely intellectual product it describes. Add in the oddity of two literature professors, one of whom is African American, serving as the infamous senator's amanuenses and the fact that the words "a novel" appear in brackets on the book's front cover (albeit in a smaller font than any of the other words), and the reader may be readily forgiven for lacking clear expectations upon opening the book.

Before arriving at the novel's first page, though, the already puzzled reader still has to contend with a farcical list of blurbs supposedly written by Abraham Lincoln ("I knew Strom and I didn't think he had this in him"), William Howard Taft, Clarence Thomas ("Finally, a voice that speaks the true black experience!"), William Bennett, and John Ashcroft. Even then the satirical metatext that frames the novel is not yet complete. The reader next encounters a tongue-in-cheek disclaimer on the copyright page (a device Everett revisits in several other books) emphasizing that even though "*there are many references to actual people, all of our interactions with those people (and the fictitious ones as well) are, in fact, fictitious.*" Although the impossibility of the real-life Everett and Kincaid having any interactions with fictitious characters should be fairly self-evident, the disclaimer reminds the reader that the versions of Everett and Kincaid—that is, the authors of the ostensible work of nonfiction that appears within this work of fiction—are fictitious and should not be mistaken for the Everett and Kincaid who are the authors of the novel the reader is holding. The disclaimer concludes with an intentionally insincere apology: "*If any of the matter of this novel should be found offensive by anyone, we understand (if not completely) and suggest you find another book to read. We wish we could say that we mean no disrespect.*" The book's Menippean degeneration has already begun before the start of what appears to be its actual text; the incongruities of the title hint at each of the first three devices from Weinbrot's list, and the disclaimer functions explicitly as a preemptive satire by incursion, directed at anyone foolish enough to have taken the title at face value—as *My Pafology*'s uncritically worshipful audience might do.

Having finally arrived at the novel's first page, the reader sees what appears to be a chatty personal memorandum to Thurmond from Barton Wilkes—identified indistinctly as "Assistant to Aide" (7)—in which Wilkes obliquely suggests that the senator take advantage of his "peculiar place in history" and consider the "production of a possible mode of transport" along "the route we have traveled to arrive" at "the new diversity" of contemporary America (7). Wilkes's circumlocutions never specify that this is the history book presaged in the title, but the reader is certainly inclined to cling to that conclusion in the wake of all the mis- and disinformation presented thus far. Dated two days after the initial memo, a three-line, handwritten note from "Strom" follows, and it indicates that his mind is failing him: "Come to think of it, I did play Mother May I. That's been a while. Who are you? What?" (8). Without any intervening or corroborating correspondence, the next letter is on Thurmond's official letterhead and consists of a blunt, half-page proposal by Wilkes—now identified as "Junior Advisor, Public Relations"—to the Simon & Schuster publishing house for a book called "A History of the African-American People by Strom Thurmond" (9). Wilkes faux-modestly denies that he "[has] been entirely uninstrumental in persuading [Thurmond] to undertake the project in its present form" (9) and insists that the senator wishes to have "no honorific titles" appended to his name in the title. The preceding two pieces of correspondence indicate not only the distortions inherent in Wilkes's self-effacing language but also that the project has no "present form" at all, except as a notion in Wilkes's mind.

The remainder of the book plays out an elaborate and increasingly absurd web of communication—public and private—primarily among Wilkes; Martin Snell, an editor at Simon & Schuster; R. Juniper McCloud, Snell's assistant; Juniper's sister Reba; and the professorial/authorial duo of Everett and Kincaid, who are approached by Wilkes to ghostwrite the manuscript that Thurmond is obviously incapable of producing himself, at least in a form that would be acceptable to the publishers. In fact, until halfway through the book, Thurmond seems only nebulously aware of the project attributed to him by Wilkes—or of Wilkes, for that matter. Thurmond's signature on the book contract—"For Cindy, With Love, Strom" (47)—suggests that Wilkes either forged his signature by copying it from an autograph or duped Thurmond into signing the contract. Thurmond's first unmistakably direct involvement with the project occurs eight pages before the novel's end, when he handwrites a note to Everett and Kincaid indicating that "it strikes my old pate that we should be getting this book done" and invites his two ghostwriters to join him for a working lunch (303). Thurmond's voice is thus comparatively absent from the book whose cover suggests that he is the (proposed) author. Kincaid noted in an interview about the novel that Thurmond "withered away to almost nothing[,] . . . more or less" as the book moved away from mocking him and "turned to issues of writing, authenticity, biography, character, and horsing around" ("Collaborating" 370). The project eventually falls apart—partly because Thurmond apparently dies while doing a headstand during his lunch meeting with Everett and Kincaid—leaving the reader to sort out the confusion arising from the fact that the real-life Percival Everett and James Kincaid finished and published a novel whose name is similar to the work of ostensible nonfiction that their fictitious counterparts within that novel ultimately abandon and leave unpublished.

Schmidt claimed that the novel represents "the perfect example [of] what Weisenburger means by degenerative satire [because] it . . . produces its own dissolution and dismantlement" (159). The novel *A History of the African-American People (Proposed) by Strom Thurmond, as Told to Percival Everett and James Kincaid* satirically frames the unfinished concept of "A History of the African-American People by Strom Thurmond"—which Thurmond retitles "*A History of the Colored People by Senator Strom Thurmond, America's Oldest Living Lawmaker*" (306) late in the book. Unlike *My Pafology,* which exists as a text-within-a-text inside *Erasure,* Thurmond's would-be history book does not appear within the novel except as a few fragments of dubious research provided by Wilkes and a five-page introduction, grudgingly produced by the fictional versions of Everett and Kincaid and rejected via a brief form letter from Simon & Schuster on the final page of the novel. *A History of the African-American People* basically tells the story of why "A History of the African-American People by Strom Thurmond" does not exist. Schmidt suggested that the novel's satire is entirely reflexive: "all along [it] has been a satirical subversion of questions of authorial identity, the defining qualities of a 'black' text, and whether only African Americans have the authority to write a history of their people. The satire of Everett's epistolary novel thus targets neither Strom Thurmond nor any other real extra-textual entity" (159).

Schmidt furthermore observed that the novel is quintessentially Menippean in posing, but not answering, the question of whether Thurmond is able (and/or suitable) to author a work of African American history, given both his race and his personal history: "Barton Wilkes asks the tandem of ghostwriters to show that Thurmond 'is, properly understood, a black writer.' . . . And while this is an outrageous thing to say about the notoriously bigoted Thurmond, it raises an important question about this degenerative satire: namely, what is a black writer, and what makes—by extension—a black text? . . . By complicating the levels of narration and narrative transmission, this satire dissimulates blackness and the question of black authorship in a text that consists of nothing but masquerades" (Schmidt 159–60). Thurmond asserts his notion of the value of black authorship in stating that Everett being "colored" is "a good thing, for my book anyway" (306); unsurprisingly, his perspective expresses the kind of "constricting fiction of identity" that Monk resents in *Erasure*. Nevertheless, given that Everett disavows Monk's obligation to write in a particular manner that others ascribe to blackness, he would not disqualify Thurmond from writing a history of the African American people simply for being white. Both the fictional Everett and his real-life analogue are unambiguous in their belief that Thurmond is essentially "nuts" (309), but *A History of the African-American People* questions whether Thurmond's proposed book would be rejected or accepted by publishers and audiences based on its reprehensible and demonstrably flawed ideas or on the "properly understood"—that is, manipulated and fictitious—racial presumptions concerning its ostensible author and/or any of the others involved in the "masquerades" to which Schmidt referred.

Formal Multiplicity

Many critics have noted that Menippean satire is distinct for its multiplicity. Most often this multiplicity has been described in formal terms, as in Frye's observation that Menippean "exuberance" is expressed "by piling up an enormous mass of erudition" to the point of creating an "encyclopedic farrago" (11). Weinbrot similarly noted the "various mixtures of genres, languages, plots, periods, and places" (5) inherent to the mode. Eugene P. Kirk echoed this, calling it "a medley—usually a medley of alternating prose and verse, sometimes a jumble of flagrantly digressive narrative, or again a potpourri of tales, songs, dialogues, orations, letters, lists, and other brief forms, mixed together" (xi). Joel Relihan elaborated on Menippean multiplicity's disruptive purpose, arguing that its "indecorous mixture of disparate elements, of forms, styles, and themes that exist uneasily side by side" preclude the reader's "coherent intellectual, moral, or aesthetic appreciation" (34).

Although Bakhtin too mentioned formal diversity, he revealed a more rhetorical brand of Menippean multiplicity: "the entire world and everything sacred in it is offered to us without any distance at all" through "unfettered and fantastic plots and situations [that] all serve one goal—to put to the test and to expose ideas and ideologues. These are experimental and provocative plots . . . full of parodies and travesties, multi-styled[, that] can expand into a huge picture" (26). For Bakhtin, this "huge picture" is directly due to Menippean satire's exploitation of what he termed the heteroglossic nature of language: "it represents the co-existence of socio-ideological contradictions between the present and the past, between differing epochs of the past, between different socio-ideological groups in the present, between tendencies, schools, circles and so forth" (291). Satire foregrounds this heteroglossia through the related technique of polyphony: "[Polyphony] serves two speakers at the same time and expresses simultaneously two different intentions: the direct intention of the character who is speaking, and the refracted intention of the author. In such discourse there are two voices, two meanings, and two expressions" (324). Polyphony is not necessarily satirical. For example, a scene in which a character repeats a phrase spoken by another character earlier could indicate homage, rather than mockery, even though the reader is meant to hear and to feel the "echo" of the previous utterance—that is, the phrase's implications in its original context—when the second character speaks the same line. When used satirically, however, the implicit authorial "voice" is intended not just to augment but also to undermine the voice on the surface of the text.

Each of the novels discussed so far in this chapter is polyphonic. In the case of *God's Country* and *Grand Canyon, Inc.,* Everett largely limits himself to only two levels of simultaneous "voicing" in dismantling a pair of toxic American cultural narratives: the "frontier myth" and the "self-made man" (see chapter 5 for additional discussion). Bubba is revealed to be the "one moral hero . . . endowed with a sense of justice and honor" (Déon 5) in *God's Country* partly because "Curt [Marder]'s naivety and stupidity are pitted against Bubba's common sense and human qualities" (Bonnemère 156). Marder's first-person narration unwittingly reveals how much of his "naivety and stupidity" result from internalizing and then uncritically repeating the dominant—and corrupt—cultural "voices" of his time. These include the "dime novels about the frontier" that Marder insists "give a fair account" (Everett, *God's* 10) of the world, as well as other traditional sources of morality: "I'd learned my frontier Christian lessons well—lie, steal, cheat, and, when all that failed, pray" (92). Marder's folly is satirized, but so is the racist cultural discourse that allows him to valorize himself even as his words and actions betray a much baser character. As Krauth noted, Marder's "attitudes are also those of all the whites in the novel . . . [and] Everett creates the unsettling interior experience of race hatred" by putting "his readers in the skin of a white racist, forcing them to hear and feel the self-vaunting pride and belittling prejudice of a white supremacist" (319). Krauth also argued that the novel "does something more than laugh at a seemingly exhausted genre" in emphasizing "the gulf between Marder and the other races around him: between his fear and their bravery, between his incompetence and their skill, and between his depravity and their goodness" (319). Krauth claimed that Everett also "recovers" to some extent the genre of the Western by undoing two of its most glaring historical omissions; in the book he depicts Native American and African American characters whose unmistakable virtues—even heroism, in Bubba's case—contradict the exclusion of those groups from the frontier's mythology except in hostile or subservient roles. In the end, "Everett's parody of the Western cheerfully demolishes its most cherished features" (321).

In *Grand Canyon, Inc.,* BB Trane embodies the authorial-satirical "voice" that remains implicit in *God's Country.* Bauer noted that Rhino Tanner's worldview—and hence the language through which he expresses it—is inherently *not* polyphonic but rather a self-centered, circular monologism: "His language implies a total coincidence between what he says and reality. His sense of reality is founded on an equation between language and facts that thus confers a performative power to language. It seems as though telling stories makes them true. . . . He invents stories throughout and invents a reality that suits him, indifferent to the world around him" ("Percival Everett's *Grand Canyon Inc.*" 260–61). In chapter 13, as BB first reveals himself as "your narrator . . . and not some disembodied entity" (83), he suggests that the ball bearing that Rhino lodged in his forehead years ago has given him a kind of polyphonic ability: "I mention the BB only because it is my defining and certainly my most special feature. The hole in my head works as a kind of third eye. . . . Imagine that I am pushing the needle into my hole, extracting it, and wiping it on the paper" (85). This oracular perspective invalidates the notion that BB's narrative stands in simple contradiction to Rhino's version of the truth. The "vision" provided by a "third eye" in Buddhism, after all, is mystical, not personal, and so when BB suggests that "sometimes . . . the BB in my head rolls into a truth," it gives greater weight to his assertion that "what happens at the end of this story is more than poetic justice; it is real justice" (85–86). Even at the moment when a massive wave—the Colorado River, freed from the dam that has constrained it—is rushing down the canyon to kill him, Tanner tries to suggest that his own desires are entirely consistent with God's: "He shouted something unintelligible at the water, then attributed the words to Jesus" (126). BB's narration is presented as less nominally divine but considerably more transcendent: "As a seer and a story-teller, [BB] is the character with the fullest apprehension of reality because he stands as a mere observer, a watcher, as he says at one point, thus refusing to translate the real into something else. He just absorbs it, in this way stressing the stillness of his position as opposed to the circulation of the world around and inside him" (Bauer, "Percival Everett's *Grand Canyon Inc.*" 266).

Both *God's Country* and *Grand Canyon, Inc.* present the reader with two "voices" and suggest a preference for the one that sides, respectively, with Bubba and BB—the similarity of their nicknames may not be entirely coincidental—over the hypocritical and self-aggrandizing voices of Curt Marder and Rhino Tanner. Importantly, though, neither Bubba nor BB offers a prescriptive truth of his own to replace the ones they deride, least of all a simple negation via diametrical opposition; they instead demonstrate the interrelated value of open-mindedness and careful observation as means to gaining understanding. The Menippean dimension of these texts arises less from their relatively mild structural polyphony than from both texts' satirical depiction of protagonists who are essentially mouthpieces for broader cultural voices: the "frontier myth" that provides Marder with his violently ignorant notion of "what this country's all about" (23) in *God's Country;* and Rhino's sense of "the *real* American Dream" (113) in *Grand Canyon, Inc.* As such, these two books are more akin to classical Menippean satires in discrediting a particular philosopher—regardless of how poorly that title fits either Marder or Tanner—as well as his philosophy. As Yves Bonnemère wrote, Everett "provokes laughter mixed with scorn for the would-be hero and the West he is made to represent" (157).

Linguistic and Philosophical Multiplicity

Glyph, Erasure, and *A History of the African-American People* all playfully experiment with form and narrative to a much greater degree, bringing many more "voices" into their polyphonic mix and thereby inhabiting even more fully capacious dimensions of contemporary Menippean satire. David Musgrave's catalog of the different manifestations of Menippean satire's "radically heterogeneous form" (22) diagnostically supports the assertion that these three novels are Everett's most representative Menippean satires. Musgrave has listed seven structural and/or rhetorical "features[, not all of which] will be present at all times in every Menippean satire" but which are distinctive enough to lead him to the conclusion that "if it looks like a Menippean satire, then it probably is" (23). The first feature is "structural heterogeneity," essentially the same jumble of genre conventions that Frye, Kirk, Weinbrot, and Relihan have observed: "Traditionally, this was seen as the admixture of prose and poetry, but essentially it can mean the insertion or mixture of different literary genres, such as letters, diary entries, scholarly apparatus such as footnotes, or a profusion of prolegomena, prefaces, and other textual apparatus or the use of different typographical forms" (22). Having discussed this feature at length earlier in this chapter, there is no need to rehash it here.

Whereas the first feature in Musgrave's schema emphasizes the formal variety of Menippean texts, three other features work together to encapsulate its linguistic and philosophical variety; these will be discussed not in the order in which he presents them but in terms of how they correlate to one another. His second feature is called "stylistic heterogeneity," which involves both the "frequent use of different languages" and the "frequent use of portmanteau words, neologisms, jargon, slang, and obscurantism" within those languages (22). The sixth feature is "encyclopedism," a totalizing worldview marked by the use of "lists, anatomies, parodies of entire world views or ideologies of belief-systems." Musgrave has stated that, in general, "the possibility of the successful encyclopedic view is ridiculed or parodied," usually by suggesting the "impossibility of systematic understanding or explanation of the world, through any of several major discourses, such as the political ([Salman Rushdie's] *Midnight's Children*), religious ([Jonathan Swift's] *A Tale of a Tub*), philosophical or sentimental (*Tristram Shandy*), or ideological ([Thomas Pynchon's] *Gravity's Rainbow*)" (23). Musgrave's seventh feature suggests the recurrent rhetorical practices of Menippean satire: "digression, lists, catachresis (or the deliberate misuse of metaphor) and enthymeme [a form of reasoning that, often problematically, omits one or more of its essential premises]" (23) These techniques all contribute to the sense of performative "spectacle" in *Glyph, Erasure,* and *A History of the African-American People.* As unconventional uses of language that call attention to themselves, they present the reader with additional interpretive difficulties beyond those of the conventional novel.

Glyph is clearly the most stylistically diverse of the three, as a quick survey of its opening chapter demonstrates. The page just prior to the chapter presents the reader with the first of many diagrams that appear in the book. This one visually implies a reciprocal relationship between a pair of concepts—"signifier" over "semantic clock" and "liar" over "time"—whose meaning is fairly opaque, even to the reader familiar with literary theory. Moreover, the diagram is attributed to the as-yet-unknown Ralph, leaving both its import and its origin unclear (*Glyph* 3). Immediately thereafter Ralph introduces himself via a simultaneously grandiose and humble statement: "I will begin with infinity. It was and is the closest thing to me. I am a child and all I see is infinitely beyond my grasp, my understanding, my consciousness" (5). If this last statement is true for the preposterously intelligent narrator, there is little hope for the poor reader being inundated with subheadings in French—"différance," "ennuyeux," and "donne lieu"; German—"bedeuten," "Vexierbild," and "umstände"; Latin—"peccatum originale," "ens realissimum," "causa sui," "vita nova," and "mundus intelligibilis"; Greek—"pharmakon," "seme," "ephexis," and "ootheca"; and formal logic—"(x)(Cx→~Vx)⊢(x)[(Cx&Px) →~Vx]"; as well as English that is scarcely more familiar or comprehensible—"unties [*sic*] of simulacrum," "libidinal economy," "anfractous," and "tubes 1 . . . 6" (*Glyph* 5–37). In addition, the actual text of Ralph's narrative is so motley in tone, subject, genre, and even typography that the reader is likely to feel relieved by the blank page that separates the first chapter from the second.

Yet for all its difficulties, *Glyph* is no more inherently incomprehensible than such celebrated "encyclopedic" novels as Cervantes's *Don Quixote*, Gustave Flaubert's *Bouvard and Pécuchet* (1881), James Joyce's *Finnegans Wake* (1939), and David Foster Wallace's *Infinite Jest* (1996), each of which exhibits similar extremes of stylistic heterogeneity, although not necessarily for similar purposes. Stylistic and linguistic diversity serves Everett's Menippean satirical ends by accentuating the difference between Ralph's difficult and erudite, but ultimately open-ended, play with the forms of language and what he terms the "gum-bumping" of his father, Douglas (7). Douglas believes he possesses a "systematic understanding or explanation of the world" (Musgrave 23), and as the mocking nickname, Inflato, that Ralph bestows on him suggests, his son intends to "deflate" (compare Kaplan, above) this belief. Ralph insists that Inflato's "yak[king] about the ongoing critique of reason" (*Glyph* 10) causes him to fall "repeatedly into the same trap, the thought that he could not only talk about meaning, but that he could make it" (7). Despite Ralph's astonishing intellect—which his father fails to recognize, believing instead that his son is "mildly retarded" (7)—Ralph remains insistent that "language was the prison and the escape and therefore no prison at all, any more than freedom is confinement simply because it precludes one from being confined. Indeed, my much regarded and remarkable relationship and facility with language had caused my incarceration, but it had also freed me" (145). Ralph's meaning in the final sentence of this passage is both literal and figurative, given that it is the written evidence of his unusual intelligence that stimulates the series of kidnappings that make up the novel's plot. The figurative intention comes through as the second "voice" in this utterance, though, reinforcing Everett's aforementioned comments about language's inherent contradiction—"It refutes itself. But in so doing, reaffirms itself"—and its indispensability to human existence.

Ralph's way of telling his story fits Linda Hutcheon's definition of historiographic metafiction, which uses a parodic accumulation of "any signifying practices it can find operative in a society" in order to "challenge those discourses and yet to use them, even to milk them for all they are worth" (133). Whereas Ralph's father would insist on imposing meaning on language, Ralph's own purely written form of language—he refuses to speak even though he can—frustrates any such effort. In essence, he forces the reader to find pleasure/satisfaction in the intellectual exercise that the text requires rather than in the hope of a definitive answer as to what it means (compare the discussion in chapter 5 about the final lines of *Assumption*). In doing so, Ralph liberates himself in his creator's preferred manner: "Everett seeks personal independence from the constricting boundaries of fixed systems, his art asserting personal identity in freely chosen, if unpredictable acts of self-creation" (Ramsey 131).

Erasure too uses stylistic heterogeneity satirically. Most of Monk's narration is in the "proper" English that one expects from a literature professor with an upper-middle-class upbringing, but Monk notes that this usage conflicts with other expectations when he recalls the puzzled reactions of opponents "on a basketball court when upon missing a shot I muttered *Egads*" (2). Languages that differ drastically from this awkwardly formal English are inserted into the text in several places. Most obviously, the two "nested" texts—*F/V: Placing the Experimental Novel* and *My Pafology*—introduce extreme parodies of "Academese" and African American dialect, respectively, into Monk's narrative. Monk clearly intends *F/V* as a hand-delivered mockery of the Nouveau Roman society's preferred scholarly argot, a point made clear by its barbed closing: "*A reiteration of the obvious is never wasted on the oblivious*" (17). The inclusion of Monk's curriculum vitae—a document whose deeper implications are indecipherable, and likely irrelevant, to nonacademic readers—injects another aspect of Monk's professional language into the story.

In regard to African American vernacular, Lesley Larkin noted that "[Monk] is careful to create in [Van Go Jenkins] a character who is bereft of the linguistic birthright passed down by writers like Hurston and Ellison. . . . Monk deliberately distances [*My Pafology*] from literary works, like *Their Eyes Were Watching God,* that (in his view) authentically represent and celebrate black linguistic ingenuity" (156). Monk's incredulous reaction to Juanita Mae Jenkins's runaway best seller *We's Lives in Da Ghetto* illustrates his awareness of her characters' debased language and its significance to his own satirical intentions: "I remembered passages of *Native Son* and *The Color Purple* and *Amos and Andy* and my hands began to shake, the world opening around me, tree roots trembling on the ground outside, people in the street shouting *dint, ax, fo, screet,* and *fahvre!* and I was screaming inside, complaining that I didn't sound like that, that my mother didn't sound like that, that my father didn't sound like that" (62). His immediate response is to "put a page in his father's old manual typewriter" and to write *My Pafology,* which is transcribed in full beginning on the next page of the novel. Monk begins his parody of African American "linguistic ingenuity" with the first chapter heading, which is spelled "Won" rather than "One," establishing a pattern of faux ignorance that persists throughout *My Pafology.*

There is yet another major nested text in *Erasure,* though, and it serves a crucial function in distinguishing Everett's methods from Monk's. Immediately after an emotional and noncomical episode in which Monk swims to the middle of a pond to retrieve his Alzheimer's-afflicted mother from a boat, the tone of the book shifts dramatically. What follows is a nine-page section with the untranslated French heading "Àppropos de bottes," an archaic phrase that literally means "on the subject of boots" and figuratively signals a sudden and/or pointed change of subject. This is a reworked and reframed version of a short story entitled "Meiosis," which was previously published in *Callaloo* in 1997 by Everett under his own name. Everett embeds it within Monk's text and in doing so transforms it into a polyvocal commentary on Monk's satirical project. To emphasize further the seeming discontinuity from the main narrative, Everett/

Monk prints this section in a noticeably different typeface, an approach he likewise uses for all of the other "digressive" texts previously noted. The story, presumably authored by Monk, though its origins are never revealed, turns out to be not a digression but rather a parable that serves both as a mirror—from Monk's authorial perspective—and as a counterpoint—from Everett's authorial perspective—to what is happening in Monk's life. "Àppropos de bottes" fancifully and idealistically echoes Monk's experience of gaining fame and fortune while masquerading as Stagg R. Leigh. It tells the story of a character named Tom who fabricates aspects of his identity in order to become a contestant on a rigged game show named *Virtute et Armis.* This phrase, meaning "by valor and arms" in Latin, is also the state motto of Mississippi, although the text does not reveal this fact. When Tom is later introduced by the show's emcee, he is announced as being "from Mississippi," an epithet that is repeated at the end of the story. These two details imply that the story resembles "The Appropriation of Cultures" (which, like "Meiosis," was originally published in 1997) in depicting a character creatively finding a means of entry into a culture that hitherto excluded him. If the story is read only as an inserted episode within Monk's journal, ignoring the inseparably double ontological frame of Everett's novel, such a figurative reading is plausible; after all, Tom's exertions on the game show resonate symbolically with Monk's ambition for literary appreciation. Within *Erasure,* though, Tom's story contributes to a Menippean commentary on particular aspects of the enveloping text.

As Tom fills out the application to become a contestant, he almost immediately feels an impulse to falsify: "The first question asked for his name and already he was stumped. He wanted to laugh out loud. Under the line, in parentheses, the form asked for last and first names. He wrote Tom in the appropriate place and then tried to come up with a last name" (169). If Tom actually has no last name, he resembles Harriet Beecher Stowe's long-suffering slave protagonist Uncle Tom, whose name has become a shorthand accusation of selling out one's black identity in exchange for white favor. This Tom, however, is not betraying his blackness; rather he is obfuscating what it suggests to others while trying to earn a spot on the game show: "He thought to use Himes, but was afraid that he would somehow get into trouble, more trouble. Finally he wrote, Wahzetepe . . . . If asked, he would say it was an African name, but he knew that it was a Sioux Indian word, though he didn't know its meaning. He didn't know how he knew the word, but he was sure of it as his name" (169–70). Although he rejects the last name of the provocative African American writer Chester Himes, he chooses a name from a Native American tribe famed for its (admittedly tragic) resistance to white domination, even though the name's significance is not consciously apparent to him. Tom's thoughts suggest that he is confident the show's white producers will neither know nor particularly care about the distinction between a Native American name and an African one anyway. At the outset of his deception, Tom is more sanguine than Monk about how to use his audience's ignorance to his benefit, though he also seems to lack Monk's desire to protest, to reveal, or to undo that ignorance. Tom completes his imposture by lying not only about his last name and social security number but also "about his address, about his place of birth, about his education, claiming that he had studied at the College of William and Mary, about his hobbies, in which he included making dulcimers and box kites out of garbage bags" (170).

Ironically, all of this absurd misinformation almost immediately proves inconsequential. He is flatly told by the show's producer, Damien Blanc—that is, "white devil"—that no one "really gives a fuck where you studied or what you studied or if you studied." Blanc informs Tom that he has been chosen for immediate inclusion on the show because of a last-minute cancellation and that the reason for his selection was his stellar performance on the brief exam that was part of his questionnaire. Tom thoroughly and correctly answers a series of questions pertaining to insect classification, nineteenth-century French ballet, the Mean Value Theorem from calculus, as well as a "boring" question about "the single-point continuous fuel injection system that the Chrysler Motor Company devised in 1977" (170). Blanc seems to validate Tom's intellect as he repeatedly tells him that he "can't believe how well you did on that exam" (172). Monk/Everett begins introducing doubt about Blanc's motives, though, when the producer also tells Tom that he should treat being on *Virtute et Armis* as a "golden opportunity" that might even land him "a recording contract or a sitcom offer" (172). In essence, he is telling Tom that it is his appearance on television, not his expansive knowledge, that matters to the world. He promises Tom the chance to strike it rich in one of the two realms of culture, popular music and low comedy, that have been comparatively open to African Americans since the dawn of minstrelsy. As Blanc and Tom walk to the studio, they pass "a black man who was mopping the floor," and Tom recognizes him as "a former contestant on the show" (172–73). This comment casts Tom's earlier recollection of "the ugly ends met by his predecessors" and his desire to "succeed where the others had failed" (172) in a new light. Whereas this comment initially seems to be an effort to boost his confidence in the face of a difficult game, the narrator's explicit mention of the race of the contestant-turned-janitor strongly hints that Tom is being set up for a fall because of the color of his skin.

This sense is amplified as Tom is prepared for the show by the makeup artist: "'You ain't dark enough darlin',' she said. She began to rub the compound into the skin of Tom's face. . . . He watched in the mirror as his oak brown skin became chocolate brown. 'There now,' the redhead said, 'that's so much better'" (173). The racial violence hitherto implicit in Tom's predicament becomes more explicit as he is made to wear a shirt with a collar that is too tight and a tie that is described as "squeezing his throat with the stiff collar [of the shirt]" (174). Tom realizes that he is being prepared for a televised lynching, and he nervously tells himself that "he had to win this game. He just had to win" (174), as though his life is literally at stake. The point that he is not expected to win, or likely to be allowed to do so, is driven home by the show's smarmy host, Jack Spades, who welcomes Tom to the set by saying, "I want to wish you luck. Just relax. I'm sure you'll do fine and be a credit to your race" (175).

To this point the story superficially parallels Monk's efforts to parody the "constricting fiction of blackness" represented by *We's Lives in Da Ghetto* in order to find a means to be judged on his own literary/intellectual merits. Tom's experience in the makeup room directly parallels an episode in *My Pafology* in which Van Go is told that "this will make you shine like a proper TV nigger" (112) while he is being prepared for his own television appearance. The "constriction" inherent in Tom's blackness is furthermore literalized by the nooselike collar of the shirt he is forced to wear. Monk's situation differs significantly from Tom's, though, inasmuch as the barriers to acceptance that he faces are not solely the work of whites. Just prior to "Àppropos de bottes," Monk recounts his failure to "talk the talk" in order to "fit in" among African Americans. Monk recalls a series of phrases such as "*What it is? You better step back. That's some shit. Say What?*" and claims that they "never sounded real" either in his usage or "coming from anyone [else]" (167). Monk's lament that he never knew "when to slap five or high five, [or] which handshake to use" (167) links him to such "post-soul" characters as Benji Cooper, the narrator of Colson Whitehead's *Sag Harbor* (2009). During the school year Benji lives in Manhattan, where he attends a mostly white prep school; this fact leaves him somewhat mystified about gestural nuances during the summers he spends among an almost exclusively African American group of friends in the Long Island beach community of Sag Harbor: "The new handshakes were out, shaming me with their permutations and slippery routines. Slam, grip, flutter, snap. Or was it slam, flutter, grip, snap? I was all thumbs when it came to shakes. Devised in the underground soul laboratories of Harlem, pounded out in the blacker-than-thou sweatshops of the South Bronx, the new handshakes always had me faltering in embarrassment" (Whitehead 43). Richard Schur has explained the possible consequences of these two characters' inability to master the use of these gestures: "Handshakes, like the use of language, are performative—conferring legitimacy and authenticity on some while revealing the supposed failings of others" ("The Crisis" 247).

Neither Monk nor Everett has much use for discourses of "legitimacy and authenticity" where race is concerned, regardless of whether they govern language or behavior. Tom's experience of being made up and costumed makes visible the show's conception of a "legitimate" black person, a fact that Blanc demonstrates through his exclamation upon seeing Tom: "Nice job, girls. Real nice. He looks just right. I almost didn't recognize you." The significance of Tom's sardonic reply, "Me, either" (174), is lost on Blanc, but it reminds the reader that Tom abandons his self-fictionalizing impulse as soon as he is told that no one cares. Monk also claims to have realized that "no one cared about my awkwardness but me" (167), but his ongoing performance as Stagg suggests otherwise.

Tom's situation on the game show also echoes another episode from Monk's teenage years. Despite "enjoy[ing] the exercise and the game" of basketball, Monk confesses that he did not enjoy "playing the game," in part because he "wasn't very good at it" (133). One day when he is seventeen, his mind begins to drift while playing basketball and he winds up "considering the racist comments of Hegel concerning Oriental peoples and their attitude toward the freedom of the self" (133–34). His distracted musings do not prevent a teammate from passing him the ball, and after Monk awkwardly throws up "a wild and desperate shot which had no prayer of going in," that teammate demands to know what he was thinking. His simple and truthful response—"Hegel . . . I was thinking about his theory of history"—precipitates a flurry of dismissive responses that threaten violence: "Get him"; offer scorn: "Philosophy boy"; or express incredulity: "Where the hell did you come from?" None marvels or otherwise positively comments on Monk's thoughts, which are clearly unusual in both subject and depth for a seventeen-year-old (134).

Thus, when Tom steps onto the set of *Virtute et Armis* to compete against the thoroughly unexceptional (and white) Hal Dullard, Monk's intended framing of *My Pafology* by "Àppropos de bottes" is complete. Like Everett, he is decrying the general devaluation of intellect—and specifically black intellect—by American popular culture, a process Monk knows firsthand, as demonstrated by his rueful inclusion of an editor's written rejection of one of his earlier manuscripts: "*Why did you bother sending it to me? It shows a brilliant intellect, certainly. It's challenging and masterfully written and constructed, but who wants to read this shit? It's too difficult for the market*" (42). Monk is desperate for an outlet in which his intellectual skills will be rewarded on their own terms, and Tom's flawless victory on the game show is a literary projection of this desire's fulfillment. Monk wants to win like Tom but does not recognize the importance of Tom's willingness to play the game "free of illusions" (264) until the end of *Erasure,* though even then his realization seems incomplete and/or inadequate.

Everett's juxtaposition of "Àppropos de bottes" and *My Pafology* reveals the polyvocal satire that he directs not just at Monk's intended targets but also at Monk himself: "[Everett] frames the longest text-within-the-text in such a way that readers are alert to its parodic register while also remaining sensitive to the possibility of meanings that exceed or contradict Monk's intended critique" (Larkin 162). Monk's attempt to resist the expectations imposed on blackness is unsuccessful not only because of the unsophisticated interpretations of his audiences but also because, as Morgan asserted, "despite his arguments otherwise, Monk is not truly attempting to write a satire" (166). Although Tom distorts his identity in order to get on the show, he reveals his lie to Blanc before he is even accepted as a contestant: "Actually that's not true. I just wanted to put down something" (Everett, *Erasure* 171). He then proceeds to win the game not by further violating its corrupt rules but rather by legitimately demonstrating superior knowledge. Admittedly, having knowledge inferior to Dullard's would be difficult, as Dullard not only incorrectly identifies the nation's first president as Thomas Jefferson but also "did not know that a gorilla was a primate. He did not know the abbreviation for Avenue. He did not know what a male chicken was called" (177). As was the case with those he was asked on the preliminary exam, Tom's questions are esoteric and obscure, involving biological cell division, tenth-century Arabic poetry, septic-system installation methods, and Ralph Waldo Emerson's poem "Self-Reliance" (175–77).

Despite the obvious unfairness of the game, Tom wins, a fact that causes the all-white studio audience to fall first silent and then dead, presumably from shock. Monk seems to expect a similar reaction from the various audiences he exposes to the literary imposture of *My Pafology,* whether by appearing as Stagg R. Leigh as a guest of Kenya Dunston—a fairly obvious parody of Oprah Winfrey, who Everett bluntly says "should stay the fuck out of literature and stop pretending she knows anything about it" (Shavers, "Percival" 49)—on her daytime talk show, or playing the same part in a business meeting with a Hollywood producer while negotiating the seven-figure film rights for the book. As the slavering readers/consumers of *My Pafology* remain unaware of having their ignorant expectations overthrown and, correspondingly, fail to be shocked—to death or otherwise—by his performance, Monk concocts increasingly elaborate, and untenable, rationalizations that make him "able to look at my face in the mirror and to accept" (209) the fame and fortune that his supposed act of protest is bringing him.

Some critics have insisted that Monk's refusal "to explain to his readers how to interpret his work" is an assertion of authorial integrity and that he therefore "never compromises his art" (McConkey-Pirie 31). This might be a defensible interpretation if Everett and Monk were as substantively similar as their superficial resemblances imply. Everett certainly denies the desire to influence *his* readers in this way, but Monk has been expressing his anxiety about his potential readers' reactions since the book's opening page. Moreover, he flatly asserts that *My Pafology* is "a failed conception, an unformed fetus, seed cast into the sand, a hand without fingers, a word with no vowels[,] . . . offensive, poorly written, racist, and mindless" (261) to his fellow judges on the selection committee for what is called "simply and pretentiously *The Book Award*" (223). In fact, he does so less than half a page after a flat declaration of his self-interested intentions: "Call it expediently located irony, or convenient rationalization, but I was keeping the money" (260). The hypocrisy on display in these passages buttresses Lavelle Porter's claim that Monk's success requires him to accept covertly the same oppressive discourse of authenticity that he lambastes overtly throughout the book: "Monk is able to sell *My Pafology* by concealing his actual identity as a learned man, and an author of more intellectually rigorous fiction. . . . Monk was able to convince them of his authenticity by concealing his identity and assuring them that his writing was the product of the streets and not the library. This reality points to the fact that the sale and marketing of authentic art as a commodity is contingent upon the 'organic' quality of the author herself. Too much formal education (real or perceived) corrupts that authenticity" (155). Monk is doubtlessly constrained by the expectations of a "normative society, both black and white, [that] refuses to let him speak, to let Monk successfully involve himself in representation" (Hogue 121), but he also keeps the money once it becomes clear how well conformity pays. Consciously choosing to "sell out" is the exact opposite of Tom's victorious exhibition of actual knowledge or the Swiftian satirical protest staged by the protagonist of Paul Beatty's novel *The Sellout* (2015), who attempts to reinstitute segregation and slavery in his California hometown as a barbed commentary on how little has actually changed.

Morgan added that Monk's impersonation of Stagg becomes an example of the "grotesque, caricatured blackness" he claims to be resisting, and the more he allows the suggestion of Stagg's reality to go unchallenged, the more it reinforces the fact that "*My Pafology* has all the signifiers of a work to be taken seriously, at least when presented to an audience already largely inured to a complex signification regarding black masculinity." Everett's polyvocal and satirical framing—whether of *My Pafology* by "Àppropos de bottes" or of Monk's journal by *Erasure* itself—assures that "Monk's text is unable to function as a fully articulated satire because Monk is unable to establish any distance between himself and his narration; satire presumes authorial understanding of the situation being satirized, while providing space for simultaneous audience awareness of authorial distance from the actual plot as it occurs" (Morgan 166).

Musgrave's three features of linguistic and philosophical multiplicity play major roles in *A History of the African-American People* as well. The interplay of voices speaking and writing publicly to one another in the formulaic jargons of politics, publishing, and academia readily conveys the self-conscious linguistic variety of stylistic heterogeneity. The novel adds another layer, though, in the form of private communications transacted in more intimate and less regimented forms of language, the idiosyncrasies of which tend to reveal the very traits that the book's more public forms of discourse attempt to disguise. Although the book has no overarching narrator, there is an implied editorial presence that curates the novel's fragments in a manner that is essentially omniscient. This invisible quasi-narrator uses that omniscience to juxtapose public and private communications satirically, exposing the concealed contradictions, nonsensicalities, perversities, and other sources of linguistic instability. This technique ensures that the text's lack of formal concord mirrors its rhetorical incoherence. In essence, the book becomes a series of ultimately self-negating digressions.

The hand of this hidden omniscient compositor/narrator is already apparent in Barton Wilkes's first set of interactions with the two members of Simon & Schuster's editorial staff who are responsible for handling his ludicrous book proposal. Wilkes writes his unsolicited proposal in a matter-of-fact style that could be taken straight from an online template. Although his letter meets the most minimal formal requirements of such a document, Wilkes displays his lack of understanding of the publication process by providing nothing more than the name of the book and an extremely premature request to respond to him with "such things as: 1. publicity plans 2. advances 3. royalties" (9). After a month with no response, Wilkes sends a follow-up letter that not only exposes his lack of sophistication regarding the process of manuscript review in the publishing industry—a somewhat esoteric topic, after all—but also begins unleashing the disjointed language and excessive familiarity that will soon become absolute hallmarks of all his correspondence:

> Dear Sir/Madam:
>
> In ref. to mine of the 13th inst.
>
> Ha, ha. I'm just joking, of course. There's no need for such formality.
>
> However, there is need for some dispatch, as the Senator always says, when telling the story about how there was only one outhouse at the school pie-eating contest when some prankster—the Senator swears, with

a twinkle in his eye, it was not he—put castor oil in the blackberries that filled the pies (blackberry pie, the Senator's favorite to this day): "There is some need for dispatch, Sammy!" shouts one of the boys in line. I wish you could hear the Senator tell that one.

Of course it will not be appropriate to the project we are discussing. (10)

This pairing of documents shows that Wilkes is basically capable of mimicking the form of a business letter, but that he barely comprehends the context in which that form is relevant.

His correspondents at Simon & Schuster have their own communicative issues, though, emphasizing the point that the satirical impulses of this book are not simply focused on Thurmond and those affiliated with him. The first response to Wilkes from the publisher is an unsigned form rejection that is dated nearly a month after Wilkes's second letter and misaddressed to "Blanton" Wilkes. Wilkes responds within three days, incredulous at what he believes must be a "joke" and condescendingly proposing to "get down to business, shall we?" (12). The next document is an internal memo from "Snell to McCloud," two names without any referent at this point in the book. This memo, dated two weeks after Wilkes's last letter, is a hodgepodge of chatty interoffice niceties and business: "Ask the guy for a proposal, but tell him the usual about how we aren't interested. Make that emphatic. Don't leave any room for doubt. Do you keep a cat? I find a well-groomed cat a great comfort. My ex-wife hated cats" (13). The next document, a formal business letter addressed from McCloud on behalf of Snell, follows the instructions laid out in the memo and, in doing so, clarifies who Snell (an editor) and McCloud (Snell's assistant) are. Wilkes's response is predictably off-kilter, filled with overly presumptive statements, such as "Surely not coincidental that we are both Assistants to important people"; quotations from Poe; lectures about excessive formality, for example, "Now it's easy to see why you're being standoffish"; even-more-presumptuous denials of being presumptuous, such as "Neither of us is quite his own person"; a restatement of the fact that the title of the book "can stand as description and what you call proposal"; and an invocation of southern aristocratic camaraderie: "Puissant name, 'R. Juniper.' Are you from the Charleston McClouds? My own name is a matter of pride to me, as yours is to you. Someone at your place called me 'Blanton.' Oh my" (15). The (d)evolution of Wilkes's language can be measured by comparing the relatively informal valediction of this letter—"Yours for now"—with that of his first—"Most sincerely"; within a few more exchanges, this morphs further into a catalog of bizarrely intimate sign-offs and pet names—for example, "Love, *Bark*" (26); "Devotedly, *Button*" (36); "Here ya go, bud! *Bar-bar*" (47); "Yours fondly, *Barthes*" (52); and

"Puss-puss, *Big Blan*" (128)—that mark a corresponding change in the tone and content of the letters themselves.

The initial memo from Snell to McCloud hints at the fact that the book's oddities will not be confined to Wilkes, and the next set of memos and letters establishes that there is a plague on the house of Simon & Schuster as well. Snell is every bit as unprofessional and intrusive as Wilkes in his communications with McCloud. Snell's initial awkwardness is magnified in his second memo to McCloud: "We have reason to believe this guy [Wilkes] is connected to Thurmond, but he doesn't seem to have many tines in his fork, does he? . . . Do you wear boxers or briefs? Also, you haven't answered my question about kitty" (16). Not long thereafter Snell sends a memo filled with double entendres that seems both to admonish McCloud and flirt with him:

> I am not going to get ahead at this place if I ride projects like this one and blister nothing but my own ass! Don't forget that there is a paradox here: I am the smartest fuck here and also the youngest. I expect you are already toting up dates and saying, "Well soul-kiss your sister, he isn't the youngest at all." But you know what I mean, Juney. Don't be an idiotic literalist. I am the newest and most vulnerable. Don't take advantage of that vulnerability, please. Others have, but I thought you were different. And if I'm fired, I'm taking you and that cute ass with me. Cats? (24)

This bifurcated tenor pervades Snell's subsequent messages to McCloud, and he begins making explicit advances toward his assistant even as he projects his attraction onto Wilkes: "I don't see anything kinky or out of line in his letter. Probably you are just timid, McCloud, sexually repressed. I'm not saying you should offer yourself to him or he to you. Nor should either of you find a third party, male or female" (92).

McCloud initially seems as though he might be a voice of reason or at least a naïf caught between two lunatics; he describes himself in an early letter to Wilkes as something of a babe in the woods: "Here I am just out of NYU, an English major lucky to get a job, or so I thought" (25). The rapid dissolution of his coherence and propriety is typified, however, by a letter he sends to Wilkes that spends four lines describing an editorial disagreement about the project and nearly another page and a half wildly oversharing personal details: "My sister was caught masturbating. I mean really caught. And really masturbating. My sister is two years older than me, you see, and really gorgeous, if I do say so myself. I mean, she is also pretty much a raving bitch, if you ask me, but she hides that very well around anyone except me" (62). Every character who becomes involved in the expansive correspondence surrounding the Thurmond book—including the fictional versions of Everett and Kincaid—demonstrates this sort of digressive spiraling descent into madness, strongly suggesting that one would have to be crazy to take such a project seriously in the first place.

Even the contract that Wilkes wrangles out of Snell for the book demonstrates this linguistic insanity; tucked away amid the tortured grammar of legalese and "small print" that is conventional for such a document is a quintessentially Menippean detail that purports to describe the unwritten book for which the contract is being issued: "This publishing Agreement . . . concern[s] a work presently titled *A History of the African American People* and not described as yet to be either a factual accounting, social commentary or fictional reenactment of some era, portion of time or reflection of attitudes about or concerning people of African descent on the continent of North America" (39). This nondescription not only negates practically all of the relevant meanings of the significant words in the book's title but also reinforces the sense that this book will never become more than an idea; it is only a not-something, not a something. The real-life Everett and Kincaid, however, deliver the only such book that *is* possible under these circumstances, a metafictional novel that ironically explains how and why it could never be written/published as a serious history. What they accomplish is reminiscent of the way in which Jerry Seinfeld and Larry David used fictional versions of themselves to claim jokingly that their long-running hit show *Seinfeld* was a "show about nothing" ("The Pitch"), or the way in which director Terry Gilliam made a documentary film entitled *Lost in La Mancha* (2002) about his failure to complete a feature-film adaptation of *Don Quixote*. In each case the metafictional work forces the reader/viewer to confront the irony of beholding something that seemingly should not exist, leading to possibly unanswerable questions about the nature of what *does* exist in light of the "nothing"-ness.

CHAPTER 4

Menippean Satire through Tonal Multiplicity

Shifting the focus onto a second cluster of Everett's books, the critical center of this chapter realigns around another subset of features from Musgrave's schema for defining Menippean satire. This trio of features, outlined in greater depth below, coheres into what can be called "tonal multiplicity" and is a slightly less intrinsic marker of Menippean satire than the formal, linguistic, and philosophical forms of multiplicity discussed in the previous chapter. Tonal multiplicity undoubtedly contributes to a Menippean sensibility—or mind-set, or outlook—within a particular work by amplifying and augmenting the formal structures and linguistic/rhetorical techniques associated with the mode. However, when tonal multiplicity is the predominant Menippean trait of a given text, it insinuates the mode more than epitomizing it. Stated differently, tonal multiplicity marks Menippean satire in the way that a particular combination of spices might indicate a specific cuisine; those spices can be a distinctive marker, but the distinction is largely notable for the way it alters the flavor of something more substantial, such as meats, proteins, or vegetables. Using the parameters of Paul Alpers's definition of a mode as "the literary manifestation, in a given work, not of its attitudes in a loose sense, but of its assumptions about man's nature and situation" (50), the Menippean character of those assumptions is conveyed more obliquely through tonal multiplicity than through its formal, philosophical, or linguistic cousins.

The Menippean effects of tonal multiplicity are apparent and significant within *Suder, Cutting Lisa, American Desert, The Water Cure,* and *I Am Not Sidney Poitier,* as well as in many of Everett's other works; however, those effects are also more sporadic, diluted, and/or ambiguous than in the works surveyed in the previous chapter, in which most, if not all, of the other features of Menippean multiplicity are also at work. This chapter thus continues cataloging the tonal Menippean qualities of the five books covered in the last chapter but also broadens out to look at the way in which tonal multiplicity on its own can define the Menippean quality of another set of books by

Everett, even though these are moderately less representative examples of the mode.

Although the three features of Musgrave's schema being characterized here as "tonal multiplicity" sometimes manifest formally within a given text, their function is more to impart a transformational tone to the text than to serve in and of themselves as the tropes of a recognizable literary convention. By way of analogy, stock characters such as charming princes, distressed orphans, and greedy trolls, or conventional plots involving abductions/rescues, rediscovery of lost objects, and extrication from undesirable marriages are all common *formal* markers of the fairy-tale genre. The predominant *tonal* markers of the genre, however, rely on less embodied descriptors such as menace, deception, imposture, virtue, restoration, and/or transgression. In keeping with the musical metaphor of tonality, these are the Menippean traits that help satirically "bend" or "blue" individual notes within what otherwise might appear to be straightforward and euphonious melodies.

Thematic Heterogeneity

The first component of this subset is Musgrave's third feature, which he calls "thematic heterogeneity." He describes it as the obvious juxtaposition of thematic elements that clash with one another to the point of creating an intentional and elaborate cacology—that is, a seemingly inept choice of incompatible words comparable to the dissonant noise of a cacophony: "Menippean satire frequently uses vulgarity, coarseness, or grotesquery to provide a stark contrast to the intellectual sphere which is being satirized. Another aspect of this thematic heterogeneity is the mixture of fantasy and morality" (Musgrave 23). In *A History of the African-American People,* Barton Wilkes's letters and Martin Snell's memos—which intertwine indiscreet flirtations with professional matters—are self-contained exemplars of thematic heterogeneity. The glaring difference between Monk's cultured authorial voice and the coarsely vulgar voice he creates for Van Go Jenkins serves a similar purpose in *Erasure. Glyph* contains some of the most jarring contrasts in all of Everett's work, as the narrative frequently veers between high-flown scholarly utterances and discussions of Ralph's bowel functions: "I sat on the potty while Rosenda watched. A sad scene, but I had grown accustomed to such indignities. As I sat there ignoring the woman, I closed my eyes and considered my mother. Actually, I considered Lacan, as was my wont when doing what I was doing. At that moment, I contemplated his restatement of the Freudian Oedipus Complex" (164). This contrast emphasizes that the "entire tone and flow of the novel follows from the incongruity . . . between Ralph's [adult] mind and [infant] body" (Schur, "The Mind-Body Split" 77–78). The book's thematic heterogeneity thus results both from its extreme fragmentation—which seems, literally and figuratively, like child's play when compared to *The Water Cure* (see below)—and from Ralph's simultaneous status as a physically dependent baby and a mentally autonomous polymath.

In a different way, Everett satirizes George Armstrong Custer's bloody historical legacy in *God's Country* partly by contrasting it with an absurdly comical set piece more reminiscent of *Blazing Saddles* (1974) than of *They Died with Their Boots On* (1941). Marder initially encounters Custer after stumbling into a Seventh Cavalry encampment and meeting one of Custer's soldiers with the childishly scatological name of Rip Phardt. Marder tells Phardt that he has information that will allow Custer to ambush Big Elk, an Indian chief who has been frustrating Custer's racist imposition of Manifest Destiny. Custer expresses his motivations to Marder: "It's the American way. I'm talking about our way of life, man. And they're trying to take it away from us. From *me*. First the slaves wanting to be free and now these red heathens. It's enough to make you spit in bath water" (Everett, *God's* 128). Although Marder has been invoking the "mythology [that] was invented for the West" throughout the novel to this point, Custer's words bring its underlying genocidal implications clearly to the fore. Everett noted in an interview that this myth "is really the American story. Not the story itself but the fact that it was needed" (Birnbaum 37). Presuming, with good reason, that Marder is already sympathetic, Custer tells him the unsavory part of this "American story" that is elided from the ennobling accounts of Western "settlement." When Custer and his men finally attack Big Elk's village, Marder repeats his behavior from the novel's opening scene and regards the carnage from a nearby hiding place: "They wasn't interested in taking prisoners. They shot this way and that and blindly into tepees and they was high on the killing. I could see it in their eyes. I saw a couple of soldiers grab Happy Bear, who was already wounded, and stake him to the ground. They laughed while they stood over him, then one of them sliced open his belly" (169). Marder's shamefulness in this instance is compounded not only by his complicity in betraying Big Elk—who had helped him earlier in the book—to Custer but also by the fact that the only thing he does while hiding and watching Custer's men destroy Big Elk's village is to knock Bubba unconscious with the butt of his gun to prevent him from intervening.

Disgusted by this display of violence and the underlying mind-set that justifies it, Bubba goes to a whorehouse in the town of Cahoots with a simple goal in mind: "I'm gonna kill and scalp that Custer" (178). When Bubba and Marder find Custer there, Marder initially mistakes him for a whore, which is a reasonable misapprehension given that Custer is in a bordello and "wearin' ladies' unmistakables" (182). Custer's feminized appearance triggers a rather sentimentally Oedipal reaction in Marder, who asks Bubba, "Are you really gonna kill that poor man what's dressed like my departed mama, or are you just gonna give him a little bit of a scare?" (183). When Bubba seems intent on following through with his deadly intentions, Marder reverts to his default morality; he pulls out his gun and points it at Bubba, saying, "I'm afraid I'm gonna have to do my American duty and stop you and then turn you in as a nigger what's gone wild" (184). Bubba easily wrests the gun from the cowardly Marder and knocks Custer out cold before deciding that "killin' is too good for him." Instead, Bubba issues a kind of malediction that recasts Custer's subsequent death at Little Bighorn as righteous vengeance against a coward rather than the glorious sacrifice in service of the nation as it was framed in the press and in histories: "Man like him ought to die in a special way, seeing it comin' and scared to death" (186). Custer's men burst into the room at this point, and Bubba, Marder, and the actual prostitute with whom Custer was consorting all jump out the window and flee, with the soldier in pursuit absurdly yelling, "Stop 'em! Stop 'em! . . . They done tried to kill the colonel by dressin' him up like a woman" (187). These scenes satirically undermine Custer—and Marder, who is more than willing to support Custer, tacitly and actively—not just by showing the awfulness of his actions but also by robbing him and his quintessentially (white) frontier narrative of the nobility and gravitas—"My name is George A. Custer. Perhaps you've heard of me" (127)—that Custer clearly believes he and it richly deserve.

This Menippean characteristic is hardly a development of Everett's later career, though. Thematic multiplicity is already evident in his first novel, *Suder,* in which the seemingly serious themes of existential crisis, parental insanity, and pervasive racism are paired with farcical episodes involving a sassy nine-year-old runaway named Jincy, flashbacks to Craig Suder's childhood in which he has to fend off his mother's frantic accusations of "pull[ing] on [him]self" (13), and a scene in which a now-adult Suder wins five hundred dollars in a carnival game by hitting an elephant—who also becomes his boon companion later on in the novel—in the testicles with his baseball bat. Jacqueline Berben-Masi described the tone of these latter scenes as "slapstick . . . drawn from an animated cartoon for adolescent entertainment" and suggested that they temporarily displace the book's narrative into a "realm of strange happenings that now and then exceed both the patience of a sophisticated reader and the experience of ordinary mortals" ("Getting" 25). She also contended that Everett alternates between "the basest of animate comportment and the highest of spiritual experience" and, in doing so, blends "the prosaic with the poetic" (25) as he tells "the tale of the adult protagonist's failing athletic career coupled with his haphazard itinerary towards self-discovery and fulfillment" (23). Simultaneously accentuating the book's formal, rhetorical, and thematic forms of multiplicity, she concluded that "*Suder* is parody, pastiche, intertextuality, mythic quest, and post-postmodernism—all of them rolled into one" (28).

One of Everett's most striking, but also subtle, uses of thematic multiplicity occurs in *Cutting Lisa*. The novel's resolution intertwines seemingly dissonant thematic strands—for example, beauty and revulsion, love and violence—that are established in the novel's opening pages and recur throughout the book. For the bulk of the novel, doubts have been building in John Livesey's mind concerning his daughter-in-law's possible infidelity toward his son, and therefore also the parentage of the child she carries in her womb. These doubts have been mostly confined to internalized narratives, though, many of which overlap with scenes involving three relatively breezy domestic subplots: John playing with his granddaughter, Katy; the burgeoning friendship between John and the Turners, the quirky older couple who live next door; and the unexpected romantic/sexual escapades between John and a considerably younger woman named Ruth Spencer. Although the novel is narrated in an omniscient and depersonalized third-person voice similar to that of *Walk Me to the Distance*, the narrative's focus is nearly always on John's experiences and his thoughts. The narrator rarely offers direct commentary, but the manner in which details are related to the reader results in a frequent sense of disjunction arising from both the juxtaposition of tonally dissonant details and John's curious lack of reaction—directly expressed or indirectly reported—to these dissonances.

For example, near the middle of the book, John and his new friend Oliver Turner take a trip into Newport, Oregon, the town nearest to his son's isolated coastal home. As the two older men walk down the town's main street, John sees a kite store and speaks aloud his mental note to return and buy a toy for his beloved granddaughter. Oliver responds simply with "Good idea. Now, let's drink," and the two of them walk into an "excessively nautical bar" that is immediately thereafter described by the narrator as "a room full of homosexuals." Oliver makes a mildly off-color joke—"This place is full of semen"—and asks John if he is uncomfortable. John claims not to be, remarking, "I'm from Staunton, Virginia; we don't have places like this." Oliver remarks that it is likely more accurate that "you just don't know about them" and offers to go somewhere else, but John declines, since neither of them expresses any particular concern one way or the other about the setting:

> "What do you make of all this?" John asked.
> "All what, exactly?"
> "The affectation, all this show?"
> Oliver shrugged. (66)

They order several rounds of drinks and talk for a while rather superficially about their immediate environment and their lives until a comedian named Denny takes the stage. John again asks Oliver a seemingly pointed question, "What do you think of this guy?," and Oliver again wordlessly refuses to answer. Denny's raunchy performance sets the crowd off, leading John to quip that he "feel[s] like an anthropologist," to which Oliver replies, ominously, "I feel put upon" (68). His comment comes as even more of a shock since only a few lines above, the narrator notes that Oliver has watched their waiter walk away while commenting approvingly, "Many women should have his butt" (68). The sudden change in Oliver's demeanor possibly suggests that his significant alcohol intake has lowered his inhibitions to the point that he is feeling ashamed of some repressed homoerotic impulses; at the very least, his heretofore jovial acceptance of his surroundings has been revealed as a facade that masks an underlying homophobia now free to manifest itself.

Whatever the case, Oliver soon shouts at an especially raucous fan of Denny's, "calling the man a sissy" in a manner that the narrator describes "as if [it were] an afterthought" (69). What has been a largely uneventful scene suddenly adopts a tone of danger and hatefulness: "[John] became more afraid when he looked into Oliver's terrified eyes. . . . The man's size and the alcohol made John angry and belligerent—later he would admit to being stupid and suicidal as well. John raised his fists and said, 'Come on, pretty boy. Let's see if you can take it in the face the way you take it in the butt'" (69). Oliver throws a pitcher at the man, and they run out of the bar, almost immediately resuming their jocular tone upon realizing that no one is chasing them:

> "I forgot to leave a tip," Oliver said.
>
> "That's tacky."
>
> "That was actually sort of fun," Oliver said.
>
> As they prepare to drive away, John sits for a moment behind the wheel and they revert fully back to their earlier mode of disengaged non-conversation:
>
> "What is it?" asked Oliver.
>
> "Nothing." John turned the key. (69)

By itself this scene is not especially central to the novel's plot, but it reveals both the degree to which John is capable of having his thoughts troubled and how quickly and effectively he represses those troublings when they occur. Rather than question why he might be uncomfortable when he realizes that they have entered a gay bar, he first denies that he is and then ironically deflects further by asking Oliver his opinion of the "affectation" in the room. When Oliver's hostility toward Denny and his admirers begins building, John feels "hollow and fearful" as he notes the "strange inebriated glow he thought he saw in Oliver's eyes" (68). However, when Oliver provokes a fight, John acts like Marder in *God's Country* and reverts unthinkingly to his familiar moral code: "John did the only thing he could think to do; he stood with his friend" (69).

Although the consequences of this incident for John and Oliver are negligible—the narrative perspective is notably unconcerned with any repercussions for the men toward whom Oliver hurls his taunt of "sissy"—the incident's rapid tonal shifts from the easy sentimentality of buying a grandchild's kite, to sublimated and euphemized discomfort in the presence of "affectation," to drunken fear and hostility, to lighthearted jesting, and finally back to sublimation are premonitions of the even more rapid shifts that mark the book's conclusion. John's lack of knowledge concerning the existence of gay bars in either Newport or Staunton is revealed not to be a matter of unfamiliarity—which is both understandable and perhaps even excusable—on his part. Rather, it is a symptom of his reflexive practice of excising, either by rejection or by willful ignorance, from his consciousness anything that threatens his ethical worldview. Ultimately the rapid changes in tone leave him saying and possibly feeling "nothing," a state that recurs in numerous other emotionally charged situations throughout the book.

This process of excision becomes literal in the novel's final scene, which also hearkens back strongly to the prologue. The prologue is a flashback to years earlier, when a newly widowed John was still practicing as an obstetrician. The book's opening passages describe a morning that initially fulfills John's desire for unchanging routine: "John Livesey always walked early. . . . Stopping at the steps of the porch, he looked across the street at the pastor of the Baptist church. The young minister was there every Tuesday at the same time to place the title of his next sermon in the bulletin case. John approved of this sort of regularity" (1). His leisurely morning is interrupted by a call from a colleague at the hospital in which he works, imploring John to come in early to deal with a curious case. He quickly learns that a young husband named Thompson has performed an impromptu emergency caesarean section on his pregnant wife before bringing her to the hospital to recover. John's shocked reaction contains a range of contradictory emotions: "he was angry that someone could be so stupid, appalled that a person could be so careless with the life of another, and uncomfortably impressed that anyone could pull it off" (4). When he confronts the young husband, the man replies calmly, "I did what I had to do," which sends John into a rage:

> "Jesus, man, you could have killed your wife and baby."
> "They're okay."

> "You don't understand what I'm saying, do you? That's not the point. . . . You were lucky." He took a step away and came back. "How did you know what to do?"
>
> "I figured it out." (5–6)

Although John is ultimately able to "find a certain empathy with the man" because of his "emotionless response" to the situation, John "said nothing to anyone at the hospital" and drives away, returning to his morning of following the "strict routine [that] would be the easiest way to care for himself." Upon arriving at his home, he finds that he "wanted to think about Thompson, but he didn't know how. There was something attractive about the man, yet he couldn't isolate what it was." Unable to cogitate on the ethical dilemma presented to him, John turns instead to puttering around his house and then to painting, a practice described in wholly utilitarian terms: "He had taken up painting at the suggestion of his daughter-in-law. He painted fruit. That was all he painted, fruit on tables, fruit in bowls, groups of like fruit, bunches of different fruit." Painting is a purely mechanical activity for him, rather than an opportunity to develop any new thoughts: "He claimed not to be exercising some highly developed aesthetic peculiarity but only painting to get better at it." The prologue ends with another evocation of John's conflicted emotional response to Thompson's words and deeds: "He was not so much bothered by the fact that he had just seen a woman so badly mutilated, nor was he terribly disturbed by the fact that a man could have done such a thing. What bothered him was that he was finding Thompson's action somehow beautiful" (6–7). The awkward interplay of the words "mutilated" and "beautiful" in these passages sums up the cacology that threatens to disrupt John's habituated existence by forcing him to "figure out" something that "he didn't know how" to think about otherwise.

Superficially, the ending of the book suggests that John has concluded that cutting into his stepdaughter Lisa to abort her unborn child is likewise a "somehow beautiful" act of "mutilat[ion]." Everett's juxtaposition of these two acts, though, is importantly not parallel. The thematic heterogeneity of scenes such as the one at the bar in Newport ethically distinguishes John's act—the result of a monologic reversion to his established understanding of how he believes the world should be—from Thompson's shocking, but ultimately creative, act of "figur[ing] out" what needed to be done to deliver his baby and to save his wife. Everett is undoubtedly aware that Thompson's deadpan avowal that "I wanted to bring my child into the world. . . . It's as simple as that" (5) is unlikely to persuade most readers of the righteousness of his actions, but the narrative construction of the novel's final chapters makes it abundantly clear that John's impending act is ethically indefensible unless one agrees a priori with John's reasoning. In short, there is no way to "figure out"—that is, deduce—a valid justification; one can arrive at one inductively only by begging the question and ignoring the flaws in his moral premises. In this manner Everett's conclusion becomes a Menippean satire of John's "bad philosophy," specifically his inflexible thought process and the flawed premises on which that process depends.

The extended buildup to the novel's conclusion begins when John's son Elgin is severely injured while climbing a beachside bluff with his friend Greg Yount. John rightly suspects Yount of being Lisa's partner in an extramarital affair but never voices this suspicion openly before the accident. While Elgin is confined to the hospital in Newport, Lisa confesses the affair to her husband, though she does not name Yount as her lover, a situation that John finds intolerable:

> "Oh, Dad. I know you're worried about me, but . . . it's over. She told me it's over and I believe her."
>
> "Is it your child?"
>
> Elgin closed his eyes and pinched the bridge of his nose. "I don't know."
>
> . . .
>
> "You need to know."
>
> "Why? Why do I need to know? The affair is over. We're trying to get it together." (118)

John is horrified to realize that Elgin not only does not know with whom Lisa has been having her affair but also, in his ignorance, still trusts and relies on Yount as a friend and confidant. Instead of informing his son, he essentially repeats his gesture from the earlier scene outside the bar in Newport: "He looked at his son but said nothing before leaving" (118).

John does not, however, have a shortage of ethical judgment about the matter, as the start of the next chapter reveals: "It was the betrayal, not the lies nor hurt nor the ignorance that smelled so badly. The stench of rancid souls, thought John. . . . John could just picture Greg Yount listening to Elgin's woes and nodding sympathetically, being the supportive friend, then laughing later while he held Lisa in his arms. He hated Yount, and as he thought of him, he became like the target at the end of a rifle barrel, flat and without history, just a place where the bullet would go. This man was destroying his son, his family" (119). Not long after the narrator shares these violent thoughts, John sees Yount's car in the parking lot of a bar and decides to go inside. The bar is described as though it "could have been a bar in Staunton," suggesting that John feels more comfortable here than at the "excessively nautical" bar to which he went with Oliver previously. This sense of comfort and recognition also takes on moral overtones since it is clear from the passage quoted above that John wants to confront Yount over his behavior and feels entitled to do so; he is literally and figuratively on familiar turf. The conversation that ensues between the two men is superficially chummy at first, with John even buying a round and proposing that they drink a toast "to these sad times" (125). John tries to hint obliquely to Yount that he knows about the affair via an elaborate anecdote about a protozoan parasite that uses its genetic mutability to transmit an incurable disease to humans: "The trypanosome, however, has a talent. You see, the human body produces specific antibodies for specific antigens and this parasite apparently has a mechanism for altering its antigenic coat" (126). The highly specialized biomedical vocabulary that John uses to veil his blunt accusation of deception, subterfuge, and marital infidelity unsurprisingly leaves Yount "frown[ing] in puzzlement," and the two men leave the bar for a walk out onto a nearby jetty, where John tries again along a different, somewhat more direct tack: "I assume you know that Lisa's had an affair" (127). When this too fails to get a rise out of Yount, he becomes yet more direct, though still stopping short of an outright accusation:

> "You know, I don't think that Elgin is the father of this new baby."
> "You don't?"
> "No, what do you think?"
> "I don't know." Yount looked at the rocks at his sides, the waves pounding them. "You could be right."
> "Yep," John said and sighed. "Elgin really trusts you." (128)

Perceiving no sign of guilt or regret in Yount, John looks at him and oddly "felt none of the hatred he'd experienced earlier. He felt hollow, disappointed," and he once again leaves by saying nothing and sitting in his car for a moment before departing (128). He seems genuinely confused at the fact that Yount neither understood him nor took responsibility for his actions. As with Thompson at the start of the book, his inability to get another man to agree with his ethical censure leaves John unable to speak or think.

His disappointment and sense of betrayal finally do find their release, though, once he can direct them at Lisa. After his encounter with Yount, he returns home and immediately begins drinking heavily, perhaps an intentional echo of the earlier scene with Oliver in Newport. This scene's ominousness is initially somewhat disguised; right after noting that alcohol "quenched no desire but took care of everything," John walks into his granddaughter's room and "watched her sleep for a while. So beautiful. He wondered about her dreams, if they were sweet, if he were in them." The narrator, seemingly reporting John's thoughts, describes Katy's sleeping form using the same adjective, "beautiful," that appeared in John's difficult thoughts about Thompson's actions at the beginning of the book; this repetition helps explain why the impulse to save a child by cutting into a woman seems to take root in him at this precise moment. After all, he has already expressed the thought that Katy, as part of his son's family, is in danger of being "destroy[ed]" by Yount and the affair, of which the unborn child is a revolting reminder (119). Since he can seemingly think of no way of dealing with Yount, he turns to Lisa instead. John carries his drink into Lisa's room and takes a seat next to her bed, drinking his bourbon while she sleeps. When Lisa wakes up in understandable fright, he observes that Katy is "exquisite" and adds that he would "do just about anything to protect her." Thereafter he directly confronts Lisa about the affair without any of the verbal subterfuge he has used previously with his son or with Yount. He tells Lisa that he "had it in [his] mind to kill" Yount earlier but "couldn't do it. Or wouldn't do it" (132). He rages at her for a while longer and ultimately suggests that there is still time for her to abort the baby. When she protests, "Greg wants it. He wants me," John explodes at her, "Fuck him. I do not want to hear about *him*" (133), and angrily goes off to bed.

Upon awaking the next morning, he cheerfully greets Lisa as though nothing has passed between them and instead manipulates her through her daughter: "He could see the fear in her face. He knew she was terrified of losing Katy" (134). He takes Katy with him to see Oliver, and the three of them drive up the mountain to pay a surprise visit to John's girlfriend, Ruth. When they arrive at her cabin, though, John goes in by himself and discovers her in flagrante delicto with another man, the sight of which reduces him to an expressionless state even deeper than those previously depicted: "He felt his entire weight, the weight of all his years, of everything he had come to know, settle where his stomach used to be. He felt nothing in his head, nothing in his heart, just that heaviness. He backed away, knowing that later what would bother him most about the scene was the tenderness" (136). Whether the physical metaphor is intentional or not, the language of this passage suggests that the shock of this additional betrayal has reduced John to relying on his metaphorical gut—"where his stomach used to be"—since there is nothing in his head or heart anymore. He corrals Oliver and Katy, and they drive off in silence "all the way [back] to the Turners'" (137).

Once there, John receives yet another shock when Oliver informs him that he has been diagnosed with gastrointestinal cancer, an ailment of the gut more literal than John's. The two friends exchange expressions of sympathy, but the most important development in the scene comes when John finds out that Oliver's wife has taken sleeping pills to help her deal with the stress related to her husband's diagnosis. Moments after commiserating with Lorraine by telling her that he too feels "helpless, angry, hollow," John goes into her bathroom and steals several doses of Seconal, though his reason for taking them is not yet clear. John and Katy return to their house to find Lisa gone, and John retreats to his room to process the three interrelated pains he feels: "Down in his bedroom, John lay on his back and looked at the ceiling. Some day, he thought. And it was not yet over. Indeed, it had just begun. His head was swimming but he held his direction. Nothing was clear, but he was sure. He recalled the sight of Ruth with that man. He hurt. But he felt no anger. He wanted to cry about Oliver, but he needed to put that aside" (142). The ambiguous diction at the start of this passage reinforces the fact that "nothing" in his thoughts at this moment "is clear," and it calls into question the certainty of the latter half of the passage. John is not "figur[ing] out" how to respond to his difficult feelings; he is repressing them to the point of numbness and reverting to what he is "sure" is the right thing to do.

The next chapter, which is also the next-to-last one, begins with a scene of domestic familiar concord. Lisa and Katy are happily playing a board game, and Lisa reports positive news about Elgin from the hospital. John even "smiled as he watched Katy count her move aloud," but the warmth of the scene evaporates almost instantly when that observation is followed by the narrator's report that "when Lisa looked over and caught his eye, [John] wanted to say, felt like saying 'Oliver Turner is going to die.' But he didn't say it. He didn't know why he would say it. He finished his coffee" (143). The Nick Adams–esque elocution again reveals that John has reined in his thoughts to the point that he cannot conceive of expressing his sorrow at the potential death of his friend to Lisa. Instead he drives to the hospital and unloads his feelings onto a sleeping Elgin. He expresses his love for Katy and for the Turners and declares his "interlude" with Ruth to be at an end before moving on to a darker revelation: "On the way here I determined that life was devised by the enemy. 'Let's allow them to live,' he said. 'See how they deal with that.' Dealing with it. We stumble through the years, trying to take care of our own. We do what we have to do. Sacrifices must be made" (144). John's near-jeremiad echoes Job, Gnosticism, and the Protestant work ethic, but he ends with a compassionate litany that seems to presage forgiveness and reconciliation: "I love you. I loved your mother. I'm not trying to make up for anything. You know that's not my way. Just realize that I love you. I love Katy. And now I love Lisa" (144).

The opening of the final chapter adopts a tone that continues in this direction, as John returns home, playfully scoops up his granddaughter, and offers to "make the famous Livesey cocoa" (145) for both Katy and Lisa. Everett even risks cliché as "the three sat at the kitchen table, sipping the hot drink" and John proposes adding marshmallows and singing songs together. Lisa is described as "stud[ying] his face anxiously" but goes along with it, and within less than a page before the novel's close, all seems to be well: "They . . . traded off singing songs, some they knew and some they made up. . . . They finished the cocoa. Katy yawned once more and was soon sound asleep" (146). When John proposes that Lisa have a drink with him, she "laughed and was puzzled," but she is soon cajoled by his mild manner into having a "light bourbon and water" with him. The narrator notes that John "seemed to shake clear of something" as he "offered a smile" to Lisa, the significance of which becomes clearer when she notes that her drink "tastes bitter" (146). The full realization of what he has done and what he intends to do—foreshadowed all along, of course, by the book's title—dawns on the reader at the very end as the narrator relates that John has drugged her with the Seconal he stole from the Turners' bathroom: "Lisa was trying to gain her legs. She held a hand to her head and tried to take a step." The book closes with an understated declaration whose implications are horrific: "He switched on the overhead light in the kitchen and cleared the table" (147). The oscillation between bliss and dread that has pervaded the final few chapters reaches its apex in the novel's final line and accentuates the diseased way in which John's inability to "figure out" how to deal with his grief and anger leads him to fall back on what he knows both practically—obstetrics—and ethically— that Lisa has a "rancid soul."

Everett uses the untenable—for the reader, though not for John—dissonance created by the extreme tonal fluctuations in the novel to convey his noncomic satirical critique of the means by which John unbendingly maintains his belief in the rightness of his worldview, and by extension of the grotesque act of purported love that such belief justifies. *Cutting Lisa* thereby exemplifies Frye's claim that Menippean satire is directed toward "mental attitudes" and both literally and figuratively undermines the "occupational approach to life" that John brings to his interactions with others. It is not the inherent principles of his literal occupation as an obstetrician that Everett calls into question, but rather the manner in which he ultimately puts those principles in the service of what Frye would call "a maddened pedantry" (9–10). His act of "cutting" Lisa serves no obstetric purpose but instead misuses obstetric knowledge outside its intended context to impose his ethical view—that is, to "save" his family—onto the world around him. His final act eradicates all sense of adherence to the Hippocratic Oath, and John cannot even lay claim to the debatable ethics of Thompson's decision to cut into his wife from the start of the book. He retreats into silence and routine rather than doing the difficult work of subjecting his ideas to critical evaluation, a thoughtlessness that the narrative suggests is a reliable predictor of, if also perhaps a necessary precondition for, the inhumane act with which the novel ends.

Grotesque

Musgrave's sixth feature is "grotesque iconography," a somewhat more tangible relative of the comparatively abstract concept just discussed; in fact, grotesques often contribute prominently to conveying a sense of thematic heterogeneity. Musgrave has asserted that this feature involves the use of such curiously amalgamated things and situations as "comic mésalliances, giants, talking machines, dwarves, talking animals, odd combinations of human with non-human, transformations, strange powers, and so on" (23). Leonard Cassuto claimed that the literary "grotesque is born of the violation of basic categories. It occurs when an image cannot be easily classified even on the most fundamental level: when it is both one thing and another, and thus neither one." Cassuto's assertion that the "grotesque [should] be understood as a social construction rather than as an absolute value" (6) is supremely relevant to Everett's brand of Menippean satire. Given their inherent paradoxicality, grotesques disrupt social discourses that are intended to establish or to maintain categorical divisions within reality. In this way they become "the heterogeneity of the form [made] evident in its images" (Musgrave 23), a phrase that itself is a succinct encapsulation of the general Menippean mind-set: "We behold . . . a cool and detached mind playfully exploring a moral topic. The reader's interest is not in rediscovering that greed is a bad thing or that deceit is to be avoided but in working through (with the satirist's help) the implications of a given moral virtue . . . , the contradictions between one virtue . . . and another . . . , or the odd similarities between a vice . . . and a virtue" (D. Griffin 37–38). Both Musgrave and Dustin Griffin have implied that Menippean satire is inherently a form of intellectual grotesquery, productively repurposing the anxiety or revulsion that results from unresolved paradoxes to stimulate a reexamination of conventional wisdom.

The grotesque hybrids and chimeras that inhabit Everett's works are sometimes combinations of seemingly disparate physical characteristics. For example, Alice Achitophel in *Zulus* is both a morbidly obese woman and a lissome beauty; neither reality is privileged over the other: "Alice miraculously begins to grow even larger to the point where she literally explodes, splits from her 300-pound body, and emerges as a more attractive and slender woman. However, the shell of Alice's fat body remains in rebel hands, even as she roams freely in her new slender body. Moreover, the thin Alice can psychically sense what the fat Alice's discarded head perceives as it lays [*sic*] supine in the middle of the rebel camp" (Schur, "The Mind-Body Split" 77). Alice's confusion regarding her "real" identity arises in part because her transformative explosion happens while she is in a "hallucinatory state," during which the language of the book becomes even more convoluted than it has been. These passages frustrate any attempt at strictly rational interpretation by suggesting that she gives birth to herself in a manner that evokes mammalian biology, fairy tales, and Lovecraftian horror fiction all at once: "Her thoughts spilled with shards of her brain down her body and into her lungs and became sparkling cities, fat with the hope of success and clear of the poison-planet air which she sucked in. Her ovaries shined and sang vulgar songs; and standing in the glass case of her uterus, fully developed, frozen still, was a thin Alice Achitophel, waiting to awake, her eyes dead with the promise of coming life, growing, growing, growing to the size of life" (Everett, *Zulus* 108).

The inability to explain or to reconcile what has happened initially confuses both Alice and her protector/lover Kevin Peters, though, on one hand, both of them eventually concur that simply believing it as a matter of fact is preferable to doubting: "I don't understand, but I believe that you at least think you are Alice Achitophel. Which is all that matters" (112). On the other hand, Kevin discovers that the rebels who initially appear to be Alice's refuge from the oppressive, bureaucratic city in which she lives at the beginning of the novel have "worked [themselves] up into a religious frenzy" over what happened to Alice: "I was told that an insane young woman killed Alice Achitophel, blew her wide open with dynamite and fled, that the fat woman swelled larger than her confinement, burst open and a beautiful maiden came out with her blood, and that God came down and exploded the evil one and left a minor evil for humans to exterminate. All crazy, but all convinced" (117). Kevin's conclusion that their interpretation is another sign that "this planet is sick and strange" foreshadows the novel's cataclysmic ending, in which he and Alice apparently eradicate themselves and the remnant of human life in order to cure this "sick[ness]." The grotesque oxymoron contained within Alice's vision of "eyes dead with the promise of coming life" echoes the novel's next-to-last line, in which Alice and Kevin prepare to press down together on the lever that will exterminate humanity: "She questioned him with her eyes, then closed them" (245).

Employing the grotesque in a more abstracted manner, each of the three stories within *Assumption* (which is discussed at length in the final chapter) involves Ogden Walker being misled by an act of imposture related to a crime, a situation that stimulates the one essential trope—the "mystery" in need of a solution—of conventional detective fiction. Everett creates situations in which Ogden is fruitlessly chasing after a series of red herrings rather than solving the mysteries with which he is presented. Few of the characters in this book are who and what they appear to be—or at least what they represent themselves to be—a process that ultimately extends all the way to Ogden himself in the unexpected climax of the third story. This irreconcilable instability upsets the fundamental logical premises of the genre and thereby constitutes a major part of Everett's "toying with the assumptions we have when we enter into that kind of story" ("Author Percival" 188).

Glyph presents the reader with yet another form of grotesque, one that incorporates both the literal/corporeal version that appears in *Zulus* and the more figurative/conceptual version that appears in *Assumption*. Although his intellect is exceptional for any human being, Ralph's grotesqueness is partly physical, as evidenced by the reaction of almost all the adults in the book to the precocious writings produced by an infant still bound to his crib:

> It wasn't until I was near done writing that I looked up to see the completely stunned and befuddled face of Inflato floating over me. What I wrote:
>
> 1) Mixolydian is not misspelled.
>
> 2) Though the writing is young and, perhaps, overly exuberant, the story is solid and thoroughly and absolutely readable.
>
> 3) Da-da is full of shit.
>
> Inflato looked at my eyes and then to Mo, swayed for a second, then fainted. (Everett, *Glyph* 25–26)

Just as the physiological response of fainting is an analogue to the emotional confusion engendered by Ralph's note, the physical dimension of Ralph's grotesqueness accentuates the novel's other, more abstract forms of multiplicity: "the reader must suspend disbelief that a child could be born with the innate ability to read and write at a post-doctoral level . . . even if he has yet to discover elementary lessons of day-to-day living, or the wonders of his own body . . . . The protagonist must retain the attributes of childhood, adolescence, and adulthood" (Berben-Masi, "Jailhouse" 50, 53).

Theodore "Ted" Street's undead status in *American Desert* is likewise a mixture of physical and ontological grotesques. It is, after all, the sight of his presumed-dead body coming back to life during his funeral that stimulates not only "a terrible riot which spread from the church and into the streets" (16) but also a sense of thematic heterogeneity through the clash of funereal and farcical elements:

> Then, as the choir ended its final *amen* with a harmonious hum, Theodore Street sat up in his coffin. A hush filled the church, as one might expect, but it was not long-lived. . . . Gloria Street fainted but remained frozen upright with wide-open eyes. Gloria's sister made a break for the door, her large feet tripping her near the end of the aisle's red carpet, causing her to roll to a stop at a blind man's feet with her dress over her head. Orville Orson farted and farted again. The dean prayed, loudly. The *Beowulf* woman reached into her bag and readied the pepper spray her fiancé had bought for her. (11)

It becomes clear after he is examined by a doctor a few days after his seemingly miraculous resurrection that Street realizes he has few, if any, of the usual signs that would normally indicate being alive:

> "I don't know why I'm doing this," [Dr.] Timmons said. "I can't find a pulse in the first place. . . . No blood pressure"
>
> . . .
>
> Ted looked at the woman's face and could see her fear. . . . "What now?" he asked.
>
> "I can't really tell anything here," she said. "I need to find out if there is any brain activity."
>
> "My speaking to you doesn't count," Ted said.
>
> "As odd as it sounds, no," she said. (65)

Neither the doctor nor Street can articulate what this contradictory set of signs means: "'It seems I'm dead,' Ted said to his wife. 'Obviously you're not dead, Mr. Street,' Timmons said" (66). The doctor's comments to the press as she leaves the examination demonstrate that this indeterminacy stimulates neither curiosity nor wonder but rather dread: "This man is dead, yet he is alive. His heart is not beating, but his brain continues to function. I don't understand it, I don't have any answers for you. He's frightened, I think. I too am frightened . . . . Maybe we should all be frightened" (68). As Michel Feith pointed out, "[Street's] re-animated body, unable to feel physical pain but endowed with new gifts of empathy and mind-reading, is a paradox," and he gave this state a specifically grotesque/Menippean interpretation when he argued that it "makes him akin to a trickster figure" when "associated with his sense of humor and parody" (Feith, "Blueprint" 10).

Street remains unsure throughout the rest of the book about how and why he has returned from nonexistence, and neither of the two discourses—science and religion—that would presumably have ready answers to those questions proves useful. Their mutual inadequacy is exemplified by a man named Oswald Avery, whom Street meets while escaping from incarceration in a government research lab. A parody of the classic "mad scientist" character, Avery is trying to combine religion and science in a manner laden with potential significance: "We're here trying to uncover the secrets of reanimation. Perhaps the most famous reanimated person is Jesus Christ. . . . The fifth wound to the Christ was a cut delivered by a Roman soldier named Longinus. The staff of the spear is in Rome, but the blade, well, no one ever knew where the blade was. Until about fifty years ago when Hitler's men found it in a cave. . . . Anyway, we ended up with the blade and on the blade are blood stains, the blood of Jesus. From the stains we isolated the DNA and using the DNA we tried to clone Christ" (197).

These efforts ultimately re-create not a world-redeeming heroic figure but only "twenty dark-haired, drooling men dressed in jumpsuits," many of whom are "badly deformed" with "faces [that were] twisted, with cleft palates, crossed eyes, long drooping lobes" (196–97). As Feith pointed out, this is just one of "many episodes of the novel [that] seem to have been beamed piecemeal from paranoid action and [science fiction] series: the black helicopters, the underground base and laboratory at Area 51, the secret military experiments therein conducted, ring the *X-Files* bell of government conspiracy." This observation led him to assert that "Everett engages in cultural critique, through the satire of cliché fragments of popular culture," which seemingly produce nothing more significant than the shambling pseudo-Christs of Avery's underground laboratory (Feith, "Blueprint" 11). Feith furthermore suggested that "the very pleasure derived from their reactivation and recombination in a comic, surrealist-inspired narrative may well redeem" these otherwise stale narrative fragments.

The conclusion of Street's life story supports this claim, even as it stops short of offering any explanation for what has been happening or why. Street actively participates in the rescue of a group of children from a charismatic, David Koresh/Jim Jones–type cult leader and is hailed as a hero because of it. Although this act might seem to justify his return from the dead, Street gains no insight by the end of the book that would mitigate his status as a grotesque in violation of his (and our) understanding of the categorical distinction between alive and dead. Street films a farewell interview in the book's final pages in which nearly all of his assertions about what has happened to him are grammatically and/or existentially negative: "I am dead. I died and I am dead and I can tell you no more about the meaning of life than I could when I was alive. . . . Now I am nothing but pain. To myself, my family, and to you. . . . I am no hero. . . . I am no angel. There is no god for which I might serve as an emissary. I am no savior. I am no messiah. . . . I wish that I had no mouth, so that my silence would mean as much as my words. I wish that my words had no meaning" (290). In keeping with Everett's possibly ironic goal of "knowing nothing at all" (Medlin and Gore 159) through his writing, Street's (after)life has become a Menippean rejection of almost all positive interpretations other than Street's emphatic relief at being "*finally,* in this life, a decent man" (290). When Street removes his head from his body—the same cause that failed to kill him permanently after he was in a car accident while driving to commit suicide—after concluding the interview, he "stayed dead" (291). Although there is no sentimentalized redemptive significance to his return, as in such iconic "second-chance" films as *Heaven Can Wait* (1978) or *Ghost* (1990), Street at least gets to fulfill the promise, stated on the novel's opening page, of telling a galloping story that describes how "in a most profound way, he stood—or stands even—outside himself, not so much on the parapet of consciousness but of life itself" (3).

Despite this list of fairly literal examples, Everett's grotesques just as frequently operate in more figurative psychological, philosophical, and/or linguistic realms. For example, in the course of analyzing *Suder,* Anthony Stewart explicitly referred to Cassuto's definition of the grotesque as he outlined the novel's plot:

> *Suder* is . . . a test of the title character's abilities to converse across boundaries and, in the face of the failure of a conversation, to find emancipation in some other way. . . . It represents multiple attempts at such conversations: black/white, male/female, representative/individual, technical/vernacular, stereotype/cosmopolitan, sane/insane, and the binary that perhaps contains these others: conventional/unconventional. . . . Suder intuits his stereotyped subjectivity and attempts to escape this position . . . by becoming "grotesque," as Leonard Cassuto uses this term, defining the tension created in the space between categories. ("Do you mind" 116)

The only overtly physical grotesque in Craig Suder's characterization involves his literal interpretation and subsequent incarnation of a hybrid identity that is unconsciously attributed to him by various figures throughout the book. In the opening chapter, as Suder returns to the dugout after yet another hapless strikeout, his manager suggests that the way out of his slump is "to straighten up and fly right" (Everett, *Suder* 5). While Suder is a child, he meets the famed jazz pianist Bud Powell, who deepens the complexity of the youngster's association with flying creatures: "He looked at my face and said, 'You remind me of Bird.' . . . 'Charlie Parker,' Daddy said to me. I didn't know this name either, but I liked that he said I looked like Bird" (31). After taking his leave from baseball, his home in Seattle, and his family, Suder becomes profoundly invested in Parker's explicitly bird-themed song, "Ornithology," going so far as to carry a record of it and a phonograph with him everywhere, in addition to buying a saxophone on which he attempts to learn how to play the song. Uzzie Cannon has described this last development explicitly as a tonal—in a musical sense as well as a more figurative literary one—shift: "Through his appreciation of 'Ornithology,' the freedom and flight imagined in Parker's song become, for Suder, synonymous with life. . . . Suder's encounter with 'Ornithology' begins his transformation from blues-child to jazz free-bird" (101).

All of these references to flight and birds converge in the final scene of the novel, when, "having had his fill of being seen only as a black baseball player . . . Suder decides that the most thoroughgoing escape from such limitations is to take to the air, to momentarily become something entirely different . . .

that only Craig Suder can become—namely a man who flies like a bird" (Stewart, "Do you mind" 121–22). Initially he does so by manifesting his would-be avian identity in the most superficial ways: "As his resolve strengthens, Suder begins to do what he feels is necessary to become closer to bird-like: he starts to eat worms, he tries to raise his body temperature by deliberately catching a cold and attempts to increase the flexibility of his neck" (Stewart, "Do you mind" 123). With the assistance of his cranky nine-year-old ward, he uses an assemblage—that is, a material grotesque—of objects to construct the means by which he intends to take his coach's words at face value and "fly right": "I've built the frames of the wings with plastic tubing. Each frame is like a big horseshoe, about as tall as me, with slats running across the width. I've sorted out the strongest trash bags and cut them into strips and wrapped the strips around the frames. The feathers are going on one at a time" (Everett, *Suder* 164). It is with these artificial wings that he "step[s] off" the mountain on which he has been living with Jincy and Renoir the elephant—whom he adopted after their comically violent first encounter—in a situation that parodies the conventional nuclear family. Unlikely yet happy quasi-familial combinations recur throughout Everett's fiction, further complicating the idea that grotesques are intended solely to disgust or to censure. Suder begins flying, albeit only after an initial terrifying free fall. At the novel's end, not only is he "making big circles and . . . pretty much in charge," but he is also sporting an erection, signaling an end to the literal impotence that has accompanied its figurative twin since the opening pages of the book (171).

Berben-Masi associated Suder's transformation with the transcendent mythic hero pattern cataloged in Joseph Campbell's *The Hero with a Thousand Faces:* "the plot line proceeds from the hero's motivated departure . . . [and is] completed by the eventual fulfillment of his true nature as predicted during his childhood by recognition of and reunification with his 'Bird' heritage, or consecration by the divine father figure" ("Getting" 24). Although Campbell did not define such a "reunification" specifically as a grotesque, Berben-Masi suggested such an interpretation in calling Suder a "successful human bird" (26). Using "human" as an adjective to modify "bird" in this way is not only linguistically unusual but also ontologically grotesque and wholly appropriate: "Suder's refusal to play by the rules of taxonomy [the zoologist Richard] Beckwith tries to impose on him signals the shift in Suder's quest, from one of understanding to one of grotesque autonomy. . . . The crucial point here is not that [Suder] expects to *become* a bird, but that he . . . heighten[s] our realization of his violation of the basic categories, a violation upon which he begins to thrive" (Stewart, "Do you mind" 123). Suder's rejection/expansion of Beckwith's biological classification in the book's final line resembles Ted

Street's experience with scientists—mad or otherwise—in *American Desert*. Beckwith embodies a rigidly scientific worldview, as shown by his insistence on referring to all animals by their Latin taxonomical names; yet he cannot explain Suder's flight in an ultimately meaningful way, leaving it up to Suder to define it for, and as, himself: "And I'm flying, goddamnit, I'm flying. Then I see Beckwith on a ridge with the hunters and he's pointing up at me. I imagine him to say, '*Homo sapiens.*' And I says, 'Craig Suder'" (171). His name now denotes a hybrid individual who has "become the 'Bird' that Bud Powell had once called him, the 'Bird' soaring in Charlie Parker's 'Ornithology,' and the literal bird that flies off Willet Rock" (Cannon 110).

There is some critical disagreement concerning the extent to which Everett intends Suder's flight to echo the "quintessential metaphor for freedom" that recurs "in modern and contemporary African American literature, music, and art" (Cannon 112n8). The comparison with Toni Morrison's oft-cited adaptation of the "flying African" folktale in *Song of Solomon* (1977), published only six years before *Suder*, can be suggested readily in case one is so inclined. I tend to side more with Stewart's view on the novel's conclusion, which is that Suder is in greater need of "an assertion of the aggressive and radical autonomy available in the grotesque" than of a liberation that simultaneously solidifies a racial or ethnic bond: "At this point he is not 'too black' or 'not black enough.' . . . He is only Craig Suder, and this is his great accomplishment. As he flies over the group of people watching from the ground, to say anything else about who he is can only miss the point" ("Do you mind"124). Stewart further argued that "miss[ing] the point" in this manner would be to sidestep the novel's "requirement that we interrogate our habitual interpretations. One need not be able to take flight like a bird to be able to commit oneself to questioning the associations we tend to make through habit" ("Do you mind" 124–25). His interpretation of the ending allows Suder to become and to remain a sui generis figure; it does not invalidate habituated readings, but it certainly points out their ultimate limitations.

Such limitations become apparent once again in *I Am Not Sidney Poitier*, the curiously named protagonist of which is both a material and a nominal grotesque as he gets older in the novel and starts physically resembling the famed actor after whom he is (not) named: "'I can't get over how much you look like Sidney Poitier. A young Sidney Poitier.' 'More every day, it seems,' I said" (83). Sarah Mantilla Griffin has suggested that this resemblance does not necessarily constrict Not Sidney's identity because of what Sidney Poitier represents as an actor: "Sidney Poitier's movies are famous for boldly exploring race relations. . . . In exploring these relations, Poitier has to signify in many different ways in order to challenge the meanings attached to signifiers like blackness, criminality, wealth, education, and so forth. Through divorcing signifiers from meaning and henceforth changing meanings, Poitier's characters were often able to change understandings of those signifiers" (27). The difference between Sidney and Not Sidney becomes confused on a narrative level, though, as Everett deliberately incorporates scenarios that parody scenes from some of Sidney Poitier's best-known films: "When Not Sidney Poitier gets himself into such scenes, the distinction between him and the actor becomes blurred. Not [Sidney] does not have his own identity; the one he has been given is just a negation, defined by what he is: Not" (Gretlund, "Black" 44). For a while Not Sidney proves to be able to emulate Sidney Poitier, which Griffin argued "change[s] the signifying fields of Poitier's films," thereby allowing him to become a similarly "multifaceted, malleable signifier" (S. Griffin 27).

Any positive aspect to this malleability is soon undermined by the fact that Not Sidney appears to be fated in his life to replay the same scenarios that Poitier played as an actor. Given that many of Poitier's films featured happy endings for the characters he portrayed, this might not initially seem like a bad thing, but Sharon Willis has offered some insight into Everett's methods by contending that Poitier's films ultimately were expressions of a "fantasy of racial understanding and 'assimilation' that requires no effort on the part of white people." In her view, the "Poitier effect . . . functions as a defense, or a compensatory gesture, averting or deflecting the possibility of a kind of critical thinking that would involve a serious reciprocal interracial exchange" (5). Not Sidney's ultimate inability to break away from Sidney Poitier despite being nominally his diametrical opposite reveals the invariable and extremely limited system of signification that is available to him.

He clarifies early on in the telling of his story that his mother—whom, it should be noted, he also describes as "absolutely, unquestionably, certifiably crazy" (4–5)—gave him his name apparently without consideration of the famous actor: "One might have thought that my mother imagined that our last name, rare as it was, was enough to cause confusion with Sidney Poitier. . . . But her puzzled expression led me to believe that my name had nothing to do with the actor at all, that *Not Sidney* was simply a name she had created, with no consideration of the outside world. She liked it, and that was enough" (7). His mother's unlikely, but seemingly genuine, disconnection from external signifiers contrasts with a phenomenon that Willis has articulated in regard to the real-life Sidney Poitier. She noted that as he became more successful and recognizable as an actor, his appearances in film were increasingly marked by a doubled identity in which he and the characters he portrayed were simultaneously present: "As the only black male lead in Hollywood in this period . . . he was always appearing as himself alongside whatever character he was playing

. . . . To the extent that both his casting and his roles depend on and reinscribe his iconicity, he is always playing himself" (24). Furthermore she noted that Poitier's participation in the rhetoric of "magical reconciliation" that pervades his films not only creates a self-reinforcing confusion between himself and his characters but also radiates outward to subsume African Americans in other contexts: "But as his roles conflate the image and the man through repetitions of his familiar presence, his returns also help guarantee the exclusion of other black actors. Besides securing the authenticity of his performance and, by extension, of his films' stories and their magical resolutions, Poitier's performance also stands in for an entire race even as he emerges from it as an exception. His cinematic presence . . . recall[s] a population largely absent from his films' on-screen worlds" (25). If Sidney Poitier himself is caught up inescapably in a representational process that blurs the lines between his real-life self, the characters he plays, and all of black America, then Not Sidney hardly stands a chance of escaping that same gravity; in essence, his name protests too much for most people—especially most white people—who come in contact with him to take seriously, since what Sidney Poitier represents to them is so reassuring and comfortable that it does not make sense for a young black man *not* to be him—or to be *Not* him.

One of the few people who accepts that Not Sidney has an identity that is meaningfully separate from Sidney is, ironically, Ted Turner, the media mogul. Not Sidney's mother had believed in Turner's company before it became successful and struck up a friendship with the future billionaire: "Turner saw my mother's substantial investment in his dream as the kind of symbol and charm for his success. My mother was the kind of grass-roots, if not proletarian, person he wanted to imagine his media world touching, however tangentially, on his way up to great and obscene wealth" (8). After Not Sidney's mother dies, Turner comes to get him and takes him away to Atlanta, where he lives in one of Turner's mansions. Unlike Rhino Tanner from *Grand Canyon, Inc.,* though, Everett's fictional Turner is neither bumpkin nor bullshitter. He is fully aware of the "scenario of the rich do-gooding white man taking in the poor little black child" that was popularized on television during the 1980s: "You ever see that kidney-sick little boy who can't grow on that *Diff'rent Strokes* show? Well, I think that's just obscene, Not. Not him, but that picture, that model of the black child being raised by some great white father. I'm not that arrogant" (12). Not Sidney confirms Turner's rejection of this clichéd role when he notes that he was not actually raised by Turner after his mother's death, but rather that he "lived at one of his houses and was left pretty much to my own unformed devices" (8). Despite his quirky demeanor and proclivity for homespun turns of phrase, Turner reveals himself to be a fairly open-minded thinker, one who even has something of the satirist's bent to him in how he intends to undermine the "Arnold and Webster" model he deems "obscene": "I'm going to take over television and air that trash every day several times a day instead of only once a week. That way we'll all become desensitized to its harmful and consumptive effects by sheer overexposure" (12).

Everett, of course, knows that this was not the real Ted Turner's intent in developing the syndication-based programming model for his much-imitated TNT network, but his fictional Turner is in many ways a more astute observer of reality than most of the people with whom young Not Sidney interacts. Although Turner's worldview is far from clear-eyed and infallible, his willingness to accept Not Sidney's identity as something entirely distinct from Sidney Poitier makes him exceptional within the novel: "I imagined that he considered Not to be an actual name and couldn't believe that it would be simply the single syllable it was. So, it came out *Nu'ott,* the same way god became *ga'awd* for the evangelist on the street in downtown Decatur" (11). Whereas almost everyone else overdetermines the latter portion of Not Sidney's two-part first name, Turner accepts and emphasizes the former portion and makes *Nu'ott*—which would also be, more or less, the pronunciation of "new art" in Turner's southern drawl—out of it; if Not Sidney could find a way to do the same, it would validate his mother's claim that his name was entirely sufficient to identify him on its own.

While he is in high school, though, Not Sidney's name continues to be a source of confusion and consternation for him:

> To my teachers my name was odd, but to my classmates I was Sidney or Not Sidney or something other than Sidney. My *real* name became a mystery to be solved for many. Still, I was beaten often, but now in an attempt to have me give up that prized bit of information, namely my name. There was some upside, as some of the looser girls would offer to kiss me if I told them my name. I would gladly agree to the arrangement. I would receive the kiss and then say, "My name is Not Sidney." Unfortunately, the *looser* girls often would and could be more violent and fierce than the boys, and so they would offer up an entrée of whup-ass with sides of hair pulling and scratching. (29)

Sidney claims, in an echo of Turner's earlier comment regarding his plan to inundate audiences with episodes of *Diff'rent Strokes* and *Webster,* that a "steady diet of humiliation leads to a kind of immunity or desensitization to abasement and discomfiture," after which the beatings taper off for lack of interest, having not left "any perceptible marks—physical, physiological, or neurological" on him. Ominously, he remarks that "psychic damage . . . is far more difficult to assess," though he also believes himself to have been inoculated against it by his "sense of irony" (29–30).

The possibility of such damage intensifies, though, when his history teacher, Miss Hancock, takes an interest in him for more than his savvy answers to her in-class questions: "There were clearly codes in her employ that fell short of my understanding, but it soon became evident that my emerging resemblance to Sidney Poitier was not lost on her and that an inappropriate and, I must say, welcomed relationship began to surface" (30). Not Sidney initially enjoys her attention and their awkward sexual encounters, but when he begins feeling uncomfortable and tries to end their affair, she threatens to turn him in, mockingly noting that the authorities will hardly believe him, "a kid without a proper name, angry because he couldn't live out his fantasy with the hot teacher" (36). Essentially she is pointing out that by not being Sidney Poitier, the unthreatening and desirable image of blackness for whites such as Miss Hancock, he will doom himself. Having recognized from the beginning that her interest in him is due precisely to his uncanny resemblance to Sidney Poitier, Not Sidney knows what breaking that spell means for him, but he decides to do it anyway. When Miss Hancock flunks him, Not Sidney reports her to the school's principal and the district superintendent, neither of whom takes his complaint seriously. Far from being dismayed, though, he understands it as his cue to leave and, in doing so, invokes another fictional character with few, if any, possible connections to Sidney Poitier: "I was fairly clear in my desire to become a high school dropout. I decided right then to light out for the territory, as it were, to leave my childhood, to abandon what had become my home, my safety, and to discover myself." He punctuates this revelation with two further literary allusions—"I was a fighter of windmills. I was a chaser of whales"—before ending with a *Suder*-like self-affirming exclamation: "I was Not Sidney Poitier" (43). The comparisons with Huck Finn, Don Quixote, and Melville's Ishmael all suggest that Not Sidney's self-authored bildungsroman will not be entirely devoid of external patterns, but all the ones he alludes to are at least definitively *not* Sidney Poitier. The life story he proposes for himself may not be wholly "new art" at this point, but in that regard he is not so different from most other adolescents.

Although Everett mines his protagonist's complicated identity for a substantial amount of slapstick humor, its damaging existential consequences are made clear by the middle of the novel, when Not Sidney begins showing signs of having a mental breakdown caused by the strain of maintaining the boundary between himself and his nominal not-self. Not Sidney's journeys upon leaving home immediately begin resembling episodes from Sidney Poitier's films. This does not seem to be planned ahead of time, nor does Not Sidney appear to recognize the similarities; nevertheless, these parallels undermine his ability to "discover [him]self" in the manner expressed by his soliloquy upon departing from his high school. Not Sidney finds himself agreeing to build a church for a group of nuns in the backwater town of Smuteye, Alabama, a plot development that parodies Sidney Poitier's Academy Award–winning role in *Lilies of the Field* (1963). While there, Not Sidney avails himself of a bathroom at a truck stop with a "lot full of big rigs and Confederate flags" and has a moment of anxiety: "There I shaved while truckers in undershirts brushed teeth and washed hairy pits. No matter how much they scrubbed they looked nothing like Sidney Poitier, but I looked just like him and so they stared." Not Sidney's mention that the presumably white truckers with whom he shares the bathroom cannot scrub themselves to look like Sidney Poitier initially seems like a wry twist on the old racist joke about the inability to wash the blackness off one's skin. The looks they direct toward him—and the implicit threat thus conveyed—reinforce this interpretation. However, a second level of dissociation develops and involves his reflection: "They stared at Sidney Poitier's face in the mirror and I stared at it, too. The face was smooth, brown, older than I remembered, handsome. The face in the mirror smiled and I had to smile back" (191). Not Sidney seems to perceive the face in the mirror as that of Sidney Poitier, and the sense of compulsion expressed in the final sentence again echoes Willis's observations about both the manner in which Sidney Poitier's self and cinematic image are intertwined and the way in which he becomes a stand-in for "largely absent" others. Not Sidney is in the midst of literally reenacting a scene from one of Sidney Poitier's movies as he slips into a state of confusion regarding his identity. As Sarah Griffin noted, this is the first slip down a slope that eventually results in an almost complete out-of-body dissociation: "Not Sidney recognizes a separation between himself and the self that smiles at him from the mirror, but is comforted in seeing this other. Only just before his psychotic break does it become clear that this other may be harmful to Not Sidney's mental well-being. At that time, Not Sidney dreams that he is dead and looking down upon his dead body" (28–29).

Whereas Craig Suder's combination of human and birdlike—and Birdlike—qualities imparts to him "a sense of autonomy and purpose he lacks before" (Stewart, "Do you mind" 123), Not Sidney's unresolved fusion of identities has the opposite effect. By the end of the book, the resemblance between Not Sidney and Sidney is as much metaphysical as physical, and Not Sidney's dream death has become disturbingly close to becoming a reality, at least as far as his distinct personality is concerned. He attends an Oscars-like awards show to accept a "special award for Most Dignified Figure in American Culture" (234) as Sidney Poitier. His interactions with various people who believe he is the actor point out the extent to which his identity has become blurred: "[A] young woman came up to me and asked for my autograph. She said 'I just love you, Mr. Poitier.' . . . I wrote: *For Evelyn, All the best, Not Sidney Poitier.* She was puzzled as she read. 'You're not Sidney Poitier?' 'I am'" (232). This exchange repeats a gag regarding his name that has recurred throughout the novel; although his signature indicates that he retains his understanding of himself as being separate from Sidney Poitier, his response to Evelyn's question is both grammatically and typographically ambiguous, and the conclusion to the book confuses the issue even further.

By the time he has schmoozed—as Sidney Poitier, of course—with Elizabeth Taylor and Harry Belafonte before the show, he faces a conundrum of identity that has no easy resolution: "Was I Not Sidney Poitier or was I not Sidney Poitier?" (233). Both of these propositions are, of course, true, and yet everything in the moment suggests instead that he *is* Sidney Poitier—and therefore is *not* Not Sidney Poitier—by virtue of the fact that everyone perceives him as such. In giving his acceptance speech, Sidney/Not Sidney offers his audience and Everett's reader one last multileveled mordant joke in this regard, indicating that he wishes the epitaph on his gravestone simply to read, "*I AM NOT MYSELF TODAY*" (234). Whether this grave will bear his name or that of Sidney Poitier is unclear, though the statement chiseled onto the tombstone would be equally true in either case because of the toll that the unresolved conundrum has taken: "although Not Sidney appears to be 'normal' throughout the novel, his final delusion reveals that he had been compensating [because of the confusion of identity resulting from his name]. . . . This does not mean that he is completely psychotic; it suggests only that he is partially delusional due to a rupture in his symbolic order" (S. Griffin 31). Everett's satire in the novel is not primarily directed at Not Sidney for failing to break free from the gravitational pull of his famous partial namesake; rather it is aimed at the various people and processes responsible for narrowing Not Sidney's opportunities to make "*Nu'ott*" out of himself.

In a similar—albeit far less comedic—manner, Ishmael Kidder's identity in *The Water Cure* is both multiple and seemingly unstable, much like the structure of the book. Depending on the context, he is: 1) the narrator and protagonist of a highly literary, if also extremely disjointed narrative; 2) a father grieving his daughter's sexual violation and murder; 3) the torturer of the man alternately identified as Reggie, Art, and W., who he believes is guilty of his daughter's murder; or 4) a female romance novelist named Estelle Gilliam. Jonathan Dittman has explained one of the effects of this particular multiplicity: "While markers, such as husband, father, and son, can refer to the same individual, these markers cannot independently define a person—more comprehensive qualifiers are necessary to even scratch the surface of identity . . . . While there is an underlying and perhaps 'genuine' description of an individual, the layers of meaning encoded in all of these symbolic representations make it impossible to truly identify a person" (16). Everett confessed in an interview to being "fascinated by" the manner in which names function as "rigid designators," and *The Water Cure* resembles many of his other recent works in exploring the "literal misunderstandings and desired misunderstandings" that arise from the way names are used (Champion 166).

Kidder echoes these observations when he expresses his sense of the inherently contradictory nature of names fairly early in the book: "Naming functions as a device for distancing as much as an emblem of connection" (Everett, *Water Cure* 33). The manner in which Kidder presents his simultaneous distance from and connection to the identity of Estelle Gilliam reveals the significance of this particular grotesque to Everett's serious play with the "layers of meaning encoded" in names. In explaining his "understanding of the novels that I made using the name of another person," Kidder pointedly "refuse[s] to consider [her] an alter ego," saying only that "somehow Estelle Gilliam found a voice and life, such as it was" (65). Earlier, though, he complicates that assertion of separation when he claims, "I simply am of course who I am, Ishmael Kidder, but I am better known as Estelle Gilliam." Such declarative utterances establish his claim to be Ishmael Kidder, but this passage's allusions to the opening line of *Moby-Dick,* to the "Popeye" cartoons, and to the punning evocation of Popeye's signature phrase by the narrator of Ralph Ellison's *Invisible Man*—"I yam what I am" (201)—all remind the reader of its constructedness by overtly signaling its fictionality; the fact that his ostensible last name is Kidder—that is, jester, jokester—only serves to deepen the reader's doubt regarding the veracity of the outermost layer of his narrative self-presentation. He goes on to claim that the only three people who know "who I am and am not" are his ex-wife, who "lives far away in another life on that other planet"; the local sheriff, to whom Ishmael is obliged to reveal his secret in order to forestall suspicion—arising from his lack of "visible means of support"—that he is a drug dealer; and his agent, whose income is dependent on Estelle's output, not Ishmael's (25–26).

About Estelle's formulaic output, Kidder writes, "The structure of my romance novels was confining" (62), which hearkens back to Margaret Russett's claims about Everett's "unrelenting assault on constricting fictions of identity" (366). However, Kidder recognizes that his "business" as a writer of romance novels "was not art . . . in any way," resulting in a situation in which he cannot imagine "when form and structure [would] not confine me, not constrain me" (Everett, *Water Cure* 62). *The Water Cure,* which is simultaneously Everett's novel and Kidder's memoir/meditation/disquisition, is an extreme example of such an unconfined, unconstrained narrative, one that allows Kidder to "find some kind of freedom" and challenge those who would dictate to him "what the form will allow" (62). Albeit in a radically different format, this same structure and intention are present in *Erasure* as well, and in his own way Kidder is as much an outspoken critic of bad writing and reading practices as Monk Ellison is. Kidder continues his thoughts in this fragment by angrily ranting against the "stinking corrupt dumbass morally de-centered president and his greedy slimy ass-breathed henchmen" (63), in the process marking his text as the diametrical opposite of the implied romance novel he normally writes—but of which no explicit trace appears in *The Water Cure* beyond a few book titles. He longs to be able to interrupt "during some steamy removal of some hat or cape or bra and simply tell the lost and lonely woman who is reading my formulaic, predictable, though albeit well-written, novel" about all the ghastly things her "beloved country" is doing (147).

Kidder thus presents his assertion of an identity as an author separate from Estelle Gilliam as a productive response both to perceived artistic limitations and to his abiding sense of powerlessness resulting from the violence inflicted on his daughter and the violence of the novel's geopolitical setting. However, as Dittman noted, it also involves an attempt at reclaiming his masculinity, which is publicly threatened when he is forced to reveal the female aspect—that is, Estelle—of himself to the sheriff. In order to confirm his own innocence and reestablish his manly bona fides, he has to demonstrate the very type of violence he seems to abhor when it is perpetrated by his government or his daughter's killer: "Kidder goes along with the sheriff's suggestion and waits for the drug dealers in the woods. In order to defend his masculine identity, Kidder must conform to the 'American way' [of vigilantism] alluded to by the sheriff. As a result of this challenge, Kidder plays into the conventional assumption that masculinity equals violence" (Dittman 13). As is the case with the text of the narrative being read as Everett's novel, "Kidder's statements about guns and killing are diametrically opposed from the thematic elements of Gilliam's romance novels. . . . Violence toward others, while antithetical to Estelle Gilliam, becomes a necessary tool for Kidder's reclamation of the masculine identity lost through his appropriation of a feminine alter ego" (13–14). In short, the multiplicities of identity within Kidder function like the "series of narratives that exist both within and in contradiction with each other" that Kimberly Eaton has contended destabilize meaning in *Erasure* (224).

The fictional characters named Percival Everett in *A History of the African-American People, I Am Not Sidney Poitier,* and *Percival Everett by Virgil Russell* destabilize identity not by showing the multiplicity of meaningful layers within a single person but by questioning the value of names, one of Dittman's most "categorically significant linguistic markers" (16). The real-life Everett implies this technique in describing the origins of *Percival Everett by Virgil Russell:* "It comes out of Frege's Puzzle, the problem that you have reconciling sense and reference. And so it's really about that, about two things that can have the same name and not be the same thing. That's not very helpful, is it?" ("Author Percival" 189). Like René Magritte's famous painting *The Treachery of Images* (1929), which playfully reminds its viewers that a representative image of a pipe is still not a pipe, Everett's semantic grotesques—whether they are one thing/person with many names or one name that signifies multiple things/people—are intended to remind his readers that "linguistic systems of representation can be altered or amended to form new meanings in society" (Dittman 16). The linguistic and semantic grotesquery associated with naming in *Percival Everett by Virgil Russell* reaches its bewildering apex near the book's end: "My name is Name. My name is my name and the name of both the word *name* and Name, my name. I am not the only one with the name Name and there are also other names" (219).

Grotesques of various sorts appear elsewhere in Everett's work as well. For example, nearly all the characters in *A History of the African-American People* are grotesquely "doubled" in some way, whether through the contrast between the real-life versions of Thurmond, Everett, and Kincaid and their fictional selves; the gradual revelation of McCloud's sister Reba, who increasingly draws Wilkes's attentions away from the *other* R. McCloud in the book; or the dozens of ridiculous appellations—for example, "Toodle-oo, *Beeuuttee*" (127) or "Call me Lars, *Barton*" (199)—with which Wilkes closes his letters. His inconsistent self-reference further destabilizes the ability of both his correspondents and the reader to understand who and what he is—and, therefore, what he is saying. Wilkes furthermore inflicts this destabilization onto his various correspondents by constantly altering their names. For example, he addresses Everett and Kincaid variously as "Percival and James, James and Percival, Jacival and Perames" (117); "Perce and Jim" (178); and "Percy and Jimbo" (254), and he is constantly trying to pry loose the meaning of the initial R. in McCloud's name—"Roman? Reynard? Rilke? Raz?" (48). This overt play with names echoes Dittman's claims about Everett's technique in *The Water Cure*. It also shakes the most fundamental indicator of identity of a character whose entire significance to the book—his putative status as Thurmond's aide—is already suspect as early as the book's second piece of correspondence, when Thurmond asks, "Who are you?" Wilkes's claims become wholly doubtful by the book's middle, when Thurmond asks Everett and Kincaid, who have never met Wilkes in person, if "he [is] the one who wears those light blue outfits?" (151).

Although Thurmond's mind is far from sharp, Wilkes's assertion of being his close aide and collaborator is rendered unreliable by Thurmond's complete ignorance of his existence. The irony of this situation is magnified by the horde of individuals implied by the catalog of names Barton assigns himself in his correspondence. If Barton himself is of dubious reality, what does that suggest about his self-referential entourage?

The intentional layering—and resultant confusion—of texts, authors, and characters in *Erasure* likewise results in a grotesque of polyvocal multiplicity that contributes to the novel's Menippean disruption of authorial significance: "Everett, in his portrayal of the reception of Stagg Leigh's work, shows that the existence of a writer in reality has no bearing regarding the creation of a narrative" (Eaton 224). As discussed in the previous chapter, the meaning of *My Pafology* is absolutely dependent on the reader's ability to discriminate among the book's would-be authorial voices at any given moment, a situation that results in "an ambiguity about to whom this narrative actually belongs" (Eaton 223). It is at once a fictional part of Everett's novel, a document within Monk's nonfictional journal, Monk's fictional parody of *We's Lives in Da Ghetto,* Stagg's nonparodic fictional expression of a supposedly "authentic" black aesthetic, and Van Go's nonfictional memoir of growing up in the ghetto.

Issues of (self-)representation are prominently featured in *Grand Canyon, Inc.* as well. Sylvie Bauer noted that Rhino Tanner "materializes and gives shape to an abstraction, a chimera" ("Percival Everett's *Grand Canyon Inc.*" 258) in "lay[ing] claims to the American Spirit" (Everett, *Grand Canyon Inc.* 113). She argued that Tanner's transformation of the Grand Canyon from a natural wonder into an expression of himself "not only legitimizes his position but also legitimizes the absurd reality he creates, in which the American spirit he claims is symbolized by the Ferris wheel [with which] he mars the Grand Canyon's rim" (Bauer, "Percival Everett's *Grand Canyon Inc.*" 260). The creation of a nominal/philosophical grotesque prefaces the physical transformation of the landscape:

> At the age of ten, the boy already has a goal in life, inscribed in bold letters in his sidekick's notepad: "Acquire the Canyon." In the process, the name of the place is maimed—deprived of the adjective "grand," it loses its nature as a proper noun and becomes another reality, an abstraction figured by its ultimate transformation into a brand. . . . The canyon is thus de-realized and given a new identity, that of a mere adjectival modifier defining the now real object embodied in the truncated word "Inc." In other words, the series that moves from "Grand Canyon" (the original), to "the Canyon" (its transcription in the notebook), and then to "Grand Canyon Inc." (its

> mutilation to become an amusement park) finds its ultimate transformation when it becomes "the Grand Tanner Canyon." (Bauer, "Percival Everett's *Grand Canyon Inc.*" 258–59)

Moreover, within a few pages of the book's end, Tanner's notoriously ignorant worldview seems on the brink of transforming more than just the canyon:

> Rhino Tanner and the Sultan of Brunei sat in Tanner's special glass room stuck in the side of the canyon overlooking the amusements. . . .
>
> "I am amazed at what you have accomplished," the Sultan said.
>
> "It took vision, my friend."
>
> "It has given me hope that I can take over as much of New York and San Francisco, just as you have succeeded here."
>
> "It just goes to show: If you want it more than they want it, you get it. Jesus said that." (Everett, *Grand Canyon Inc.* 123)

Bauer noted that "what has happened here is a sense of confusion between reality and its representation, representation being the only sense of reality that survives Tanner's plans" ("Percival Everett's *Grand Canyon Inc.*" 259). Thus, when Everett does to Rhino's plans what Bubba symbolically does to Custer's—Everett even links the two by calling Rhino's futile act of shooting at an onrushing wall of water "Tanner's last stand"—it is by completely transcending human representation and, in doing so, removing the physical and nominal grotesques from reality: "Everything he had built was completely defeated, washed away forever, no pieces ever to be found. The canyon became what it once was. There was no dam, no lake, only river, the mighty Colorado" (126).

The narrator Vlepo functions as a metafictional grotesque in *Frenzy* because of how Dionysos uses him invasively to observe other characters. The "grotesque mutations" of Vlepo's character are "partly a display of self-definitions, leading us to wonder about how we imagine ourselves and possibly depict ourselves" (Tissut, "*Frenzy*" 287, 288). Vlepo's initial self-presentation even breaks down the categorical distinction between himself and Dionysos: "For as long as I have known that there is time and a life to know, I have been with the god. I am not his creation, but I cannot claim a life away from him. My experience is, of a kind, my own, but it is shaped by what is chosen for me to see" (3). Initially, Dionysos chooses for Vlepo's self to be translated into various inanimate objects and animals, often in order to aid with Dionysos's own efforts at human self-presentation: "Dionysos stood at the canal edge, having disguised himself first as a mortal and further as a country man with a tethered goat. I had been made the goat and so stood on four feet, shaggy" (4). The limitations of this dislocation of identity are described in a manner that parallels Dionysos and Vlepo as author and narrator, respectively: "The god would have me in this goat but not as a goat, it being a limit of his power; he could not propagate out of nothing the matter of the beast, but he could insert me. And in the beast I was, smelling my vessel and tasting in my own mouth what it chose to eat" (5–6).

As the book progresses, though, Vlepo begins to inhabit a multitude of other human characters within the novel, sometimes riding along as a passenger physically attached to their bodies and at other times as a presence within their psychological consciousness: "Dionysos put me upon the head of Agave. The window into her thinking was buried beneath her grey hairs, but I found stable footing and observed" (43). Essentially, Dionysos empowers Vlepo to *represent* the identity of the things and people into which he is "inserted," but neither Dionysos nor Vlepo can *create* them. Everett described his own authorial relation to reality is similar terms: "Every one of my novels is a complete and accurate representation of the world around me. I don't believe they're abstract at all. I think they're concrete and absolutely real. . . . The only constraints that are sometimes annoying, or maybe it's just one constraint, is that the world I create has to exist between the covers of the book" (Champion 172). Vlepo's usefulness as an observer in the text is thus less a result of his shrewdness in describing reality from the perspective of an individual consciousness and more because of his ability to enter into a kind of mythic gestalt consciousness comprised of anyone whose thoughts or internalized sensations Dionysos wishes to know. Vlepo incarnates the inherently grotesque (in Cassuto's definition) situation of the quasi-divine omniscient narrator, gifted with the limited ability to be others but consequently cursed by an attendant diminishment of the self.

Collectively these manifestations of the grotesque in Everett's work perform the "straddl[ing of] the nihilistic, the affirmative, the speculative[,] and the silly" that Musgrave has seen as a defining condition of Menippean satire. He claimed that it "ultimately resists systematic definition precisely because it is . . . characterized by a structural principle of radical heterogeneity," enabling it to serve as "an inspiration for imitation and parodic investigation" (31), as it does in so many of Everett's stories and novels.

Madness

The last remaining feature from Musgrave's list—fifth in his original ordering—is applicable to practically every one of Everett's books from *Suder* to *So Much Blue:* "Eccentricity, madness, foolishness, extreme behavior or abnormal states are frequent in the narrator and/or characters of Menippean satire" (23). Given that eccentric or insane characters are in no way unique to Menippean satire, this trait is perhaps the least intrinsic among those in Musgrave's schema. Such characters can, however, play a crucially Menippean part when used to critique a "bad philosophy" that is otherwise perceived or believed to be wisdom. For example, the unshakably optimistic philosophy espoused by Pangloss—and sanctioned by the Westphalian court of Baron Thunder-ten-Tronckh at which he serves—in Voltaire's *Candide* (1759) certainly seems like madness when juxtaposed against a world filled with extreme violence, deceit, treachery, natural disasters, and disease. Likewise, Peter Profitt, the narrator of Edgar Allan Poe's story "The Business Man" (1840), presents himself as a wholly reasonable figure at the outset of his first-person tale. The reader is surely intended to doubt this assertion—as well as the "method" whose merits he touts—once Profitt confidently discloses that his keen business sense is due to a prominent bump on his head that he received as a child when his nursemaid smashed him into a bedpost. Even a wholly noncomic character such as Raskolnikov in *Crime and Punishment* (1866) is at least partly Menippean in his murderous and self-justifying eccentricity, inasmuch as Dostoyevsky used him to illustrate what he saw as the glaring flaws in the philosophy of Friedrich Nietzsche and the politics of Nikolai Chernyshevsky, both of which were gaining proponents in Russia at the time the novel was written. In contrast, Robin Mookerjee has argued that sociopathic, hyperviolent contemporary characters such as Tyler Durden from Chuck Palahniuk's *Fight Club* and Begbie from Irvine Welsh's *Trainspotting* serve a Menippean satirical function in their "reject[ion of] beliefs considered assumptive" (102) within their societies; in Mookerjee's view, they are at least as much the vehicles of those books' satirical energies as they are the targets of them.

The eccentrics, fools, and madmen/-women who appear in Everett's books—many of whom have already been discussed in different contexts above—fulfill a wide range of functions, from the conventional to the unexpected; the majority of them are in some way targeted by Everett's satire as the embodiment of or mouthpiece for a philosophy whose "madness" is its downfall. Some of his characters—for example, Douglas/Inflato and nearly all of Ralph's series of kidnappers in *Glyph;* Monk Ellison in the latter stages of *Erasure;* Barton Wilkes in *A History of the African-American People;* and Theodore Street in the earlier stages of *American Desert*—are mocked as "educated fools" in a manner that hearkens back to the earliest Menippean satires. Characters in another group that includes Curt Marder in *God's Country,* Rhino Tanner in *Grand Canyon Inc.,* the vain television journalist Barbie Becker in *American Desert,* and the hick residents of Smuteye, Alabama, and Peckerwood County, Georgia, in *I Am Not Sidney Poitier* are considerably less educated in their foolishness and, accordingly, are satirized more for their uncritical acceptance/invocation of bad philosophies than for their formulations thereof. Another group that includes John Livesey in *Cutting Lisa,* Ishmael Kidder in *The Water Cure,* and Ogden Walker in *Assumption* departs from the two groups above by shocking the reader in noncomedic ways with unexpected acts of violence. These outbursts—and their justifications, or lack thereof in Walker's case, for them—undermine or at least trouble these characters' external appearances and/or narrative assertions of rationality and respectability.

Another set of characters with altered mental states provides Everett with a different sort of satirical tool, one related to William Ramsey's assertion that "irrationality and madness appear frequently in [Everett's] fiction" because the American society he depicts "is such an arbitrary assault on individual dignity that often it is mentally disruptive" (132–33). In the opening chapter of *Suder,* Craig Suder recalls a childhood memory of his father bluntly telling him and his brother, "Boys, your mother is crazy" (7). Her behaviors in subsequent flashbacks—going jogging in hot weather wearing a full winter coat, speculating with increasing paranoia that her husband is having an affair, constantly berating both of her young sons for their presumed masturbation—do little to contradict this diagnosis. However, the novel also gradually reveals the extent to which Craig's mother is defined by others, specifically other men, including her well-meaning but aloof husband and the racially bigoted, religiously zealous, and medically incompetent Dr. McCoy. Everett described the novel as "an African-American's internal search for emancipation. Craig Suder is obsessed and terrified by the craziness of his mother, an insanity which is a metaphor for the American experience as she is taunted by white religion which fights her own attempt to find freedom" ("Signing to the Blind" 9). Both as a child and in the novel's present, in which his baseball career and his family life are falling apart, Craig is "scared to death that whatever sickness was loose in my mother was also loose in me" (Everett, *Suder* 82). Everett certainly gives the reader reasons to question Craig's sanity as he withdraws further from his life into the isolation of the mountaintop cabin/bird's-nest that he shares with Jincy, the runaway child, and Renoir, the battered/rescued elephant.

As Stewart observed, it is Bud Powell—the same character who suggests Craig's connection to Bird—who offers a more positive interpretation of the mother's seeming insanity: "Powell's assessment distinguishes itself from that of the rest of the family: 'He said that maybe Ma was just different. I was searching for "just different" in the woman dashing back and forth, back and forth, but all I saw was crazy'" 82). Powell exhibits "a . . . willingness to approve of—or at least accept—Kathy on her own terms. He brings a different language to the family's habitual practices and is able to reinterpret these practices as a result. He doesn't convert; he converses" (Stewart, "Do you mind" 120).

Cannon specifically related this "different language" to Powell's background as a jazz musician, noting that the philosophical underpinning of jazz as a musical form becomes the metaphor for Suder's liberation from the "blues" he is suffering from at the novel's beginning: "The blues seems to designate hopeful resignation, while jazz appears to emphasize movement and action to overcome that resignation. . . . At any given moment, the performer can choose his approach to the music of his life; this is what Suder does when the blues has given him no recourse and he turns more earnestly to jazz for inspiration" (Cannon 104). Powell's articulation of the merely "different" state of Kathy Suder's mind removes the constrictions that seem to cause her suffering; likewise Craig has to do something irrational in attempting to fly with his artificial wings. As unorthodox as this act of willful madness may be from a therapeutic standpoint, the novel's conclusion does not condemn it.

Daniel Barkley's willing embrace of the Confederate flag in "The Appropriation of Cultures" likewise leaves many of the people he interacts with—both black and white—puzzled about his sanity. Travis, the man from whom he buys the pickup with the massive "rebel flag decal covering the rear window of the cab," is described as "lost, scratching his head and looking back at the house for his wife" (*damned* 96–97) when Daniel not only refuses to haggle down the asking price but also offers him two hundred dollars more. Similarly, Daniel's friend Sarah assumes that he has "flipped" (98) because of his idleness when she hears his claim that he bought the truck *for* its decal, not in spite of it. When Travis delivers the truck and Daniel expresses his delight at finding a vehicle "with the black-power flag already on it," his uncomprehending reaction highlights Daniel's eccentricity in regard to the flag's presumably monological symbolic power: "'What?' Travis screwed up his face, trying to understand" (100). After a period of "confused" (101) reactions, the "strange looks and expressions of outrage changed to bemused laughter and finally to open joking and acceptance" (102) of Daniel's "mad" gesture of reverse appropriation. When the story ends with "the piece of cloth [being] quietly dismissed from its station with the U.S. and State flags atop the State Capitol," it is without either "ceremony" or "notice" (103), suggesting that Daniel's complication of the flag's symbolism has devalued it for its primary audience. His action has in no way eradicated the underlying racist mind-set, but it employed madness to accomplish a powerful symbolic goal—removal of the flag from the South Carolina Capitol—that seemed impervious to reason at the time Everett wrote the story. Ted Street's development of limited omniscience as a seeming, if also unexplained, result of his dead-alive status in *American Desert* and the insightful "nonsense" offered by Not Sidney's strange surrogate father-figures—Ted Turner and Percival Everett—in *I Am Not Sidney Poitier* likewise serve as positive examples of alternative mental states that raise questions about conventional wisdoms that have become either stale or unreasonably restrictive.

In a wholly different tenor, the slow descent of Monk's mother into Alzheimer's disease provides a frequently grim backdrop to *Erasure*'s parodic and comic play with literary conventions. She is certainly not "mad" in the usual sense, but her loss of memory and personality becomes a mirror for aspects of Monk's characterization as he simultaneously fragments into his literary alter ego and unearths long-buried family secrets that radically alter what he thinks he knows about his parents and his siblings. Marc Amfreville has gone so far as to argue that Monk is "carefully constructed as what could be viewed as a pathologically depressive character." Exacerbated by the extent to which he "is confronted with actual loss"—including his sister's murder, his brother's marital difficulties and identity crisis, his mother's mental health problems—during the course of the novel, this condition has progressed to "a stage . . . where action is mechanical, creation no longer a source of satisfaction, and self-loathing pervasive" (182). Such a premise radically alters the interpretation of Monk's dissolution as the book progresses; rather than being the comeuppance for an act of callously hypocritical egotism, Monk's fragmentation into Stagg and Van Go instead becomes a cautionary tale about the unforeseen psychological consequences of rigid stereotyping—another potentially distressing "loss" of meaningful identity—on already unsettled personalities. Not Sidney's breakdown in *I Am Not Sidney Poitier* likewise issues a satirical warning about the traumatic effects of overly rigid external impositions of identity. In less comedic ways, Alice Achitophel's almost infantile simple-mindedness—which disappears along with her body fat when she mysteriously transforms—at the beginning of *Zulus* and the titular "dance that [Dionysos] had spread like disease throughout the hills of those nostalgic lands" (3) in *Frenzy* become metaphors for Everett's philosophical musings on the mental and physical aspects of altered states.

In short, although it is perhaps the weakest of Musgrave's Menippean traits on its own, "madness" combines productively with various other, more substantial techniques both to amplify and to signal more explicitly Everett's satirical intentions. Rather than continuing to catalog further the extensive range of eccentricities and insanities of Everett's major and minor characters across thirty books—a process that has already been accomplished to some extent in piecemeal fashion thus far—it is perhaps more useful to move on to a case study of another interlinked subset of Everett's texts that includes additional explication of the role that madness plays in his work even as it extends the discussion further.

CHAPTER 5

The Menippean West

Portions of the previous two chapters discuss in passing how Everett satirically treats certain aspects of the mythology of the American West in *God's Country, Grand Canyon, Inc.,* and *American Desert.* Several critics have noted a contrast between those three books and the remainder of Everett's fiction set in the mountains and deserts of the West. For example, Leland Krauth began his comparison of *God's Country* and *Watershed* by noting that the two novels "are radically different, the one an uproarious comedy, the other a troubling mystery" (314). Similarly, William Handley suggested that "if Everett's other westerns, *God's Country* and *Grand Canyon, Inc,* are mischievous re-workings of generic conventions that call to mind Mark Twain, then *Watershed* is a non-formulaic but equally revisionist western more like John Sayles'[s] soberly searching film *Lone Star*" (304). The predominant critical opinion has been that the "naturalist mediation of frontier experience" (Munby 323) found in such works as *Walk Me to the Distance, Watershed, Wounded,* and *Assumption* stands somewhat apart from the overtly satirical and predominantly comic tenor of the aforementioned trio of novels. This chapter, however, demonstrates that Everett's Western—that is, set in the West, not necessarily conforming to the genre conventions of the "Western"—fiction remains intrinsically satirical, as well as specifically Menippean and degenerative, even when its form and/or tone make it less immediately discernible as such.

The key to this assertion lies in considering these novels not only as a subset of related works (as several of Everett's critics have already done) but also within the wider context of his entire body of work. Krauth suggested the value of such an approach in noting that *God's Country* and *Watershed* "make a natural pair that reveals how Everett's engagement with the West—the West of fiction as well as actuality—provides a medium for the expression of some of his most fundamental concerns. . . . The two novels disclose both characteristic gestures of his sensibility and essential values deep in the grain of his art" (314). Handley further outlined the contours of Everett's complex, sometimes even contradictory depiction of the West, particularly in terms of any perceived obligations to represent the region and its history in prescribed ways:

> Seen together, Everett's western novels both exhibit and tackle one of the central literary problems in literature of the American West: how does a western writer free his imagination and at the same time respond to the demand for historical authenticity that readers for two centuries have brought to this cultural landscape (whether real or imagined) . . . ? These works of western fiction are historical in the deepest sense: not because they offer up "facts" or because they "faithfully represent a bygone era," but because they are self-conscious about the way in which the "truth" of history is never objective but always subjectively imagined. Moreover, "history"—especially the history of American racism—is itself a record of discourses. (Handley 304, 306)

Everett uses "self-conscious" repetition of various tropes of Western exceptionalism in all four of the works of fiction examined in this chapter. In these "unpredictable acts of self-creation" (Ramsey 131) he engages in a mostly noncomic yet fundamentally Menippean satirical critique of conventional Western constructions of identity. William Ramsey noted that "the West in Everett's stories is never a complete release from the cage of racial oppression. . . . In one way or another, [his] fiction often focuses on individuals who do not 'know their place' in a socially hierarchical American culture" (132). The troubles that Everett's characters experience in the West become a synecdoche for their struggle with belonging in the country as a whole; they satirically reveal the flaws in a "record of [American] discourses" pertaining to both individual and collective concepts of identity.

Frontiers, Old and New

The majority of *God's Country* takes place in a physical world whose constituent parts—for example, a one-street town prominently featuring a general store, a saloon with a swinging door, a brothel, and a jail—contribute to an intentionally clichéd representation of the nineteenth-century West. Everett described *God's Country* as having arisen from a desire "to exploit the fact that there is a mythic West. . . . It has nothing to do with any reality" (Birnbaum 37). Although his other two comic satires set in the West depart from the intentionally formulaic setting of *God's Country*, they still tinker with "mythic" and/or "invented" aspects of the West. Rhino Tanner's story of self-absorbed capitalism in *Grand Canyon, Inc.* plays out in an iconic landscape with a multitude of symbolic layers that comment on the relationship between American identity and nature. *American Desert*'s title alone signifies the literal and metaphysical lifelessness that Ted Street encounters throughout that novel, whether in the suburbs of Los Angeles, in Big Daddy's fundamentalist enclave/arsenal in the wilderness, or in the Area 51–like government research compound far beneath the surface of the southwestern desert. Although Everett has bristled at times at the critical overdetermination of his works set in the West—"I hate that the presence of Native people, mountains, or even a horse causes people to call a work a western" (Goyal)—he also has delineated it as a region with a distinct cultural dynamic that he finds both useful and liberating: "I set things in the West because I know it very well. I have a level of comfort that gives me freedom. It's a place that's known for the self-sufficiency of its inhabitants but where people actually depend on each other profoundly. You can live in your apartment in New York and never see anybody for years and survive. You can live on a ranch in Wyoming, but you're gonna need somebody sometime, and the people who live around you are there. That's part of the landscape" (Dischinger 46). His nuanced, and far from uncritical, appreciation for the region's cultural history and geography—both real and imagined—provides Everett with ample opportunities to explore the mimetic and the satirical potentials inherent in it.

The books under consideration in this chapter are set neither in the mythic western territory of Zane Grey novels and John Ford films—or the simulacral versions depicted in the cinematic and serial versions of *Westworld*—nor in the familiar spaces of *Beverly Hills 90210, Weeds, Breaking Bad,* or countless other television serials set in the contemporary urban/suburban West. Instead they take place in the sprawling ranch country of Wyoming, the rough plateaus of rural New Mexico, and the snowy mountains of northern Colorado; such realms have been featured only sporadically in contemporary pop culture—for example, Clint Eastwood's "revisionist western" film *Unforgiven* (1992) or Craig Johnson's series of crime novels that subsequently spawned the television series *Longmire* (2012–17). As spaces with fewer readily available preconceptions for reader to bring to the text, these settings allow for more intimate and psychologically engaging portraits of how prejudice roams the West than do those that appear in Everett's overtly parodic work. The symbolic significance of these places is simultaneously less complex and less rigid than that of an iconic landscape such as Monument Valley or a prototypical "Western" town such as Deadwood, South Dakota; this affords Everett greater freedom to play with the largely unexamined assumptions—again, the "constricting boundaries of fixed systems" (Ramsey 131)—that adhere to these places and the people who inhabit them, ultimately "reveal[ing] the black ranch to be a compromised sanctuary in an environment capable of nurturing as much bigotry as anywhere else" (Munby 323). In these works Everett satirically "recuperates" reality in a manner akin to that which Krauth has seen at work in *God's Country:* "at the same time [Everett] dismantles the traditional Western, he recuperates it, infusing into its clichés some gritty realities and exploiting its abiding mythic power to create a Western paradoxically truer to life than the conventional one but still larger-than-life" (321).

As is true in *God's Country, Grand Canyon, Inc.,* and *American Desert,* race is relevant to the satirical tenor of each of these four books without being the overriding concern of any of them. These books' geographically remote and sparsely populated settings are contemporary analogues of the malleable "frontier" that has contributed to racialized constructions of American identity since the earliest days of European settlement:

> As a much repeated ideological narrative in American culture, the frontier myth has most often served the interests of the dominant race, class, and gender, providing a mythic justification for the positions of power held by middle-class white males. The myth is based on a racial opposition between the "civilized" (white) and the "savage" (nonwhite, usually American Indian but often African American or even lower-class whites or white immigrants) and tells the story of the evolutionary inevitability of the triumph of civilization over savagery and the dominance of the white race over all other races. The frontier myth is the narrative of the civilized individual's journey westward into the savage American wilderness. (M. Johnson, *Black* 7)

Compared to its foregrounding in *God's Country* or *Grand Canyon, Inc.,* the frontier myth is relatively diluted in the contemporary settings of Everett's realistic Western fiction, as can be inferred from the narrator/protagonist John Hunt's description of the town near his ranch in *Wounded:* "I was never quite prepared for it, though I'd lived outside it for twenty years. Even when it had been tiny, its abrupt appearance after the bend always made it seem large. Now, with a couple of housing developments and the new community college campus and the strip malls that followed, it was damn near urban sprawl" (11). Despite this description of a borderland that has been "civilized" and homogenized, Everett's characters still interact with their distinctly western environments in ways that reveal the ongoing influence of the frontier myth.

Everett's most significant Menippean gesture across these four books involves the simultaneous subversion of a pair of interrelated notions. First, he questions the veneration of individualism—generally of the "rugged" variety—that has been embedded in the mythology of the frontier in general and of the West in particular at least as far back as the trope of the "strong silent type" embodied by Gary Cooper in *High Noon* (1952) or John Wayne in *The Searchers* (1956). Second, he explodes the idea that the frontier has become an egalitarian space in which everyone is free to participate: "If identity through place is as fictional a construct as identity through race, Everett's characters nonetheless sometimes find an empowering sense of self through faith (if troubled) in that particular identity script. . . . [They] start with a strong sense of belonging to a western community and with a solid sense of identity . . . that becomes troubled as the story progresses" (M. Johnson, *Hoo-Doo* 194). This troubling sometimes takes place in an explicitly racial or ethnic context, but it just as often plays out on a more idiosyncratic level.

Alexa Weik Von Mossner has reminded readers that Everett "often insists on the fluidity and indeterminacy of race, confronting his audience with characters who defy racial stereotyping and broad generalizations" (76). The characterizations of the protagonists of these four books bear out her assertion, though there are also significant differences among them in terms of how and why their racial identities are complicated. David Larson's race in *Walk Me to the Distance* is never specified, though numerous critics have argued (in general, unconvincingly) that he is black based on various circumstantial details in the text. It seems unlikely that Everett intended David's race to be an issue, given that his initial description already negates various presumptions about who and what he is:

> It wasn't that David Larson returned home from Vietnam to find that his girl had taken up with another man; he didn't have a girl when he left. He'd spent his time in the army telling people that he was from Georgia, then trying to explain to them and, with time, to himself, why he didn't have a southern accent; finally coming to "I guess I never had one." . . . David hadn't had the good sense, the keen foresight to get wounded and lose a limb, and though certainly affected by his tour, he did not come home emotionally or mentally scarred, suffering from flashbacks or a fear of thin people on bicycles. He returned as unremarkable as he had been when he left . . . just a soldier, a man without the courage, conviction, or cowardice to have run north to Montreal or Toronto. (3)

Described from the start in apophatic terms—that is, that which he is not—he soon arrives in Slut's Hole, a place whose very name evokes emptiness. Not long after his arrival, he meets a cantankerous yet kind local woman named Chloë Sixbury, whose distinguishing features are a wooden leg and a son named Patrick who is described simply as being "an idiot" (6) and "retarded" (7). After Sixbury asks David where he was born, she tells him that he should "settle there [in Georgia]. People should live where they have a history," to which David replies simply, "Don't like it there. Never did" (8). Although his initial stay in Slut's Hole and at Sixbury's ranch is intended to be only temporary while his car is being repaired, David quickly finds an unexpected sense of home there, and the remainder of the novel examines how and why he arrives at the conclusion that "he couldn't be any place else" (207) despite a number of developments that would seemingly contradict such a conclusion.

Michael K. Johnson insisted that "*Walk Me to the Distance* is in many ways paradigmatic of Everett's western fiction" in its "use of disabled characters and metaphors of disability" (*Hoo-Doo* 187). He suggested a Menippean interpretation in observing that the physical and material grotesques that Everett's protagonists encounter subvert foundational aspects of their identity: "[His] stories often turn on . . . encounters with the otherness of disability, deformity, or poverty [that] result in or foreshadow moments of existential crisis, disintegration, and fragmentation during which the character becomes aware of . . . the illusory nature of both his sense of wholeness and his sense of successful integration and belonging" (195). There is little doubt that David arrives in Slut's Hole in need of something to fill the grammatical and existential negatives by which he is defined at the book's outset, but Everett intends the reader to remain dubious about the reasoning that David employs in choosing his new home.

For example, early in the novel David sees Sixbury's son "fucking a sheep" while wearing hip waders into which the animal's legs are tucked to keep it from running away (22). This absurd image initially seems like a puerile mockery of rural life, an impression that is reinforced when David awkwardly recounts the scene for a neighbor, who responds with incredulous mirth: "Howard laughed harder. 'Don't shit me'" (29). David tries to redirect Patrick's sexual urges by paying for a prostitute to visit him, but the encounter (predictably) goes poorly. Patrick's next sexual indiscretion is less laughable, inasmuch as it involves an assault on a human, specifically Butch, the abandoned Vietnamese girl who has by this point in the novel become David's de facto ward. Patrick runs off into the wilderness and is tracked down by a posse of local men, including David. When the men find him, they dispense a form of "frontier justice" that also has powerful and indelible racial overtones: "David went into the cabin and kicked at the low flame and embers. He was scared to death. He wasn't sure what was going to happen, but of course he knew. . . . There was no hangman's noose. Just a slipknot. . . . [Patrick] just hanged there and died" (126–27).

Troubled by his participation in this killing, David seeks solace at "the one church, the Lutheran Church of Slut's Hole" (134). The sermon he hears there invokes aspects of the frontier myth in proffering excuses for the brutality of Patrick's extralegal summary execution:

> The thing about this country is—well, it's relentless. It doesn't let up. It goes on and on, with this enormous sky for a face. It goes on and on, with

> this oppressive beauty. . . . And the longer it lets us live, the more we have to love it. As we trust God, so we must trust this land. We have no choice. We are alone here. We must trust ourselves and our faith. . . . There are bad things . . . and there are evil things in this world. But a bad thing need not be evil. A bad thing need not be wrong. Many a right action is unpleasant. God judges us as much by our intentions as by our deeds. Here, in this harsh environment, we must be men. Even our women must be men. (136)

Immediately after this sermon, David seems to be almost unconsciously "whispering the words, rolling them into the sea of mumbling as the entire congregation joined in the recitation" (136). This suggests the extent to which he has become receptive to the self-justifying and constricting logic that apparently demands (among other things) complete self-negation from women. Thus this logic is invalidated as neither an ethical nor a grammatical improvement on the negatives that constrained David prior to his arrival in Wyoming.

Everett never wholly undermines David's embrace of Slut's Hole and/or the West as his new home, but he certainly questions the extent to which it requires willful ignorance—that is, acceptance of a version of the frontier myth—on his part. David never confesses to Sixbury what he helped do to her son, although the text hints that she understands and even accepts it. Furthermore he and his fellow vigilantes escape prosecution because the investigating officers subscribe to a frontier ethics similar to that espoused by the sermonizing pastor:

> David went to the Lowe ranch and told Joshua what Sixbury had said to the state police the night before. Lowe sat in his big chair and looked at David on the sofa. David came to the end of his report. "And so Baker just left."
>
> "You say it was Baker?"
>
> "Yes."
>
> Lowe nodded. "A good man."
>
> "They're not just dropping it like that, are they?" asked David.
>
> "You sound like you're not satisfied."
>
> "I just don't think they're finished."
>
> "I figure they probably just needed a reason to let it go." (206)

David continues to question his own morality, though, wondering out loud if he, unlike Baker, is "a bad man," to which his friend and fellow vigilante tidily responds, "If you have to wonder, chances are you're not" (206). Though this scene thoroughly lacks the comedy of *God's Country* or *Grand Canyon, Inc.*, it is not difficult to imagine Curt Marder or Rhino Tanner invoking a similarly uncritical perspective to justify their own reprehensible actions. Moreover, if

Everett does intend the reader to perceive David as black, his ultimate acceptance of what essentially is a lynching of a mentally disabled man potentially becomes an even more perverse act of denial. Even without that inherently racialized interpretation, though, Everett leaves the reader less comfortable than David about the answer to the rhetorical question he poses to Sixbury on the novel's last page: "So this runs pretty smoothly, now that we have a routine. No problem at all, huh?" (208–9). If we recall Sixbury's early advice to David about settling "where [he has] a history," then we also have to question the extent to which he acknowledges that history truthfully in his new home.

Watershed Moments and Historical Wounds

Whereas in *Walk Me to the Distance* David Larson begins as a character defined by what he is not, the narrator/protagonist of *Watershed* begins his story with an assertion of his individuality that also concurrently refutes any form of collective identity: "My blood is my own and my name is Robert Hawks" (1). He continues by noting that he "would seem [to be] a pretty faithful copy" of his father and grandfather, inasmuch as all three men "hated America, policemen, and especially churches" (3–4). It is not until after he recalls being told why he should not rely on the police "if some KKK grabbed your grandfather right now" that his race becomes unmistakably clear to the reader: "The police will stop you and search you and, if they don't shoot you, they'll take you in and say you look like another 'nigger.' They may not use that word, but that's what they'll mean" (14). Despite subsequently recounting incidents that validate his grandfather's prediction, Hawks repeatedly asserts that race is of minimal importance to his self-conception and seems either mildly annoyed or nonplussed when other characters notice his blackness. Given his recollection that his grandfather "put the barrel of his over-and-under shotgun in his mouth and pushed the trigger" because of his inability to live with people who "believe in one way, their way" (72), Hawks's withdrawal—symbolized by his frequent efforts at physical and emotional escape from Karen, his admittedly unstable girlfriend—seems more a psychological avoidance strategy than a principled affirmation.

This withdrawal becomes more significant in light of the narrative control—Hawks is far from "dead" in Barthes's sense—that he asserts at the book's opening: "That I should feel put out or annoyed or even dismayed at having to tell this story is absurd since I do want the story told and since I am the only one who can properly and accurately reproduce it. There is no one else in whom I place sufficient trust to attempt a fair representation of the events" (2). Not long after this declaration, Hawks also acknowledges a tendency to "simply and stupidly fall . . . into something out of convenience" (6) in his relationships with women and admits that he reflexively lies to Karen to placate her when they argue. These details cast doubt on Hawks's conviction regarding his own "accuracy" and "fairness." Moreover, Hawks's choice of the word "fair" to describe his "representation of the events" recalls—perhaps intentionally—Curt Marder's misplaced trust in the "fair account" (Everett, *God's* 10) of the West that he receives from dime novels, as well as the title of Everett's short-story collection *The Weather and Women Treat Me Fair,* whose protagonists, like Hawks, "seem stymied by the injustices they observe and are unable or unwilling to create alliances across boundaries of racial, ethnic, or other forms of difference" (M. Johnson, *Hoo-Doo* 207).

Hawks's initial account of retreating to his cabin in the mountains of northern Colorado makes clear not only that the cabin is a place of refuge for him but also that his motivations for seeking such refuge are bound up with avoidance of unpleasant realities: "Before I came out here to the cabin, to fish and think and be alone, I was in the city with Karen, a woman I had been fucking. . . . Her voice grated on me, as did her attitudes and disposition, and finally her smells, but still I would lie between her legs again and again, pathetically seeking release or simply seeking" (4–5). As Karen tries to convince him not to go fishing, he realizes that he wants "to tell her that I was not in love with her, never had been in love with her and, further, believed completely that she was too insane to be capable of love herself," finishing his line of thinking by noting that he "genuinely detested her." Rather than express this admittedly unpleasant—but seemingly genuine—feeling to Karen, he instead tells her another noncommittal half-truth about his reasons for going fishing:

> "Why!?" she had screamed, her voice much louder than her size. "Because you need to get away from me? Am I that awful?"
>
> "No, because I want to go fishing. I like fishing. It relaxes me." (5)

The staccato cadence of Hawks's answer is consistent with his relatively taciturn conversational affect throughout the novel, but it also contrasts dramatically with his narrative voice, creating a tonal multiplicity that calls attention to itself. Everett uses this distinction to set up his Menippean satire; Hawks the character, heading out to his cabin for a "relaxing" stretch of being on his own, does not possess the same sense of "self-sacrifice and moral commitment" that Hawks the retrospective narrator has developed by living through the events of the novel. Hawks's veneration of the cabin as a site of uncomplicated succor from the world becomes another form of false place-oriented mythology, not only because his own avoidant behavior is a necessary precursor to his presence at the cabin in the first place but also because of the cabin's proximity to the disputed watershed that becomes the reason for novel's main conflict.

The cabin's status as a symbol of Hawks's mind-set is further established after he arrives there in the early stages of the book. While Hawks is stopped at a store on his way to the cabin, his truck fails to start. He is saved from being stuck by a woman named Louise—he learns her full name only later—who "jiggle[s] a do-hickey" under his hood. He offers her a ride, and she accompanies him part of the way toward his cabin. He notes that her canvas sneakers do not seem sufficient for the snowstorm that appears to be imminent, but he quickly suppresses his concern when she unconvincingly insists she has a pair of boots in her backpack: "I felt her uneasiness and so I backed off, attending to my driving, putting both hands on the wheel. I hoped that I had not made her feel that I was interested in her" (11). Although his ambiguous word choice in this final sentence might be interpreted to Hawks's benefit as not wanting to scare her into mistaking him for a sexual predator, a line from the next scene suggests a less charitable reading.

Upon his arrival at the cabin, Hawks unleashes a lengthy and mechanical-sounding paragraph describing the minutiae of his routine at the cabin in a manner reminiscent of Ernest Hemingway's "Big Two-Hearted River." Much as John Livesey attempts to impose a routinized control onto the world around him at the outset of *Cutting Lisa,* Hawks tries to reduce the sum of his responsibilities to just himself and the upkeep of the cabin: "I climbed down, put away the ladder, and collected a load of wood from the pile I'd chopped earlier. I went into the house and dropped the fuel by the stove, then went back outside and secured the tarp over the stacked logs beside the house before taking in another lading of wood" (13). Once his chores are completed, though, he finds himself "thinking . . . about that little woman Louise out there someplace in the cold without proper gear." He almost immediately severs any emotional response he might have to this mental image, though, in the process absolving himself of any possible ethical entanglement: "It was her business though. I didn't care who froze to death from their own witlessness or considered deliberation" (13). The first few pages of the novel make it clear that Hawks does not allow himself to feel any potentially unsettling emotions, whether they pertain to his personal life, his familial history, or his work as a hydrologist. The wholly utilitarian language he uses to describe his life at the cabin becomes the verbal manifestation of this unencumbered personal utopia, echoing David Larson's willful self-deception that everything "runs smoothly" now that he has "a routine" at the end of *Walk Me to the Distance.*

The reassurance that routine provides is satirically undermined not just by the tonal juxtaposition with Hawks's more knowing narrative voice but also by the novel's underlying formal multiplicity. Hawks insists that he has attempted to keep his unique brand of geological expertise—documentary fragments of which are interspersed throughout the narrative in quintessentially Menippean form, along with excerpts from historical accounts, treaties, and other seemingly nonfictional texts—free from any ethical entanglements: "I had done so much to remove all things political from my life. Even in my work as a hydrologist I seldom involved myself in the use of my findings for any kind of agenda promotion; rather, I saw myself as a hired gun." Moreover he reveals that he has attempted to include racial issues within this neutrality: "I didn't talk about politics, didn't respond to talk about politics, didn't care about what I read in the papers, and didn't feel any guilt about my lack of participation in those issues of social importance. I did not know or associate with many black people. . . . I didn't need Christianity to dismiss people and I didn't need them to be white" (152). Just as Hawks flees to the cabin to escape admitting to Karen not only that he does not love her but also that he has actually come to loathe her, he retreats to the emotional safety of largely unexamined beliefs regarding his own impartiality. These positions become increasingly untenable as Everett satirically degenerates their constituent premises; as the solitude of his cabin is increasingly breached by visitors both friendly and hostile, his emotional isolationism is revealed as unsustainable self-deception.

When his hydrological knowledge helps uncover evidence of a lethal conspiracy against the Plata, Hawks is forced to question the putative nonalignment of his work. The increasingly frequent and intrusive presence of FBI agents—particularly a special agent named Gladys Davies, whose interest in him seems equal parts prurient and professional—pushes Hawks further into a "new, if accidental involvement with the American Indian Revolution" (153). This association intensifies to the point that he voluntarily sides with the Plata during an armed standoff against the FBI, further opening the door to Everett's subversion of the isolationist philosophy by which Hawks has been living: "If apathy and noncommitment are self-protective stances, so is distancing oneself from the issue of race. . . . The first step in that evolution [from apathy to commitment] for many of Everett's characters is to acknowledge (or discover) the real effect fictions of race play in their lives" (M. Johnson, *Hoo-Doo* 193). Hawks comes to realize that he is driven primarily by "a longstanding [*sic*], unanswered, personal quest to understand my grandfather" (Everett, *Watershed* 153). Acceptance of such a quest requires Hawks to acknowledge the truth of the claims of racialized injustice made by his grandfather and by the Plata, whose water is being both stolen and poisoned: "Understanding the struggle led by Louise Yellow Calf and Hiram Kills Enemy is, for Robert Hawks, understanding that his father and grandfather had been fighting for rights that were claimed and denied all the time" (Clary 171).

The narrative begins to draw more explicit parallels between the racism that Hawks's grandfather faced and the situation of the Plata; this occurs at roughly the same time that Hawks uncovers evidence that agents of the federal government have been diverting the flow of Dog Creek, the water of which is necessary to the tribe's survival and legally theirs by treaty. He recalls an episode from his childhood in which his grandfather "risked everything, his life, his career, and his family to keep 'blacker than black' Bunchy Cooke from frying in the chair in the Peach State," an act for which he is hailed as a hero by the black community. However, it also resulted in his disbarment for a legal technicality, presumably in retribution for challenging the racist order of things. Young Robert does not understand his grandfather's resulting sadness and hopes only that "things are going to work out . . . [because] all this means is that Grandfather will have more time to fish, right?" (157–58). His language echoes Hawks's attempt to avoid a necessary confrontation with Karen by invoking his love of fishing; the salient difference, of course, is that the child's hopeful invocation of fishing stems from naïveté, whereas the adult's is a conscious side-stepping of unpleasant reality.

Immediately after this flashback to Hawks's childhood, the narrative shifts to what appear to be fragments from early eighteenth-century legal codes. These excerpts from a series of four decrees cluster various nonwhite peoples together in ways that testify to their fundamental lack of freedom:

> *1706—All and every Negro, Indian, mulatto, or mestee bastard child who shall be born of any Negro, Indian, mulatto, or mestee, shall follow the state and Condition of the Mother and be esteemed a slave.*
>
> *1712—Any Negro or Indian slave, or any other slave can be baptized but is not free.*
>
> *1712—No Negro, Indian, or mulatto hereafter made free shall enjoy any houses, lands, tenements within the colony.*
>
> *1740—All Negroes, Indians, mulattoes, or mestizoes and all their issue are absolute slaves, and shall follow the condition of the mother.* (158)

These two scenes are narratively part of Hawks's stream of consciousness, but they are also—and more importantly—part of his stream of conscience. When the narrative switches back to his involvement in the "business with the FBI and AIR," Hawks's decision to grab his "reports on the Plata Mountain drainage"—that is, the evidence of illegal actions by the government—and "my grandfather's shotgun" on his way out the door speaks to both his new commitment to taking sides and his realization of the broader historical context of his choice. He notes that he "didn't know what the Indians were planning and how I would fit in, but it was clear that somehow I would" (158–59). Although he is not yet fully comfortable with this situation, he no longer feels the need to challenge its fundamental truth.

The incontrovertible "proof of bad shit" (199) that Hawks risks his life to carry to Denver at the end of the novel forces him to abandon his withdrawn individualism at least temporarily and associate himself more meaningfully and more personally with the targets—literal ones, in the case of the deadly shootout that both opens and closes the novel—of the predominantly white-associated power of the present-day version of the frontier. As Krauth observed, the novel's resolution

> folds together . . . the practical need for political action in the present with the mythic sense of heroic individualism enshrined in the past—the past of the Western. . . . Robert Hawks . . . has crossed a personal watershed from self-protective apathy to dangerous commitment. He has learned to act on behalf of others—as well as for truth. He does not face anybody in a shoot-out . . . nor does he ride off into the sunset, having set things straight—having, as the Old Western stages it, achieved some justice beyond the law . . . . His heroism [instead] becomes a matter of moral resolve. (325)

This "moral resolve" specifically involves a fuller acknowledgment of his personal past and the way that past interrelates with that of the same people—the Plata—toward whom he initially intended to maintain a dispassionate attitude, as first illustrated by his claim not to care about Louise's fate in the cold weather. The uncomplicatedly "relaxing" narrative that envelops his cabin at the novel's beginning has now been revealed as another soothing myth associated with the West that cannot and should not be maintained, lest one tacitly support what are essentially genocidal acts of treachery.

A character abandoning his logically flawed moral apathy to form a sympathetic and mutually protective community among the endangered is the overarching plot structure of *Wounded* as well. John Hunt features almost every trait that recurs in the pantheon of narrator-protagonists who populate Everett's realistic fiction of the West. In fact, although they arrive in rural Wyoming on very different trajectories, the basic parameters of Hunt's life in Highland are those that one might extrapolate for David Larson after a few decades of living in Slut's Hole. A horse trainer by profession, Hunt is equally comfortable reading a book or welding a tractor blade. He peppers nearly all of his conversations with a sardonic humor that stops just short of misanthropy; he has been carrying for many years a psychological wound resulting from the untimely death of his wife; and he shares his author's preference for the companionship of animals over that of humans—with the exception of his elderly uncle Gus and his flirtatious neighbor Morgan. As Marie-Agnès Gay observed, the way

Hunt tells his story reveals his inner state at the novel's beginning: "The narrator's description of life on the ranch teems with detailed descriptions [that] make use of a precise, discriminating and sometimes technical vocabulary. Language comes easy and straight when John Hunt evokes the reassuring routine of material life. However, his well-ordered everyday life with his Uncle Gus is put to the test by a series of crises" (Gay 2). Some of these "crises" are positive, such as Morgan's ultimately successful romantic pursuit of him; others are unmistakably negative, such as the murder of a gay college student named Jerry Tuttle and the subsequent suicide of Hunt's ranch hand Wallace Castlebury, the prime suspect in Tuttle's murder. All of these plot developments, though, push both Hunt and his narrative language "out of safe boundaries and familiar territory" (Gay 2).

Like the notable distinctions between the utterances by narrator Hawks and by character Hawks in *Watershed,* the linguistic contrast that Gay notes becomes an example of Menippean tonal multiplicity by calling attention to Hunt's tendency to shape reality to conform to his relatively simple but inflexible emotional needs. Hunt is also like Hawks in presenting himself as a man aloof toward both demographics and history. His love for the ranch country of Wyoming is unmistakable, but it is framed in mostly geographical terms: "It was dramatic land, dry, remote, wild. It was why I loved the West. I had no affection necessarily for the history of the people and certainly none for the mythic West, the West that never existed. It was the land for me. And maybe what the land did to some who lived on it" (45). This panegyric to the landscape immediately precedes a scene in which Hunt discovers a pair of baby coyotes who, unlike their mother, have survived an unjustifiably cruel act of human violence: "I knew what had happened. Someone had poured fuel down into the animal's den and tossed in a match. . . . I felt sick. I was confused, near tears, angry. No one was keeping sheep there, so the lame excuse of protecting stock didn't even make sense" (45). One of the pups survives and is adopted by Hunt and his uncle after being nursed back to health—albeit after having part of a leg amputated. This speaks to Hunt's capacity for compassion in certain circumstances, but the sickening feeling he has while observing the burnt coyotes' den exacerbates his generalized sense of being "endangered when it comes to human relations in general, and emotional involvement in particular" (Gay 4).

As Michael Johnson observed, Hunt's love for the land and its potential to affect people echo the "idea that the American West is an exceptional place, fundamentally different from the rest of the country" as well as being "one of the oldest and most repeated tropes of western writing." He went on to note that "it is typical of Everett's fiction that he repeats *and* critiques that trope, his characters cynically realistic about western racial relations but also idealistically hopeful that the West is indeed (or could become) . . . a haven" (M. Johnson, "Looking" 29). As he does in the scene with the burnt coyotes, Everett closely juxtaposes expressions of this cynicism and this optimism to emphasize the tension between them. For example, a gay-pride rally in the aftermath of the student's murder brings a large group of outsiders to Highland, including David, the gay son of one of Hunt's friends from college, and David's boyfriend Robert. Hunt and the two young men go out to lunch, during which the Vermont-raised, Illinois-educated Robert asks Hunt if he has ever encountered any racial "problems" in this rural Wyoming town. Hunt's answer contains both of the impulses Johnson mentioned: "Of course I have, son. This is America. I've run into bigotry here. Of course, the only place anybody ever called me nigger to my face was in Cambridge, Mass. . . . There are plenty of stupid, narrow-minded people around. They're not hard to find. There are a lot of ignorant people, a lot of good, smart people. Is it different where you come from?" (52).

Hunt notes that by saying this to Robert, he "felt a little like a bully and didn't like it" (52); he attributes these feelings to being put on the defensive by Robert's presumptions about Wyoming's cultural backwardness. On a deeper level, though, his emotional response is consistent with the cognitive dissonance arising from a desire to "repair or preserve the exceptional places that they simultaneously doubt can exist" (M. Johnson, "Looking" 29), a trait that Johnson has attributed to many of Everett's characters. After all, Hunt has already been defensive about the "implication, if not outright accusation" in the "Eastern papers" that Tuttle's murder is "symptomatic of some rural or Western disease of intolerance." As he does later in the diner with David and Robert, Hunt claims that such intolerance is a wholly national trait and wonders pointedly "why the reported rash of fifty rapes in Central Park was not considered a similar indicator of regional moral breakdown" (34). The simplest answer is that there is no comparable mythology extolling "what the land did to some who lived on it" that is pertinent to New York or Cambridge.

Everett weaves this basic conundrum into the entire novel. Testifying to the prospects of repair and preservation, Hunt's ranch becomes a warm, nurturing home not only for him and his uncle but also for the rescued coyote, for Morgan, and for David; much as he does in *Suder* and *Walk Me to the Distance,* Everett creates an unconventional yet basically functional family structure that transcends biology and conventional social bonds. The doubts about the exceptionality of the place, however, are reinforced when Hunt *is* called "nigger" to his face by white neo-Nazis right there in his hometown (200) and also when Hunt overhears his friend Duncan making bigoted comments about David's sexuality. Although he claims to be neither "disappointed" nor "surprised"

(188) by Duncan's comments, the lack of compassion they evince is magnified by having been uttered during a manhunt for David, who has gone missing and for whose safety Hunt rightly fears. These incidents complicate Hunt's assertion that where he lives is no worse than anywhere else in the country, and they also redirect back onto Wyoming his efforts to subvert the moral superiority of other, more presumably liberal parts of the country. Everett gently but unmistakably satirizes Hunt as an unrequited lover of the West; he is willing and able to overlook and to excuse its unsavory aspects, but the favor is never fully returned.

The novel's violent resolution is reminiscent of Patrick's hanging in *Walk Me to the Distance,* both in its brutal interpretation of what constitutes justice and in the unsatisfying justifications offered for such brutality as an inevitable part of life on the frontier. Hunt's uncle Gus is dying of cancer and frustrated by a lifetime of miscarried justice, especially the eleven-year prison sentence he served for "kill[ing] the [white] man who was raping his wife" (9). Near the book's conclusion, Gus apparently executes the three neo-Nazis with whom Hunt has had multiple run-ins; he kills them in retaliation for their numerous hate crimes, the last of which is kidnapping David and beating him to near-death. Importantly, he shoots the first one immediately after being racially slurred by him:

> Gus entered the cabin.
>
> "Fuck me," the redhead said. "What is this? Nigger heaven?"
>
> What happened next was and still is a blur. I recall a flash and a loud pop and the red beard expanding and breaking, the chair falling over, the weasel sliding across the floor to the wall and Gus, standing there with a .45 in his hand.
>
> "Fuck, fuck, fuck," the remaining tied-up man kept saying.

As Hunt begins to process what has happened, he bluntly states the obvious: "You killed him"; and Gus replies equally matter-of-factly: "It would seem so." When he follows that up by saying, "I've got two left," Hunt observes, "At first I thought he was talking about bullets, but then I realized he meant them. Gus's face was tired, hard" (202).

Although Gus's lack of emotion might initially imply his acceptance of righteous violence in a normative manner comparable to that of the preacher in *Walk Me to the Distance,* Gus—who moved to Wyoming only after the death of Hawks's wife—is not acting in order to protect any existing idealized notion of "his" West. After Hunt discovers David unconscious and bleeding heavily but still alive, he returns to the cabin to get Gus so that all three of them can go to the hospital together. Gus makes it clear, though, that he intends to finish evening the score, not just for David's wounding but also for the injustices he has suffered in his life, which are as responsible as his cancer for the tiredness and hardness in his face at that moment: "Gus gave me a hard look and I felt the differences in our years and experiences. He put his hand on my shoulder and said, 'Take David to the hospital. Tell the cops you found David anywhere but here or near here'" (204). Hunt's reference to "[feeling] the differences in our years and experiences" marks the return in *Wounded* of the Freudian *unheimlich* that Michael K. Johnson perceived at the core of Everett's Westerns: "The central dramatic event, or the catalyst for that event, involves a moment when the homely becomes unhomely, when the familiar becomes strange, and that uncanny experience usually precedes a moment when the racialized identity that the protagonist has left behind, transcended, repressed, or that has simply become only one part of the protagonist's sense of self, returns to centrality. Concurrently, the American West that has become home for so many of Everett's characters becomes instead an unhomely place" ("Looking" 35). Hunt professes not to understand Gus's words, which suggests that he has not yet fully processed the "differences" that are driving Gus's actions. However, after David succumbs to his injuries at the hospital, the truth of the situation has dawned on Hunt enough for him to tell Morgan, "Gus killed a man today. I think he's up there killing all of them." He adds a telling narrative comment to this piece of dialogue that completes the circle of Everett's satirical critique of Hunt's previous mind-set and attendant narration: "I found it odd how easily those words came from my mouth" (206). These words do not remain "safe" or "familiar" (Gay 2) within the ethical confines of Hunt's erstwhile mythology of place; if justifications of violence are now coming "easily" to him, it is because he has learned a brutal lesson through David's death that forces him into a recognition of solidarity with the excluded that is akin to Hawks's political kinship with the Plata at the end of *Watershed*. Both men come to recognize that they have both figurative and literal "skin in the game" in ways they formerly tried to discount.

Wounded ends with Gus being brought back to Hunt's ranch by Elvis Monday, a resident of the local Indian reservation who too has been personally targeted by the neo-Nazis. When Hunt asks Gus what has happened, he says only, "Talking is over," and Monday ruefully explains to Hunt that "this is the frontier, cowboy. . . . Everyplace is the frontier" (207). Both of these comments importantly differ from the exculpatory sermon David Larson hears in *Walk Me to the Distance* because they come not from a (tacit) beneficiary of the frontier myth such as the preacher—or Curt Marder, or George Armstrong Custer, or Rhino Tanner—but rather from characters who have personally and collectively suffered because of it. Monday's lack of distinction between the local and the universal conveys a moral flattening similar to Hunt's earlier comments to Robert; if "this" is the frontier as much as "everyplace" is, then exceptionalism is no longer a viable perspective. However, if Monday's utterance is taken as a commentary on the ubiquity of violence claiming to be justice, then it contains none of the tempered optimism of Hunt's earlier attempt to balance "ignorant" and "good, smart" people. In neither case does Monday's comment allow for the circumvention of reality that Lowe offers to Larson at the end of *Walk Me to the Distance.* Monday encourages Hunt to "take care of your uncle" (207) but does not offer him absolution based on abstract notions of what the frontier considers moral. The novel simply and ambiguously ends with Hunt "nodd[ing] and stepp[ing] away" (207) in response to Monday's words, leaving unanswered the "unsettling question [of] whether the neo-Nazis represent a new force threatening to change the West [that Hunt] loves or whether he has been misreading the natural and political landscapes all along" (M. Johnson, *Hoo-Doo* 211). Both answers to what Johnson posits as an either/or question can be true without any diminution of Everett's satirical commentary, which is directed not at the actual situation of the American West but rather at the ways in which various forms of its idealization—that is, repression of the *unheimlich*—are unhelpful, even dangerous, in their willful ignorance.

Unmaking Assumptions

Assumption is perhaps Everett's most thorough—and most unexpected—disruption of the conjoined mythologies of identity and place that adhere to the West. As the three stories that make up the novel unfold and the reader learns more about their protagonist, deputy sheriff Ogden Walker, it becomes apparent that he is yet another in a series of "central character[s in Everett's work] whose sense of identity is under some form of stress, if not actually coming apart at the seams" (Stewart, "Talking" 1). This stress is already manifest in the novel's prologue. While Walker is camping in the desert near Las Cruces, New Mexico, he hears his dead father's voice berating him in his dreams: "His father spoke to him, a dead voice telling Ogden he was a fool, a fool to love the desert, a fool to have left school, a fool to have joined the army, a fool to have no answers, and a fool to expect answers to questions he was foolish enough to ask. And his father would have called him a fool for working in that hick-full, redneck county" (3). Soon thereafter the narrator elaborates that "Ogden's father would never have approved of his son's job with the sheriff's office. He wouldn't have said it outright . . . but he would have made it clear that he believed Ogden to somehow be a traitor. A traitor to what would have remained forever unclear, but it would have been tinged with the language of race and social indignation" (13). As with Robert Hawks and John Hunt before him, Walker's ancestor provides him with a troubled and contradictory history that centers on his racial identity, coupled with a westward migration that was supposed to mitigate the significance of that identity. His father had "moved to New Mexico from Maryland because there were fewer people and so, necessarily, fewer white people. He hated white people, but not enough to refrain from marrying one" (13).

In many ways Walker is more prepared than Robert Hawks or John Hunt to admit the bigotry that pervades his western home, observing early on that an elderly woman he is assisting "didn't like him because he was black" and then adding that this "was probably true for half of the white residents of the county" as well (6). In a moment of dark humor reminiscent of the Clayton Bigsby character from Dave Chappelle's television show, Walker even meets a blind white supremacist who claims to be able to "smell a nigger" (90) but who nevertheless fails to perceive Walker's race—presumably because he cannot imagine a black cop in rural New Mexico—until Walker sardonically reveals it to him as he walks away from their encounter. Almost all of Everett's exposition in *Assumption* attributes characteristics to Walker that are strongly associated with his region, race, and profession. It remains unclear both to Walker and the reader, though, whether he will define himself by opposition or acquiescence to the prejudices he faces from multiple quarters because of these various traits.

From the outset Walker expresses an existential crisis that only worsens as the book progresses: "I just wonder what I'm doing. Am I wasting my time here? I don't mean in this house. I mean in this town." When his mother somewhat surprisingly agrees that he *is* wasting his time, she tempers her criticism by adding that his father "would be damn proud" of how Ogden has turned out because "there are not a lot of good men around" (22). In light of the novel's conclusion, the irony of his mother's statement not only calls her "reading" of her son into question but more importantly also implicates the manner in which Ogden assuages his own doubts in order to maintain this sense of "good[ness]." Everett varies his narrative technique both within the novel and in comparison with *Watershed* in order to highlight the flaws in Walker's thought process: "The tripartite structure of the novel is important here because the first two sections can be read as more traditional counterstories, and the last as a radical counter-counterstory. Thus, while the novel is unified in a loose sense, the three distinctive stories offer a diversity of critical approaches to dominant ways of narrativizing race" (Mullins 467).

Taking his cue from Richard Delgado's identification of "counterstories" as "a cure for the cultural and legal ills that perpetuate discrimination based on race," Matthew Mullins argued that Everett goes one step further:

> Rather than offering a triumphant story that runs counter to predominant preconceptions or that defamiliarizes narrative conventions by making a hero out of a black sheriff in the white-dominated American West, *Assumption* builds such a counterstory only to have it collapse under the weight of Ogden Walker's guilt. . . . The question that naturally arises from such a reading is why would he undercut the counterstory? Or, in terms of the story itself: why would Everett make his black hero into a murderer? The answer to both of these questions, I argue, is that to imagine *Assumption* as a counterstory would be to acknowledge that the story is, in fact, counter, which would necessarily imply that it is counter *to* something, reifying its position as somehow secondary or at least reactionary. (459–60)

Mullins's reading of the novel aligns not only with Everett's comments about "toying with the [reader's] assumptions" ("Author Percival" 188) but also more specifically with Weisenburger's assertion that degenerative satire "reflect[s] suspiciously on all ways of making meaning, including its own" (*Fables* 3). *Assumption* is not simply targeting Walker for satirical negation as with Rhino Tanner or Curt Marder, nor is it allowing for the projection of a reawakened consciousness into the book's aftermath as in *Watershed* and *Wounded*. The ending of *Assumption* overthrows the expectations of a reader expecting either a conventional narrative or its Horatian or Juvenalian satirical counternarrative. Everett leaves the reader only with an oxymoronic resolution of Walker's existential crisis in which "nothing makes sense and that's the only way that any of it can make any sense" (*Assumption* 225). Without naming it as such, Mullins identified the Menippean and degenerative quality of *Assumption*'s satire by noting that "Everett leaves dominant narratives behind and forges an alternative reality that is not beholden to self-definition by way of opposition or negation" (467). The inherent and unresolvable paradoxicality of the "alternative reality" Everett produces in this manner implicitly warns the reader against adopting it, in turn, as a prescriptive reality—that is, a new set of assumptions—in its own right.

As is the case with many of Everett's other protagonists, Walker's preferred method of processing his anxieties is to withdraw from the world into the soothing reassurance of solitary habits. Although Walker is less brazenly assertive about the effectiveness of his form of "retreat" than Hawks is, he nevertheless insists that "the world below seven thousand feet meant nothing to him" (71). Like Hawks, he frequently expresses a desire to isolate himself whenever the stress of his job becomes overwhelming, trying to use the routine tasks associated with his bachelor's home and with fly-fishing as a means of escape. His friend and fellow policeman Warren Fragua reinforces his belief in the self-protective nature of such forms of withdrawal from the world: "You've been watching television again. I told you, just tie flies every night and your mind won't get polluted" (51). The narration initially suggests that the resistance to his attempts at imposing order arises from his subconscious and is the result of repressing, rather than confronting, his self-doubts. His strategy also appears to become increasingly less effective in staving off the identity crisis that Stewart has perceived as imminent.

Walker is quite adept at sublimating any anxieties that result from either his profession or his race. When Walker goes to a diner for breakfast and a cup of coffee early in the novel, the narrator notes that he is served by a woman who "didn't much like the idea of policemen," a sentiment with which Walker seems to agree in the abstract, if not the immediate circumstances: "He understood. He didn't much like cops either, though he did want to like himself." When he tells her, "It's okay to dislike the uniform. . . . Under it I'm just like you," the narrative reveals that both he and the woman "realized that he had just uttered a blatant untruth" (15–16), though neither of them acknowledges that fact aloud. Walker's desire to "like himself" is particularly understandable in light of the town's widespread racism and the unsettling implication of suicide that closes the prologue: "He thought about the desert around him, thought about water and no water, the death that came with too much water. . . . To drown in the desert, that was the way to die. . . . Ogden closed his eyes and thanked the desert wind that it was all over" (4). This passage appears immediately after the dream in which his father calls him a fool and not long after his observation that the "desert that he and his father had shared was not like this one" (3), giving the reader a seemingly compelling explanation for Walker's willful repression of the "blatant untruth" underlying his assertion of solidarity with the woman at the diner and, by extension, with the entire community.

Everett develops this sense of repression further through the narrative exposition. For example, immediately after his mother's assertion that his dead father would approve of him as a "good man," Walker goes into "his father's tying room, where the man had made trout flies for the last twenty years of his life" and sits down to "make something easy"; this is a passage suffused with the highly specialized vocabulary of fly-fishing: "number 12 down-eye hook . . . zug bugs . . . nymph skipping the bottom of a riffle . . . peacock herl" (22). The simultaneously meditative and somewhat obsessive tone of this passage is offset by the dream that follows immediately thereafter, in which Walker attempts to lure "ten cutthroat trout," not with the "easy" tackle he was depicted tying in the previous paragraph, but with "the largest stonefly nymph he had ever seen at the end of [a] crazily long tippet." Despite casting his fly "perfectly," the trout—whose colloquial species name provides both ominous foreshadowing and local color to the story—"ignore it, almost with disdain" (23). Even though he insists to Fragua that he is perfectly happy to "fish and not worry about what we catch" (63), this dream passage's placement links it not only with his earlier self-questioning but also with his father's accusation of foolishness in the dream sequence from the novel's prologue. The association of these various scenes reinforces Walker's profound sense of doubt, whether about his profession, his father's approval, or even just the therapeutic value of his chosen hobby.

In a scene that strongly echoes Hawks's arrival at his cabin in the opening sections of *Watershed*, Everett plays out a more subjectively focalized version of the earlier fly-tying episode: "Ogden walked into his home and looked at his walls and furniture and unwashed dishes in the sink and breathed easier. He peeled off his hat and coat, went to the gas heater, and turned it on high. He took off his shoes and slipped into the moose-hide moccasins his mother had given him last Christmas. He then turned his attention to the collection of feathers and patches of deer and calf hair and spools of thread on his desk. He sat behind his vise and secured a size 10 hook, imagined a trout on the Chama rising for the Green Drake he was about to tie." This time, though, Walker does not have to fall asleep before thoughts related to his father and his own working life intrude into his routine. Initially he recalls being ten years old and "ask[ing] his father to teach him to tie," but this quickly develops into something far more complex than a halcyon memory of childhood: "As he dubbed a mixture of yellow rabbit and tan-red fox-fur onto the olive thread he recalled his father. He no longer felt sad when he thought of him. In fact, thinking of him helped Ogden relax. They had been close, for some reason not having the conflicts his friends had had with their fathers. He wondered if his present profession would have caused a problem between them. . . . He wondered because he himself had a problem with it" (49). Walker's unspoken, but seemingly conscious, thoughts concerning his father's theoretical disapproval may strike the reader as odd, given that the book has already depicted expressions of that disapproval on at least two previous occasions—in the prologue and in the blunt accusation that Walker is a race traitor that occurs only a few pages into the first story. However, each of the previous mentions—such as the disdainful trout refusing the amazing lure—is associated with Walker's dreams, and the narrative is generally forcing him further away from the improvised (and relative) comfort of such subconscious means of deflecting the recognition that "he felt out of touch with his time, didn't feel like people his age" (49).

The image of Walker's father accusing his son of being a "fool" and a "traitor" is almost impossible to reconcile with the assertion that "thinking of him helped Ogden relax." Everett uses this cognitive dissonance to suggest that the protective dissociation that Walker has used to displace his father's anger into the manageable realm of the subconscious is falling apart; by the end of the novel, this collapse will extend to the illusion that Walker is the "good man" that his mother believes he is. Everett's Menippean brand of satire does not simply invert his putative goodness, though, with some innate iniquity that can be easily censured; instead, as he has done in each of the earlier books discussed in this chapter, Everett indicts not only the personal mythology that allows Walker to maintain his comforting fiction of himself but also, and more extensively, the various diseased cultural narratives that mandated his acts of self-protective imposture in the first place. In a novel riddled with impostors, Walker is accused neither of being unique in his ignominy nor of being the *primum movens* of a fallen world.

Everett reuses a number of proper names from his past fiction in *Assumption,* thereby implying a degree of ontological consistency across his works that turns out to be one of the potential readerly assumptions that he undermines by the end of the book. Weixlmann has claimed that the small town and county of Plata in the rugged hills of New Mexico where most of *Assumption* takes place have also been the setting for several of the stories that appear in Everett's short-story collections as well as in the short novel *The Body of Martin Aguilera* (Review of *Assumption* 511). Moreover, significant portions of the first section of *Assumption* closely parallel a story entitled "Warm and Nicely Buried," which Everett previously published in 2001 and included in his collection *damned if i do*. Although Everett makes only passing reference to Plata's name in *The Body of Martin Aguilera* and "Warm and Nicely Buried," Weixlmann was not unreasonable in presuming a shared setting based on the presence of distinctive character names—for example, Warren Fragua, Fonda's Funeral Home—and plot devices.

With almost any other writer these details would certainly suffice to suggest a stable, Yoknapatawpha-like fictional geography to which that writer might return over the space of several decades. One should bear in mind, however, that Everett uses nearly all of his next novel, *Percival Everett by Virgil Russell,* to close the "gap between text and world, fiction and reality, content and form" by making it impossible to discern whether the name "Percival Everett" refers to himself, his father, the author, the narrator, the subject, and/or someone else within that novel (Huehls 299). Everett's repurposing of names and scenarios from his past works is part of a deliberate muddling of attempts to infer a unified, stable, and "Western" world that might provide prescriptive interpretations for readers. For example, whereas the Warren Fragua who appears in "Warm and Nicely Buried" is almost identical to his namesake in *Assumption,* the character who "went to the kitchen, poured himself a tall glass of orange juice, then returned to sit behind the vise clamped to his desktop . . . [,] secured a size 10 hook and imagined a trout on the Henry's Fork River in Idaho rising for the Green Drake he was about to tie" (*damned* 109; compare *Assumption* 49, quoted above) in the earlier story is named Lem Becker and demonstrates none of the race-consciousness that marks Walker in *Assumption*. Similarly, a character with the same name and prejudices as Emma Bickers, the old woman whose violent death at the start of *Assumption* sets the book's plot in motion, appears in Everett's 1998 story "Alluvial Deposits," which was also collected in *damned if i do*. As is the case in *Assumption*, Emma Bickers has an encounter at her front door with an African American authority figure that features both passive-aggressive bigotry and gunshots, but unlike the scene in the novel, she lives in Utah, the man she interacts with happens to be a black hydrologist from Colorado named Robert Hawks, and their encounter does not end with her death. It is unlikely that Everett intends these mirror scenes to be interpreted as staggering coincidences—that is, that Fragua has had almost exactly the same conversations with two entirely different people, or that a single person named Emma Bickers had similar interactions in two small towns hundreds of miles apart with a pair of characters noteworthy for an idiosyncratic set of characteristics. Therefore these slightly skewed recurrences become yet another formal multiplicity reminiscent of his concatenated narrators and nominal doppelgängers. The familiarity of the "geographical terrain . . . to Everett devotees" (Weixlmann, Review of *Assumption* 511) becomes a highly self-referential part of Everett's strategy of playful misdirection, designed to lure the reader further into a productively satirical misreading based on the assumptions that reader brings to the table.

Whatever his motivations, in specifying the place where *Assumption* is set, Everett inarguably chose to reuse the same signifier that named the tribe and reservation in *Watershed*. Most frequently translated into English as "silver," the Spanish name Plata takes on potential ironic connotations in *Assumption* that are not apparent in *Watershed* or in any of his other earlier stories using a setting with that name. Silver's relatively modest value as a precious metal corresponds to Plata's status within the West; it certainly cannot sustain the "golden" dreams of mythic California. Plata's name also ironically alludes to the thirty pieces of silver that Judas received when Walker bemoans about the petty monetary motives (see below) that he unconvincingly posits as an explanation for the town's sudden outbreak of violence. In addition Plata's prevailing benightedness is never given much of a "silver lining" in *Assumption*, except to the extent that it usually allows Walker to achieve his oft-stated desire "only to do his job" (49). This generally entails very little, as implied by the wholly unserious initial description of his boss: "Sheriff Bucky Paz was a big man with a belly round enough that the general belief was that his suspenders not only held up his trousers but kept him from exploding. He didn't carry a side arm because he figured he was wide enough without one" (13–14). Everett may also have had another, more colloquial usage of *plata* in mind. The phrase *hablar en plata* literally means "to speak in silver" but figuratively refers to speaking plainly or directly, something which few characters in Plata other than Warren Fragua actually do on a regular basis. Thus, *hablar en Plata, New Mexico* involves precisely the opposite of what this colloquial phrase normally suggests, an ironic reversal that serves Everett's satirical ends well, given the misleading appearances that both Walker and the novel try initially to maintain.

Walker's depiction at the start of the book "position[s] him squarely in the tradition of classic lawmen of the American West." At the same time his complicated performance of "heroism and integrity" (Mullins 457) in fulfilling his duties as deputy sheriff of Plata County makes Walker reminiscent of such earnest and somewhat naive law enforcers as Marge Gunderson, the police chief of Brainerd, Minnesota, in Joel and Ethan Coen's film *Fargo* (1996), or Ed Tom Bell, the sheriff of Terrell County, Texas, in Cormac McCarthy's novel *No Country for Old Men* (2005), which was adapted into a film by the Coens in 2007. When confronted with criminal acts of extreme violence that occur in their sleepy and superficially benign communities, all three of these characters are understandably staggered; the narrator of *Assumption* communicates the overwhelming nature of the situation in a deadpan tone, stating that the "accumulation of so many dead people was unusual for the Plata Sheriff's Department, and the only place to put them was the same place a single body would have been put, Fonda's Funeral Home" (51). Whereas Gunderson rises to the occasion and apprehends her perpetrator in the act of stuffing his partner's corpse into a wood chipper, Bell walks away from his duties dejected and disillusioned after being unable to collar the brutal hit man Anton Chigurh. As Joe Weixlmann noted, *Assumption* finds Everett "working both with and against the crime/mystery tradition as he interrogates assumptions we tend to hold about life's basic issues. More fundamentally, the book focuses attention on personality and process as it critiques elements within our society" (Review of *Assumption* 512).

In the opening story, "A Difficult Likeness," Walker is confronted with the mysterious murder of a cranky, bigoted elderly woman named Emma Bickers, who is introduced while Walker is investigating an incident in which she fired a gun through the closed front door of her house at what she believed was an intruder. Only moments after leaving, Walker returns to her house because of a "bad feeling about something," having initially written this sensation off either as her "acting strange simply because she was strange, [or] because she had never liked Ogden's skin color, though she had never said as much. But he knew" (9). Upon reentering her house, he discovers not only the dead body of Mrs. Bickers but also the corpse of her cat. The senselessness of the killing leads Walker's mother to ask him, "How could such a thing happen? . . . Why?" Walker's reply is simply, "It's a cruel world out there" (20), a clichéd response with limited explanatory power, to say the least.

Walker's impression that Plata is a haven removed from everything that happens "below seven thousand feet" is revealed as a willful delusion as he and his law-enforcement colleagues get more deeply enmeshed in this crime, the parameters of which begin to sprawl far beyond Plata's boundaries. Walker openly questions his motivations for so ardently investigating the death of a woman in whom he "had had little interest . . . when she'd been alive." He furthermore observes that he "was amused at how much her death was affecting him. Perhaps it was as simple as a mystery to pass the time in a boring, sleepy village. Maybe it was some kind of sublimation for a stalled life, a life he was not pursuing. Or perhaps he just wanted to catch and stop a killer" (40). The lack of clarity in his purpose mirrors the lack of clarity Walker feels as his investigation uncovers the story's various intertwined threads but cannot weave them together into the usual denouement of a police procedural: "Ogden started the drive back home. He knew more than enough to be sure that he knew nothing. A feeling that was becoming sadly familiar. He imagined that Emma Bickers was a part of the hate group the FBI agents had talked about. She'd always been unpleasant enough, but still he couldn't believe it. He had no idea what to make of the numbers. He had learned little from talking to Robbins. . . . Perhaps the holes in the meadow up in Niebla Canyon made some sense" (92).

After a shootout at the end of the story, Walker swiftly apprehends some of the criminals, including a woman (falsely) claiming to be Emma Bickers's daughter, a corrupt FBI agent, and members of a white supremacist group called *The Great White Hope* (76). Far from being the rational and reassuring denouement of the conventional detective story, though, this resolution seems more an accident than a validation of either Walker's moral code as a lawman or his skills as an investigator. The fact that a racist hate group is involved in the crime proves to be another red herring, given that Walker's status as "the only black man in a five-hundred mile radius" (78) hardly makes him a force analogous to the boxer Jack Johnson—as the Great White Hope's name implies. Bigotry is omnipresent here, but it is also wholly tangential; it affects Walker's life, but not in ways that ultimately signify greatly. As Claude Julien noted, though, the fundamental closure of detective fiction is still achieved: "In the end, the hick town sheriff . . . puts things right and a traitorous FBI agent is dispatched.

The reader feels snugly at home in a world that runs according to conventions. Good prevails over evil. . . . Life can go back to normal" ("*Assumption*" 3). The story's title suggests that although Walker may only be a "difficult likeness" of a competent detective, he has been good enough in this instance—provided that one disregards Everett's implicit warnings about reading with the same trust in superficial appearances of reality that gets Walker into trouble.

The next two stories further unravel this already imperfect satisfaction of readerly expectation, simultaneously subverting the formulaic moralism of the detective-fiction genre and any sense of societal innocence that might be attributed either to the outwardly placid realm of Plata County or to the nation as a whole. Clément-Alexandre Ulff noted that *Assumption* repeatedly uses the "motif of relatives, their mysterious disappearance, and the sudden appearance of people pretending to be those missing relatives, thus faking their identities," which allows Everett to question "the authenticity and resilience of ties in an American society whose ravaged Dream seems a distant utopia: gun violence, prostitution, hard-drugs and con-men seem to drag the reader of *Assumption* into a whirlwind of desolation" (4). As a novel composed of three crime stories that are linked by a common setting and some common characters, Everett sets up a reasonable expectation that there will be some narrative "ties" among these stories as well. Such expectations are dashed in the opening pages of the second story, "My American Cousin," in which there is no clarifying commentary on the ragged ending of the previous story, despite the passage of six months' time. As Walker becomes embroiled in another mystery—this one involving a woman named Caitlin Alison, who arrives in Plata searching for her missing cousin Fiona McDonough—there is little reason to believe that either he or his somewhat bumbling comrades in the sheriff's department are better prepared to handle it. If, like Marge Gunderson, he somewhat accidentally succeeds in the first story, then he resembles Ed Tom Bell more in the second one. By the third story, suggestively titled "The Shift," Walker has unexpectedly transformed into something entirely outside the usual interpretive framework of a lawman.

The title of the second story is a multilayered play on signification that indicates Everett's degenerative satirical intentions. On the surface it refers to the double imposture at the story's center; neither Caitlin Alison nor the cousin she is looking for turns out to be who Walker gullibly believes them to be. It also puns on the title of the farcical drawing-room comedy *Our American Cousin*, a performance of which Abraham Lincoln was attending when he was assassinated on April 14, 1865. Everett is borrowing the inherent tonal multiplicity of that historical event to frame his story, blending moments of comic mockery with deeply disturbing scenes of deception, violence, and criminality. In the early stages of the story, Walker's assistance to the putative Caitlin in her efforts to locate her missing cousin is reminiscent of the courteous small-town police work depicted on *The Andy Griffith Show* and gives Everett a chance to mock Plata's lack of sophistication gently: "The billboard was a giant hand-painted portrait of Manny with microwave ovens for eyes and a deep freeze for a mouth. Blinky had painted the sign himself and along with it the mural on the side of the store. The mural depicted refrigerators dressed like Indians dancing around a huge, glowing red convection oven. The scene was modeled after the local corn dance and most people were offended by it, but Blinky, being Native, claimed that every detail was accurate, except for the fact that the dancers were appliances" (107). When this relatively benign story devolves into another web of lies involving hookers (both dead and alive), drug deals, and kidnappings, it only heightens the contrast to the litany of trifling jokes about shooting noisy peacocks and Sheriff Bucky Paz's eating habits.

Walker travels to Denver and Dallas while chasing down vague leads, making him feel even more out of his depth than in the first story. He questions both his professional competence and his personal motivations: "Ogden was striking out. He'd only learned what he already knew. To make matters worse, the longer he drove around Denver asking his stupid questions, the less he knew what he was doing. . . . Did he really expect to solve the murder of the woman in the cabin? . . . Or was it some ego thing, or worse, some macho thing driving him?" (150). The story concludes much as the first one does, with Walker engaging in a firefight that ends with some of the criminals injured and apprehended, but there is even less explanation of the criminals' motives or methods. Walker ends the story by expressing his puzzlement to his mother:

> "Three lives for twelve thousand dollars. I mean, I just can't wrap my mind around it. I guess it wasn't about the money."
>
> "What was it about then?"
>
> "That I don't know. Power, maybe. You know what, Mom?"
>
> "What's that?"
>
> "People scare me."
>
> "They should, son." (172)

His mother's final comment becomes the springboard by which Everett completes the transformation of *Assumption* from a seeming morality play about the incompatibility of an honest man and a corrupt world into a Menippean satire of the discourses—literary and cultural—that have encouraged an overly uncritical reader to assume he or she understands Walker: "The novel's resolution will force you to reread the whole work, scrutinizing Everett's use of detective novel clichés in order to chart the variations and modulations that alienate the novel's meaning" (Muyumba).

The final story begins with Walker at a crime scene more appropriate to his initial conception of Plata. He helps Terry Lowell, a local game and fish patrolman, arrest a poacher at a riverside fish hatchery in the New Mexico backcountry. As has been the pattern in the previous stories, this relatively quiet opening quickly changes into something much more sinister. Walker's failure to maintain custody of a boy who claims to be the poacher's eleven-year-old son leads him to a meth lab in the scrubby mountains and eventually back to the riverbank where the story began, albeit under radically different circumstances. When Lowell turns up dead, Fragua gradually pieces together evidence that points to Walker not only as Lowell's killer but also as the prime suspect in the death of several other people connected to the poacher and the boy (falsely) claiming to be his son. A puzzled Fragua confronts Walker at gunpoint on the riverbank at the end of the story: "None of this makes any sense. . . . What in the world are you into? Are you on drugs or something?" (224). Although Walker's rambling answer certainly does not discount Fragua's pharmacological suspicion, it does perform a Menippean satirical subversion of the conventional resolutions of crime/detective fiction and also of rational interpretation generally:

> Of course it doesn't make sense. What does make sense, Warren? Nothing in this damn world makes sense. Just look around. I'm out of my fucking mind. I must be. What do you think? Does that have it all make sense for you? I'm an evil man. *Live* is *evil* spelled backward or is it the other way around? I'm evil. I suppose that's what they'll say. I'm possessed by the devil, *lived* spelled backwards. Does that make any sense? I wanted some drug money. I'm hooked on meth. Do any of those reasons help this make sense? I was tired of being a good guy. Was I ever a good guy? How about that? Does that have it make sense for you? This is the way it is, Warren, simply the way it fucking is. Sad, sad, sad, sad, sad. Shitty, shitty, bang, bang. Nothing makes sense and that's the only way that any of it can make any sense. Here I am, the way I am, not making any sense. Blood in the water. Blood on my shirt. (224–25)

Warren is forced to shoot Walker dead, and the story ends without offering any additional clues to either Fragua or the reader to aid in discerning what caused Walker's titular "shift."

Anthony Stewart noted that "where Ogden leads us by the end of the novel does not, in fact, solve anything," thereby completing the disruption of the conventional plot and assuring that "we cannot find out why he did what he did" and must therefore "do our best to try [to understand] within our limitations" ("Talking" 5–6). Much as Thomas Pynchon did via the opaque resolution of

The Crying of Lot 49 (1966), Everett forces his readers to think for themselves by refusing to provide any guidance in that regard. Linking the reader's desire for understanding with Fragua's, Everett has allowed them to be led collectively to the riverbank by their assumptions; in the reader's case, these assumptions may come from familiarity with the book's apparent genre, mythic associations with the West, and/or nominal connections to Everett's larger body of work. Having shot and killed Walker in the dark, Fragua "turned his light back on and looked at the face on his boots," which is presumably that of Walker's corpse. Just as the reader is now confronted with an ending whose significance is "unknowable" by any conventional reasoning, the narrator simply—and uncannily—states that "it was not a face [Fragua] knew" (225).

Conclusion

A Post-Soul (but *Not* Post-Racial) Postscript

Anthony Stewart has contended that the ending of *Assumption* also "highlights the pointlessness of the desire for the post-racial, a desire to resolve something we cannot definitively understand" ("Talking" 6). Stewart sardonically defined this "desire for the post-racial" further as "trying to resolve questions of race once and for all, principally so they will not keep coming up and leaving some people feeling embarrassed or uncomfortable" (1). He also asserted that Everett's fiction issues numerous "challenges" that fly in the face of this desire, one of which is "the mundane, although apparently fine and difficult, balance to strike between being aware that a character is black, on the one hand, while simultaneously resisting the urge to be preoccupied exclusively and reductively by this fact, on the other" (2). At the same time that Everett is satirically "signifyin(g)"—in Henry Louis Gates's sense of the term (*passim*)—on narratives of race and identity within American culture, Stewart's observation profoundly directs us to note that he is simultaneously also *in*signifying, that is, trying to render those narratives less "exclusively and reductively" significant. This latter tendency is a mark of Everett's distinctly Menippean and degenerative approach to storytelling.

Walker's final utterance sums up Everett's career-spanning skepticism toward tidy explanation, whether of race or seemingly anything else. Like Walker, Everett has demanded throughout his career that his readers take him "the way [he is], [often] not making any sense." As this book, hopefully, shows, he also mirrors Walker in offering his audience a number of possible interpretations for his work before rhetorically asking whether "any of those reasons help this make sense." If Everett had his way, a symbolic fate similar to Walker's would befall him, inasmuch as he would undergo the "death of the author" of which Barthes wrote. Everett's work has consistently attempted to expose the folly of trying to make the world—whether real or fictional—conform to preconceived assumptions, whether related to his identity, to literary conventions, to religious precepts, or to any other rigid philosophy dependent on categorization and classification.

In his *The Grey Album: On the Blackness of Blackness,* Kevin Young offers a means of approaching the racial dimension of Everett's overarching authorial project that touches on both Menippean satire and degenerative satire without mentioning either one by name. Young's concept of "storying" bears passing resemblance to what Delgado similarly called "counter-storying." If one slightly dials back some of Young's premises, though, his version of "storying" corresponds much more with the "counter-counterstorying" that Mullins has derived from Delgado's concept (see above):

> *Storying* is both a tradition and a form; it is what links artfulness . . . with any of the number of stories (or tall tales or "lies" or literature) black folks tell among themselves. . . . By storying, or what I sometimes call here "the counterfeit tradition," I don't mean falsehood or some fake blackness. . . . The black imagination conducts its escape by way of underground railroads of meaning—a practice we would call the black art of escape. In contrast, both realness and truthiness—distinct from a funky, vernacular "troof" that's part proof and part story—miss the ineffable lyric quality found in the imagination, and in the tradition traced here. Throughout, I am interested in the ways in which black folks use fiction in its various forms to free themselves from the bounds of fact. (Young 17–19)

Young's identification of this simultaneously subversive and creative concept as intrinsic to African American culture is not what makes it most germane to considerations of Everett's work. Like "Monk" Ellison in *Erasure,* Everett does not deny his own blackness; instead he rejects the extent to which that characteristic is either prescriptive or predominant among the various traits that might define him. Although such works as *Erasure* and *I Am Not Sidney Poitier* demonstrate beyond a shadow of doubt that Everett is conscious of and deeply conversant with black literary traditions, both of those works also illustrate how he is no more or less beholden to them than any others. Rather it is Young's comment about "us[ing] fiction" to break free from the "bounds of fact" that most powerfully echoes Everett's prevailing attitude toward his own writing.

As Young develops his framework further, it continues to resonate with Everett's work in articulating a desire not just for escape from restrictions but also for transcendence of them: "To distinguish it a bit from mere fiction, *counterfeit* is a term I use to discuss ways in which black writers create their own authority in order to craft their own, alternative system of literary currency and value, functioning both within and without the dominant, supposed gold-standard system of American culture. . . . One crucial aspect of the counterfeit is a renegotiation of borders—and a freedom from insular identity itself" (24). Although Everett would almost certainly quibble with the contention that his construction of an "alternative system of literary currency and value" arises primarily from his own blackness, this passage otherwise fits his lifelong authorial project quite snugly. It is only when Young asserts that "counterfeit is the way in which black folks forge . . . black authority in a world not necessarily of their making" (24) that his conception begins to diverge from Everett's, inasmuch as Everett is loath to assert *any* kind of authority in the vast majority of his works; if anything, he actively resists the notion that such authority truly exists—black, white, or otherwise—as anything other than a discourse with the power to resist and/or to rebuff scrutiny of its premises and conclusions. As Handley has noted, Everett's stories are self-conscious reminders that "the 'truth' of history is never objective but always subjectively imagined" and that "'history' . . . is itself a record of discourses" (306). His novels do not function as counter(feit)-histories; rather they are satirical metahistories that emphasize the damage inflicted on individuals and societies by uncritical acceptance of such "subjectively imagined . . . discourses."

Young is absolutely correct in attributing a liberationist bent to the African American artists and works he surveys in his book, but Everett's own blackness has never been the focal point of his writing, even when blackness has figured prominently in the construction of his characters and authorial stand-ins. As his pointed response to Sven Birkerts's review of *American Desert* revealed, Everett considers his own race to be another form of "insular identity" for unsophisticated readers to impose on his works, insofar as it becomes "all they can see" ("Color" 4). Although he often joins them in "critiquing white-dominated past and present realities," Everett departs from Zora Neale Hurston, Alice Walker, Ralph Ellison, and the other authors Young mentions in his opening chapter by refusing to "substitut[e] an alternate black one" in their place (Young 27). Young asserts that "the counterfeit is the 'literary lie.' Which is to say, it is, in that way, *useful*" (33), but Everett does not "usefully lie"—that is, write fiction—for reasons of sociopolitical exigency or even survival in the manner that Young attributes to Hurston. Rather he does do so to maintain his integrity as an artist in the face of various cultural processes—"the dominant, supposed gold-standard system of American culture"—that would try to limit him in some way to remaining in the "bounds of fact." For Everett, this "gold-standard system" is as apparent in mainstream publishing and academia as it is in South Carolina or the American West, and the artistic strictures he faces in all these realms include race without necessarily always centering on it. He creates his own authority just long enough to remind the reader of the fleeting, imprecise, and illusory nature of such authority. He will not even be bounded by the seemingly indelible "fact" of his own name, much less the supposed signification of his race or place of origin/residence.

Despite this initial departure, Young's book ultimately leaves room for Everett within its discussion of black art without constituting a new category for him to reject. Although he does not explicitly include Everett in his discussion thereof, Young describes the "post-soul" mind-set that has developed since Nelson George coined the term in 1992: "Post-soul knows well that black is not just a color or a state of mind but also a state of being; and that black art is whatever art is made by black folks. We should not want to place any limitations on such an aesthetic, whether using white or black standards" (Young 284). Young also notes that the "post-soul" generation attempts to avoid one of the pitfalls of both the Harlem Renaissance and the Black Arts Movement: "After discarding limitations on what black art can be, it proves difficult, however well meaning, to impose new, albeit 'blacker,' ones. Once achieved, freedom is difficult to relinquish" (284). Everett's unwillingness to "relinquish" his artistic freedom in any context is perhaps the most enduring quality of his writerly career, and it is not difficult—or, one hopes, overly presumptive—to imagine him nodding in agreement with Young's assertion that post-soul authors "saw and see blackness as a given, both as a subject matter and a subjectivity. The what and how any such writer would choose to write, from epic to blues to both, are not so obvious. Or proscribed" (289).

Three separate critics—Gillian Johns, Danielle Fuentes Morgan, and Christian Schmidt—have used the expansive and inherently elastic concept of "post-soul" black identity to discuss *Erasure* and *A History of the African-American People* in a collection of critical essays entitled *Post-Soul Satire: Black Identity after Civil Rights* (2014). Like these three authors, Lavelle Porter explicitly has insisted that there is value in emphasizing the "given" of Everett's racial identity, provided one also engages in self-critical reflection on how and why such emphasis can skew a reading of Everett's work. In his 2015 review of *Assumption* and *Percival Everett by Virgil Russell,* Porter began by calling out not only would-be readers but also seemingly Everett himself: "If you haven't read Percival Everett, you are missing out on one of the greatest black writers working today. Yeah, I said it. Black Writer. African-American. Colored. Negro. Afro-American. Etc. Everett can obfuscate and complicate and subvert these designations all he wants, but to the extent there is such a thing as African-American literature, he's one of the most important writers doing it" (L. Porter).

The last sentence reveals Porter's post-soul affinities, his skepticism about the existence of a discernible "African-American literature" corresponding closely with Young's radically self-evident comment about "black art [being] whatever art is made by black folks." Porter outlined the "meta-racial" perception of Everett's work as follows: "In his entire body of work one finds an ongoing meditation on all the sloppy, simplistic, lazy, and inevitable ways that we rely upon . . . racial signifiers. Sifting through his books, and the growing critical tradition around them, we find a writer who is committed to confronting, disrupting, and just plain fucking with conceptions of race at every turn." However, Porter ironically undercut any sense that what "we find" by seeing Everett this way has created a sense of obligation in the author: "Or he might write about baseball, horses, woodworking, literary theory, and hydrology if he feels like it." Porter closed his essay by once again insisting that "Percival Everett is one of the dopest black writers around," but he also illustrated his understanding of Everett as a degenerative, Menippean figure: "go ahead and listen to him as he tells you otherwise, and while doing so understand you are hearing from the best kind of unreliable narrator." In short, Porter repeatedly lauded Everett's preeminence among "black writers" while reminding us not to believe that we can (or should) know exactly what that terms signifies, because a large part of what makes Everett so great is that he is "expand[ing] the possibilities for black literature" (L. Porter) to the point that the blackness of its creators may no longer convey any constricting forms of meaning.

Everett's particularly "post-soul" expression of blackness over the course of his career is an "existential and narrative ouroboros" (Taylor, "Lucid" 84) that both destroys and re-creates itself ad infinitum. However, it is perhaps only in the frequency of its recurrence that this particular theme is significant in Everett's work. One can remove the words "racial" and "race" in the passage by Lavelle Porter above without significantly altering its accuracy regarding what "we find" in Everett's work. As Lavelle Porter has noted, a "Percival Everett novel is never just about race, never limited to race," and this volume has hopefully illustrated the extent to which Everett's "commitment to confronting, disrupting, and just plain fucking with conceptions" via Menippean and degenerative satire encompasses myriad other realms of human thought. Stewart has suggested the ultimate value of accepting Everett's work in terms of its playful—and, in Young's parlance, "useful"—subversion:

> As often as not, when Everett's work comes to critical attention, critics succumb, even in the face of the work's encouragement to the contrary, to the temptation to make some sort of either/or choice—compromise, really—either seeing Everett's work as interesting for being the literary theoretical tour de force it often is, or discussing it in the context of African American literature and exploring how it does or (more often) does not satisfy some

> pre-existing expectation that attaches to this heavily freighted, limited, and limiting term. My question here is, Why do we succumb to this temptation? . . . His work is not "only" African American literature, nor is it "only" significant for its literary theoretical displays. It draws our attention to the infinity of the continuum in between these two categories. ("Setting" 218)

Everett's jestingly earnest rejection of categories—for example, "'Uncategorizable' is a category. Which I resent" (Stewart, "Uncategorizable" 303)—is another reminder to his readers to focus on "the infinity of the continuum" rather than *any* fixed poles therein. After all, as the narrator of *Percival Everett by Virgil Russell* puts it, using a mundanely literal definition of "lying" while echoing Young's more figurative one: "lying here like this I have learned some things about us and learned nothing at all and it is the *nothing at all* that sings to me in this cucumbery trance . . . the things we think when we know we know nothing when we know there is nothing when nothing is our last safe cave of language, and vegetable, vegetable, vegetable me, the sky's in the river, the moon's in the sea, the birds speak in riddles and dolphins tell lies, that we'll all live forever and that nobody dies" (222–23).

Bibliography

Primary Sources

Novels

Suder. New York: Viking, 1983; repr., Baton Rouge: Louisiana State University Press, 1999.

Walk Me to the Distance. New York: Ticknor and Fields, 1985; repr., Columbia: University of South Carolina Press, 2015.

Cutting Lisa. New York: Ticknor and Fields, 1986; repr., Baton Rouge: Louisiana State University Press, 2000.

For Her Dark Skin. Seattle: Owl Creek Press, 1990.

Zulus. Sag Harbor, N.Y.: Permanent Press, 1990.

God's Country. Boston: Faber and Faber, 1994; repr., Boston: Beacon Press, 2003.

Watershed. St. Paul, Minn.: Graywolf Press, 1996; repr., Boston: Beacon Press, 2003.

The Body of Martin Aguilera. Camano Island, Wash.: Owl Creek Press, 1997.

Frenzy. St. Paul, Minn.: Graywolf Press, 1997.

Glyph. St. Paul, Minn.: Graywolf Press, 1999.

Erasure. Hanover, N.H.: University Press of New England, 2001; repr., New York: Hyperion, 2002; repr., St. Paul, Minn.: Graywolf Press, 2011.

Grand Canyon, Inc. San Francisco: Versus Press, 2001.

A History of the African-American People (Proposed) by Strom Thurmond, as Told to Percival Everett and James Kincaid (with James Kincaid). New York: Akashic Books, 2004.

American Desert. New York: Hyperion, 2004.

Wounded. St. Paul, Minn.: Graywolf Press, 2005.

The Water Cure. St. Paul, Minn.: Graywolf Press, 2007.

I Am Not Sidney Poitier. St. Paul, Minn.: Graywolf Press, 2009.

Assumption. St. Paul, Minn.: Graywolf Press, 2011.

Percival Everett by Virgil Russell. Minneapolis: Graywolf Press, 2013.

So Much Blue. Minneapolis: Graywolf Press, 2017.

Poetry

re: f (gesture). Los Angeles: Black Goat / Red Hen Press, 2006.

Abstraktion und Einfühlung. Los Angeles: Black Goat / Red Hen Press, 2008.

Swimming Swimmers Swimming. Pasadena, Calif.: Red Hen Press, 2011.

Trout's Lie. Pasadena, Calif.: Red Hen Press, 2015.

Short Fiction Collections

The Weather and Women Treat Me Fair. Little Rock, Ark.: August House, 1987.

Big Picture. St. Paul, Minn.: Graywolf Press, 1996.

damned if i do. St. Paul, Minn.: Graywolf Press, 2004.

Half an Inch of Water. Minneapolis: Graywolf Press, 2015.

Other Books by Everett

The One That Got Away (illus. Dirk Zimmer). New York: Clarion Books, 1992. (children's book)

There Are No Names for Red (by Chris Abani, illus. Everett). Pasadena, Calif.: Red Hen Press, 2010.

Essays, Letters, and Other Uncollected Works

"Artist Statement." In *Percival Everett: Writing Other/Wise,* ed. Keith B. Mitchell and Robin G. Vander, 77–78. New Orleans: Xavier Review Press, 2014.

"Believers." *Callaloo* 24.4 (Fall 2001): 1000–1014.

"Bull Does Nothing." *Callaloo* 12.1 (Winter 1989): 179–83.

"Chemically Darkened Like Me." *Oxford American* 78 (August 2012): 130–31.

"The Color of His Skin." Letter to the Editor. *New York Times Book Review,* June 6, 2004, 4.

"The Devotion of Nuclear Associability." *Callaloo* 22.1 (Winter 1999): 116–20.

Foreword. In Abdourahman A. Waberi, *In the United States of Africa,* trans. David Ball and Nicole Ball, vii–viii. Lincoln: University of Nebraska Press (Bison Books), 2009.

Foreword. In George C. Wolfe and Richard Taylor, *Shackles,* vii–ix. Frankfort, Ky.: Frankfort Arts Foundation, 1988.

Foreword. In *Making Callaloo: 25 Years of Black Literature,* ed. Charles Henry Rowell, xv–xvii. New York: St. Martin's Press, 2002.

"Four." *While You Were Sleeping* 25 (Fall 2003): 72.

"F/V: Placing the Experimental Novel." *Callaloo* 22.1 (Winter 1999): 18–23.

"If (Again)." *nocturnes: (re)view of the literary arts* 1 (Fall 2001): 72–79.

"In the Dark a Blade." *Modern Short Stories* (December 1988): 93–97.

Introduction. In Laird Hunt, *The Impossibly,* xiii–xiv. Minneapolis: Coffee House, 2012.

Introduction. In Thomas Jefferson, *The Jefferson Bible,* 11–31. New York: Akashic Books, 2004.

"The Man in the Moon." *Shooting Star Review* 5.1 (Spring 1991): 20–22.

"Meiosis." *Callaloo* 20.2 (Spring 1997): 263–76; repr., *Callaloo* 24.2 (Spring 2001): 454–67.

"A Modality." *symplokē* 12.1–2 (2004): 152–54.

"909." In *My California: Journeys by Great Writers,* ed. Donna Wares, 121–25. Santa Monica, Calif.: Angel City, 2004.

"Object and Word." *Village Voice Literary Supplement,* October 19, 2004, 87.

"Raising Horses, Writing Novels." *Speakeasy* (Minneapolis) 1.4 (March/April 2003): 14–15.

"The Revolution Will Not Be Televised." *Hungry Mind Review* 45 (Spring 1998): 16.

"Riding the Fence." *Montana Review* 8 (Fall 1986): 111–14.

"Rose Nose." *Aspen Journal for the Arts* 1.2 (Summer 1982): 27–28.

"Signing to the Blind." *Callaloo* 14.1 (Winter 1991): 9–11.

"Squeeze." *Callaloo* 16.3 (Summer 1993): 24–30.
"Staying Between the Lines." *Callaloo* 23.4 (Fall 2000): 1183–88.
"A Stiffer Breeze." *Callaloo* 27.3 (Summer 2004): 616–20.
"Tesseract." *Bomb* 126 (Winter 2013–14): 98–101.
"Why I'm from Texas." *Callaloo* 24.1 (Winter 2001): 62–63.

Secondary Sources

Critical, Biographical, and Bibliographical Works

Amfreville, Marc. "*Erasure* and *The Water Cure:* A Possible Suture?" *Canadian Review of American Studies* 43.2 (Summer 2013): 180–88.

Baker, Houston A., Jr. "'If you see Robert Penn Warren, ask him: Who *does* speak for the Negro?': Reflections on Monk, Black Writing, and Percival Everett's *Erasure*." In *I Don't Hate the South: Reflections on Faulkner, Family, and the South*, 121–50. New York: Oxford University Press, 2007.

Bauer, Sylvie. "'Fracture This Bone . . . and Find the True Anguish of Speech': Disenacting the Body in Percival Everett's *Zulus*." In Mitchell and Vander, *Percival Everett* 37–57.

———. "'A good place to throw ashes to the wind': 'Revenir du pays des morts' ou les soubresauts de la pensée dans *Percival Everett by Virgil Russell*, de Percival Everett." *Transatlantica* 2013.1: 1–10. Accessed 27 Aug. 2017. http://transatlantica.revues.org/6381.

———. "The Music of Words in *Zulus*." In Maniez and Tissut 153–72.

———. "'Nouns, Names, Verbs' in *The Water Cure* by Percival Everett, or, 'Can a Scream Be Articulate?'" *Revue française d'études americaines* 128 (2011): 99–108.

———. "Percival Everett's *Grand Canyon Inc.:* Self-Reliance Revisited." *Canadian Review of American Studies* 43.2 (Summer 2013): 257–68.

———. "'Private Turbulent Seas': 'Painting the Moon' in *Cutting Lisa*, by Percival Everett." *Lectures du Monde Anglophone* 1 (March 2015). Accessed January 1, 2016. http://eriac.univ-rouen.fr/private-turbulent-seas-painting-the-moon-in-cutting-lisaem-by-percival-everett/.

Bell, Bernard W. "Percival L[eonard] Everett (1956–)." In *The Contemporary African American Novel: Its Folk Roots and Modern Literary Branches*, 323–28. Amherst: University of Massachusetts Press, 2004.

Bell, Madison Smartt. "Analysis [of 'Hear That Long Train Moan']." In *Narrative Design: A Writer's Guide to Structure*, 136–46. New York: Norton, 1997.

———. "A Note on *God's Country*." *Callaloo* 28.2 (Spring 2005): 343–44.

Berben-Masi, Jacqueline. "Getting to First Base: Baseball as Organizing Metaphor in *Suder*." In Julien and Tissut 23–28.

———. "'The Jailhouse Baby Blues,' or Literal and Literary Prisons in *Glyph* by Percival Everett: Allegory, Irony, Self-Reflection, and Socio-Academic Analysis." In Julien and Tissut 49–60.

———. "Percival Everett's *Glyph:* Prisons of the Body Physical, Political, and Academic." In *In the Grip of the Law: Trials, Prisons and the Space Between*, ed. Monika Fludernik and Greta Olson, 223–39. Frankfurt am Main: Peter Lang, 2004.

Birat, Kathie. "Ordinary Voices: The Mocking of Myth in *For Her Dark Skin*." In Julien and Tissut 81–89.

Bleu-Schwenninger, Patricia. "On the Necessity of Losing One's Head in Order to Keep It in Percival Everett's *American Desert*." In Maniez and Tissut 131–52.

Bonnemère, Yves. "*God's Country:* The Mythic West Revisited." In Julien and Tissut 149–60.

Bragg, Beauty. "History (Deposed) by Percival Everett: An Account of Race, Writing, and Post-Soul Aesthetics in *A History of the African-American People [Proposed] by Strom Thurmond.*" In Mitchell and Vander, *Percival Everett* 18–36.

Buchanan, David. "The Barely Functioning Author in Percival Everett's *Erasure.*" *Kritikos* 11 (October/December 2014). Accessed January 1, 2016. http://intertheory.org/buchanan.htm.

Byers, Thomas B. "*Erasure*'s Ethics: Everett with and against Badiou." In Maniez and Tissut 89–105.

Cannon, Uzzie Teresa. "A Bird of a Different Feather: Blues, Jazz, and the Difficult Journey of the Self in Percival Everett's *Suder.*" In Mitchell and Vander, *Perspectives* 94–112.

Carmines, Amee. "Reclaiming the Greek Tradition in the African American Novel: Percival Everett's *Frenzy.*" In Mitchell and Vander, *Percival Everett* 125–45.

Charles, John C. *Abandoning the Black Hero: Sympathy and Privacy in the Postwar African American White-Life Novel.* New Brunswick, N.J.: Rutgers University Press, 2013.

Clary, Françoise. "*Watershed* and *The Body of Martin Aguilera:* The Representation of a Mixed People." In Julien and Tissut 169–82.

De Lilly, Irene Rose. "Manifest Content without a Dreamer: A Freudian Analysis of Percival Everett's *Erasure.*" *Lux: A Journal of Transdisciplinary Writing and Research from Claremont Graduate University* 2.1 (2013). Accessed January 1, 2016. http://scholarship.claremont.edu/lux/vol2/iss1/10/.

Demirtürk, E. Lâle. "Rescripted Performances of Blackness as 'Parodies of Whiteness': Discursive Frames of Recognition in Percival Everett's *I Am Not Sidney Poitier.*" In *The Contemporary African American Novel: Multiple Cities, Multiple Subjectivities, and Discursive Practices of Whiteness in Everyday Urban Encounters,* 85–109. Madison, N.J.: Fairleigh Dickinson University Press, 2012.

Déon, Marguerite. "Clichés and Cultural Icons in Percival Everett's Fiction." *Lectures du Monde Anglophone* 1 (March 2015). Accessed January 1, 2016. http://eriac.univ-rouen.fr/cliches-and-cultural-icons-in-percival-everetts-fiction/.

Dickson-Carr, Darryl. "Percival Everett." In *The Columbia Guide to Contemporary African American Fiction,* 102–3. New York: Columbia University Press, 2005.

Dittman, Jonathan. "'knowledge^2 + certainty^2 = squat^2': (Re)Thinking Identity and Meaning in Percival Everett's *The Water Cure.*" In Mitchell and Vander, *Perspectives* 3–18.

Dorris, Ronald. "*Frenzy:* Framing Text to Set Discourse in a Cultural Continuum." In Mitchell and Vander, *Perspectives* 35–59.

Dumas, Frédéric. "The Preservationist Impulse in Percival Everett's 'True Romance.'" In Mitchell and Vander, *Perspectives* 60–74.

———. "Trout Fishing and Red Herring: The Meaning of Going Wild in Percival Everett's *Damned If I Do* [*sic*]." *Canadian Review of American Studies* 43.2 (Summer 2013): 225–42.

———. "Trout Fishing and Woodworking: Digression in Percival Everett's *Erasure.*" In Maniez and Tissut 49–72.

Eaton, Kimberly. "Deconstructing the Narrative: Language, Genre, and Experience in *Erasure.*" *Nebula* 3.2–3 (2006): 220–32. Accessed January 1, 2016. http://www.nobleworld.biz/images/Eaton.pdf.

Farebrother, Rachel. "'Out of Place': Reading Space in Percival Everett's *Erasure.*" *MELUS* 40.2 (Summer 2015): 117–36.

Feith, Michel. "The Art of Torture in *The Water Cure,* by Percival Everett." *Revue française d'études américaines* 132 (2012): 90–104.

———. "Black Bacchus? Signifying on Classical Myth in Percival Everett's *Frenzy.*" In Julien and Tissut 91–118.

———. "Blueprint for Studies in the African American (Neo)Baroque: John Edgar Wideman, Percival Everett." *Transatlantica* 1 (2009): 1–18. Accessed January 1, 2016. http://transatlantica.revues.org/4266.

———. "Hire-a-Glyph: Hermetics and Hermeneutics in Percival Everett's *Glyph.*" *Canadian Review of American Studies* 43.2 (Summer 2013): 301–19.

———. "Manifest *Death*tiny: Percival Everett's American Desert of the Real." In Julien and Tissut 183–201.

———. "The Well-Tempered Anachronism, or The C(o)urse of Empire in Percival Everett's *For Her Dark Skin.*" *Lectures du Monde Anglophone* 1 (March 2015). Accessed January 1, 2016. http://eriac.univ-rouen.fr/the-well-tempered-anachronism-or-the-course-of-empire-in-percival-everetts-for-her-dark-skin/.

———. "Working the Underground Seam: Richard Wright's 'The Man Who Lived Underground' in the Light of Percival Everett's *Zulus.*" In *Richard Wright in a Post-Racial Imaginary,* ed. Alice Mikal Craven, William E. Dow, and Yoko Nakamura, 161–76. New York: Bloomsbury, 2014.

Félix, Brigitte. "Of Weeds and Words: Percival Everett's Poetry." *Lectures du Monde Anglophone* 1 (March 2015). Accessed January 1, 2016. http://eriac.univ-rouen.fr/of-weeds-and-words-percival-everetts-poetry/.

———. "'The One That Got Away': Fabulation in Percival Everett's Fiction." In Maniez and Tissut 15–33.

Fett, Sebastian. *The Treatment of Racism in the African American Novel of Satire.* Diss. Fachbereich 2. Anglistik/Amerikanistik, Universität Trier, 2007.

Flota, Brian. "Percival Everett." *Twenty-First-Century American Writers, 2nd Ser.* Dictionary of Literary Biography 350. Eds. Wanda H. Giles and James R. Giles. Detroit, MI: Gale, 2009. 86–97.

Gay, Marie-Agnès. "'Wanted: straight words' in Percival Everett's Novel *Wounded.*" *Lectures du Monde Anglophone* 1 (March 2015). Accessed January 1, 2016. http://eriac.univ-rouen.fr/wanted-straight-words-in-percival-everetts-novel-wounded/.

Geathers, S. Isabel. "'knot / a banruptury / hove / weirds': The Crystalline Aesthetics of Percival Everett's *Abstraktion und Einfühlung.*" In Mitchell and Vander, *Percival Everett* 84–100.

Gibson, Scott Thomas. "Invisibility and the Commodification of Blackness in Ralph Ellison's *Invisible Man* and Percival Everett's *Erasure.*" *Canadian Review of Comparative Literature* 37.4 (December 2010): 354–70.

Gretlund, Jan Nordby. "Black and White Identity in Today's Southern Novel." *Moravian Journal of Literature and Film* 2.1 (Fall 2010): 43–52. Accessed January 1, 2016. http://www.moravianjournal.upol.cz/files/MJLF0201Gretlund.pdf.

———. "Percival Everett: Mediating Skin Color." *Aktuel Forskning* (Syddansk University), June 2010. Accessed January 1, 2016. http://static.sdu.dk/mediafiles//Files/Om_SDU/Institutter/Ilkm/ILKM_files/InternetSkrift/TeksterInternetskrift/JanGretlund.pdf.

Griffin, Sarah Mantilla. "'This Strange Juggler's Game': Forclusion in Percival Everett's *I Am Not Sidney Poitier.*" In Mitchell and Vander, *Perspectives* 19–34.

Gysin, Fritz. "The Pitfalls of Parody: Melancholic Satire in Percival Everett's *Erasure.*" In Julien and Tissut 63–80.

Handley, William R. "Detecting the Real Fictions of History in *Watershed.*" *Callaloo* 28.2 (Spring 2005): 305–12.

Hayman, Casey. "Hypervisible Man: Techno-Performativity and Televisual Blackness in Percival Everett's *I Am Not Sidney Poitier.*" *MELUS* 39.3 (Fall 2014): 135–54.

Hogue, W. Lawrence. "The Trickster Figure, the African American Virtual Subject, and Percival Everett's *Erasure.*" In *Postmodernism, Traditional Cultural Forms, and African American Narratives,* 101–36. Albany: State University of New York Press, 2013.

Huehls, Mitchum. "The Post-Theory Theory Novel." *Contemporary Literature* 56.2 (Summer 2015): 280–310.

Jaffe, Aaron. "The Authenticity of Jargon and Percival Everett's *Erasure:* A Set with Ten Elements." In Maniez and Tissut 73–88.

Johns, Gillian. "Everett's *Erasure:* That Drat Aporia When Black Satire Meets 'The Pleasure of the Text.'" In *Post-Soul Satire: Black Identity after Civil Rights,* ed. Derek C. Maus and James J. Donahue, 85–97. Jackson: University Press of Mississippi, 2014.

Johnson, Michael K. "Looking at the Big Picture: Percival Everett's Western Fiction." *Western American Literature* 42.1 (Spring 2007): 26–53.

Julien, Claude. "*Assumption:* From Reminiscences to Surprise, from Dream to Nightmare." *Lectures du Monde Anglophone* 1 (March 2015). Accessed January 1, 2016. http://eriac.univ-rouen.fr/assumption-from-reminiscences-to-surprise-from-dream-to-nightmare/.

———. "The Fabulous Destiny of Rosendo y Mauricio, or, Between (Good) Sense and Making Sense." *Callaloo* 28.2 (Spring 2005): 297–303.

———. "From *Walk Me to the Distance* to *Wounded,* or the Undesirable Appropriation of Frontier Justice." *GRAAT: Groupe de Recherches Anglo-Américaines de Tours* 7 (January 2010): 201–14.

———. "Introduction: *Reading Percival Everett: European Perspectives.*" In Julien and Tissut 9–20.

———. "The Real and the Unreal, or the Endogenous and the Exogenous: The Case of *Walk Me to the Distance* and *Wounded.*" *Canadian Review of American Studies* 43.2 (Summer 2013): 243–56.

———. "Settings and Beings in Percival Everett's New Mexico Fiction." In Maniez and Tissut 107–30.

———. "Text and Paratext Interaction in *Watershed.*" In Julien and Tissut 119–31.

Julien, Claude, and Anne-Laure Tissut, eds. *Reading Percival Everett: European Perspectives.* Tours: Presses Universitaires François Rabelais, 2007.

Kimberling, Clint. "Spotlight on Percival Everett." *UPMississippi.blogspot.com,* February 13, 2013. Accessed January 1, 2016. http://upmississippi.blogspot.ca/2013/02/spotlight-on-percival-everett.html.

Kincaid, James R. "Collaborating with the Sphinx: On Strom." *Callaloo* 28.2 (Spring 2005): 369–71.

———. "An Interview with Percival Everett." *Callaloo* 28.2 (Spring 2005): 377–81.

Knight, Michael. "My Friend, Percival." *Callaloo* 28.2 (Spring 2005): 292–96.

Krauth, Leland. "Undoing and Redoing the Western." *Callaloo* 28.2 (Spring 2005): 313–27.

Kurjatto-Renard, Patrycja. "*Zulus:* The Body as Otherness and Prison." In Julien and Tissut 135–47.

Larkin, Lesley. *Race and the Literary Encounter: Black Literature from James Weldon Johnson to Percival Everett.* Bloomington: Indiana University Press, 2015.

Maniez, Claire, and Anne-Laure Tissut, eds. *Percival Everett: Transatlantic Readings.* Paris: Éditions Le Manuscrit, 2007.

McCarroll, Meredith. "Consuming Performances: Race, Media, and the Failure of the Cultural Mulatto in *Bamboozled* and *Erasure.*" In *Passing Interest: Racial Passing in US Novels, Memoirs, Television, and Film, 1990–2010,* ed. Julie Cary Nerad, 283–306. Albany: State University of New York Press, 2014.

McCrae, Fiona. "Frenzy." *Callaloo* 28.2 (Spring 2005): 328–29.

McConkey-Pirie, Caitlin. "Ironist vs. Empiricist: The Political Battle Royale in Percival Everett's *Cutting Lisa* and *Erasure.*" *Verso: An Undergraduate Journal of Literary Criticism* 1 (2009): 30–37.

Mitchell, Keith B. "Encountering the Face of the Other: Levinasian Ethics and Its Limits in Percival Everett's *God's Country.*" In Mitchell and Vander, *Percival Everett* 146–75.

———. "Writing (Fat) Bodies: Grotesque Realism and the Carnivalesque in Percival Everett's *Zulus.*" *Canadian Review of American Studies* 43.2 (Summer 2013): 269–85.

Mitchell, Keith B., and Robin G. Vander. "Changing the Frame, Framing the Change: The Art of Percival Everett." In Mitchell and Vander, *Perspectives* ix–xvii.

———. "Introduction: The Work of Art in the Post-Soul Era: Percival Everett Writing Other/Wise." In Mitchell and Vander, *Percival Everett* 7–17.

———, eds. *Percival Everett: Writing Other/Wise.* New Orleans: Xavier Review Press, 2014.

———, eds. *Perspectives on Percival Everett.* Jackson: University Press of Mississippi, 2013.

Morgan, Danielle Fuentes. "'It's a Black Thang Maybe': Satirical Blackness in Percival Everett's *Erasure* and Adam Mansbach's *Angry Black White Boy.*" In *Post-Soul Satire: Black Identity after Civil Rights,* ed. Derek C. Maus and James J. Donahue, 162–74. Jackson: University Press of Mississippi, 2014.

Moriah, Kristin Leigh. "I Am Not a Race Man: Racial Uplift and the Post-Black Aesthetic in Percival Everett's *I Am Not Sidney Poitier.*" In *Understanding Blackness through Performance: Contemporary Arts and the Representation of Identity,* ed. Anne Crémieux, Xavier Lemoine, and Jean-Paul Rocchi, 221–36. New York: Palgrave Macmillan, 2013.

Morton, Seth. "Locating the Experimental Novel in *Erasure* and *The Water Cure.*" *Canadian Review of American Studies* 43.2 (Summer 2013): 189–201.

Moynihan, Sinéad. "Living Parchments, Human Documents: Passing, Racial Identity and the Literary Marketplace." In *Passing into the Present: Contemporary American Fiction of Racial and Gender Passing,* 21–50. Manchester: Manchester University Press, 2010.

Mullins, Matthew. "Counter-Counterstorytelling: Rereading Critical Race Theory in Percival Everett's *Assumption.*" *Callaloo* 39.2 (Spring 2016): 457–72.

Munby, Jonathan. "African American Literature: Recasting Region through Race." In *A History of Western American Literature,* ed. Susan Kollin, 314–30. Cambridge: Cambridge University Press, 2015.

O'Donnell, Patrick. "Racing Identity." In *The American Novel Now: Reading Contemporary American Fiction since 1980,* 92–104. Chichester, U.K.: Wiley-Blackwell, 2010.

Paquet-Deyris, Anne-Marie. "'Follow Your Heart' (NBC, 1990): The Mirage of an Adaptation of Percival Everett's 1985 Novel *Walk Me to the Distance*." In Julien and Tissut 161–68.

Phillips, Carl. "Knowing Percival." *Callaloo* 28.2 (Spring 2005): 330–32.

Porter, Lavelle. "The Over-Education of the Negro: Academic Novels, Higher Education and the Black Intellectual." 2014. Graduate Center, City University of New York, PhD dissertation. *CUNY Academic Works,* https://academicworks.cuny.edu/gc_etds/267/.

———. "Percival Everett by Percival Everett." *New Inquiry,* May 5, 2015. Accessed January 1, 2016. http://thenewinquiry.com/essays/percival-everett-by-percival-everett/.

Porter, Sha-Shonda. "Identity and Misrecognition in Percival Everett's *Erasure*." In Mitchell and Vander, *Percival Everett* 58–76.

Powell, Tamara. "Lord of Allusions: Reading Percival Everett's *Erasure* through African American Literary History." *Valley Voices: A Literary Review* 12.2 (Fall 2012): 100–107.

Powell, Tara. "Percival Everett: *Erasure*." In *Still in Print: The Southern Novel Today,* ed. Jan Nordby Gretlund, 73–87. Columbia: University of South Carolina Press, 2010.

Ramsey, William M. "Knowing Their Place: Three Black Writers and the Postmodern South." *Southern Literary Journal* 31.2 (Summer 2005): 119–39.

Raynaud, Claudine. "Naming, Not Naming and Nonsense in *I Am Not Sidney Poitier*." *Lectures du Monde Anglophone* 1 (March 2015). Accessed January 1, 2016. http://eriac.univ-rouen.fr/naming-not-naming-and-nonsense-in-i-am-not-sidney-poitier/.

Rice, Almah LaVon. "The Rise of Street Literature." *Colorlines* 11 (May/June 2008): 43–46.

Ridley, Chauncey. "Van Go's Pharmakon: 'Pharmacology' and Democracy in Percival Everett's *Erasure*." *African American Review* 47.1 (Spring 2014): 101–11.

Robinson, Timothy Mark. "Percival Everett's *Glyph* as Neo-Slave Narrative: Within and Beyond Tradition." In Mitchell and Vander, *Percival Everett* 101–24.

Roof, Judith. "Everett's *Eidolon:* The Story of an Eye." *Lectures du Monde Anglophone* 1 (March 2015). Accessed January 1, 2016. http://eriac.univ-rouen.fr/everetts-eidolon-the-story-of-an-eye/.

———. "Everett's Hypernarrator." *Canadian Review of American Studies* 43.2 (Summer 2013): 202–15.

———. "For Play." In Maniez and Tissut 173–84.

———. "Mr. Everett Anthologizes." In Maniez and Tissut 35–47.

Ruffin, Kimberly N. *Black on Earth: African American Ecoliterary Traditions.* Athens: University of Georgia Press, 2010.

Russett, Margaret. "Race under *Erasure*." *Callaloo* 28.2 (Spring 2005): 358–68.

Rutter, Emily R. "Barry Beckham's *Runner Mack* and the Tradition of Black Baseball Literature." *MELUS* 42.1 (April 2017): 74–93.

———. "'Straighten Up and Fly Right': A Contrafactual Reading of Percival Everett's *Suder* and Bernard Malamud's *The Natural*." *Aethlon* 32.1 (Fall 2014/Winter 2015): 43–57.Saldívar, Ramón. "Speculative Realism and the Postrace Aesthetic in Contemporary American Fiction." In *A Companion to American Literary Studies,* ed. Caroline F. Levander and Robert S. Levine, 517–31. Chichester, U.K.: Wiley-Blackwell, 2011.

Sammarcelli, Françoise. "Vision and Revision in Percival Everett's *Erasure*." *Lectures du Monde Anglophone* 1 (March 2015). Accessed January 1, 2016. http://eriac.univ-rouen.fr/vision-and-revision-in-percival-everetts-erasure/.

Sánchez-Arce, Ana Mariá. "'Authenticism,' or the Authority of Authenticity." *Mosaic* 40.3 (2007): 139–55.

Sanconie, Maïca. "*The One That Got Away:* A Number Adventure, or a Semantic Experiment?" In Julien and Tissut 39–47.

Schmidt, Christian. "Dissimulating Blackness: The Degenerative Satires of Paul Beatty and Percival Everett." In *Post-Soul Satire: Black Identity after Civil Rights,* ed. Derek C. Maus and James J. Donahue, 150–61. Jackson: University Press of Mississippi, 2014.

Schur, Richard. "The Crisis of Authenticity in Contemporary African American Literature." In *Contemporary African American Literature: The Living Canon,* ed. Lovalerie King and Shirley Moody-Turner, 235–54. Bloomington: Indiana University Press, 2013.

———. "The Mind-Body Split in *American Desert:* Synthesizing Everett's Critique of Race, Religion, and Science." In Mitchell and Vander, *Perspectives* 75–93.

———. "Stomping the Blues No More? Hip Hop Aesthetics and Contemporary African American Literature." In *New Essays on the African American Novel: From Hurston and Ellison to Morrison and Whitehead,* ed. Lovalerie King and Linda F. Selzer, 201–20. New York: Palgrave Macmillan, 2008.

Stewart, Anthony. "About Percival Everett: A Profile." *Ploughshares* 40.2–3 (Fall 2014): 188–93.

———. "'Do you mind if we make Craig Suder white?': From Stereotype to Cosmopolitan to Grotesque in Percival Everett's *Suder.*" In Mitchell and Vander, *Perspectives* 113–25.

———. "Giving the People What They Want: The African American Exception as Racial Cliché in Percival Everett's *Erasure.*" In *American Exceptionalisms: From Winthrop to Winfrey,* ed. Sylvia Söderlind and James Taylor Carson, 167–89. Albany: State University of New York Press, 2011.

———. "Introduction: An Assembled Coterie." *Canadian Review of American Studies* 43.2 (Summer 2013): 175–79.

———. "Setting One's House in Order: Theoretical Blackness in Percival Everett's Fiction." *Canadian Review of American Studies* 43.2 (Summer 2013): 216–24.

———. "Talking about Race, Exposing the Desire for the Post-Racial, and Percival Everett's *Assumption.*" *Lectures du Monde Anglophone* 1 (March 2015). Accessed January 1, 2016. http://eriac.univ-rouen.fr/talking-about-race-exposing-the-desire-for-the-post-racial-and-percival-everetts-assumption/.

Tissut, Anne-Laure. "*Frenzy,* Practical Philosophy, and Fictive Jokes." *Canadian Review of American Studies* 43.2 (Summer 2013): 286–300.

———. "Moments of Control: Reading Percival Everett's Short Stories." In Julien and Tissut 29–38.

———. "Percival Everett's *The Water Cure:* A Blind Read." *Sillages critiques* 17 (2014). Accessed January 1, 2016. http://sillagescritiques.revues.org/3496.

———. "*Zulus* de Percival Everett: The Abecedary of Creative Transgression." *Confluences* (Université Paris X, Nanterre) 24 (2004): 151–62.

Ulff, Clément-Alexandre. "Invisible Fathers: Investigating Percival Everett's 'Lower Frequencies.'" *Lectures du Monde Anglophone* 1 (March 2015). Accessed January 1, 2016. http://eriac.univ-rouen.fr/nvisible-fathers-investigating-percival-everetts-lower-frequencies/.

Vander, Robin. "When the Text Becomes the Stage: Percival Everett's Performance Turn in *For Her Dark Skin.*" In Mitchell and Vander, *Perspectives* 139–51.

Van Peteghem-Tréard, Isabelle. "*Jouissance* in [*damned if i do*] by Percival Everett." *Lectures du Monde Anglophone* 1 (March 2015). Accessed January 1, 2016. http://eriac.univ-rouen.fr/jouissance-in-damnedifido-stories-by-percival-everett/.

Vasquez, Zach. "Avant Garde to Old Testament: Percival Everett." *Creosote Journal*, March 30, 2011. Accessed January 1, 2016. http://creosotejournal.com/2011/03/avant-garde-to-old-testament-percival-everett/.

Von Mossner, Alexa Weik. "Mysteries of the Mountain: Environmental Racism and Political Action in Percival Everett's *Watershed*." *Journal of American Studies of Turkey* 30 (2009): 73–88.

Weisenburger, Steven. "Out West." *Callaloo* 24 (1985): 489–90.

Willis, Sharon. *The Poitier Effect: Racial Melodrama and Fantasies of Reconciliation*. Minneapolis: University of Minnesota Press, 2015.

Wolfreys, Julian. "'A Self-Referential Density': *Glyph* and the 'Theory' Thing." *Callaloo* 28.2 (Spring 2005): 345–57.

Wyman, Sarah. "Charting the Body: Percival Everett's Corporeal Landscapes in *re: f (gesture)*." In Mitchell and Vander, *Perspectives* 126–38.

Yost, Brian. "The Changing Same: The Evolution of Racial Self-Definition and Commercialization." *Callaloo* 31.4 (Fall 2008): 1314–34.

Interviews

Allen, Jeffrey Renard. "Interview with Percival Everett." In Weixlmann 100–110.

Anderson, Forrest. "Teaching Voice and Creating Meaning: An Interview with Percival Everett." *Yemassee* 11.2 (Spring 2004): 1–7. Repr. in Weixlmann 51–56.

"Author Percival Everett Talks Westerns, Serial Killers, and His New Novel." *inReads*, November 28, 2011. Web. Repr. in Weixlmann 187–90.

"Author Values Background in Philosophy." *Houston Chronicle*, June 30, 1985, 4.

Bauer, Sylvie. "Percival Everett: An Abecedary." *Transatlantica* 1 (2013). Accessed January 1, 2016. http://transatlantica.revues.org/6369.

Bengali, Shashank. "The Wicked Wit of Percival Everett." *USC Trojan Family Magazine* (Winter 2005). Repr. in Weixlmann 111–18.

Birnbaum, Robert. "Percival Everett." *identitytheory.com*, May 6, 2003. Repr. in Weixlmann 35–50.

Bolonik, Kera. "Mules, Men, and Barthes: Percival Everett Talks with Bookforum." *Bookforum: The Book Review for Art and Culture* 12.3 (October/November 2005): 52–53. Repr. in Weixlmann 93–99.

Brown, Thea. "An Interview with Percival Everett." *L Magazine*, February 3, 2009. Repr. in Weixlmann 160–62.

Champion, Edward. "*The Bat Segundo Show* #295 (Percival Everett)." In Weixlmann 165–76.

Cruden, Jenna. "An Interview with Percival Everett." *DURA: Dundee University Review of the Arts*, November 17, 2012. Accessed January 1, 2016. https://dura-dundee.org.uk/2012/11/17/percival-everett/.

DeMarco-Barrett, Barbara, and Marrie Stone. "Interview with Percival Everett." In Weixlmann 148–53.

Dischinger, Matthew. "The Construction of Place: An Interview with Percival Everett." *Virginia Quarterly Review* 91.3 (Summer 2015). Accessed January 1, 2015. http://www.vqronline.org/interviews-articles/2015/07/construction-place-interview-percival-everett.

Ehrenreich, Ben. "Invisible Man." *LA Weekly,* November 29–December 5, 2002, Features sec.: 33. Repr. in Weixlmann 24–28.

George, Lynell. "Parody That's Personal." *Los Angeles Times,* October 16, 2001, E1, E3. Repr. in Weixlmann 10–14.

Goyal, Yogita. "Coming Home from Irony: An Interview with Percival Everett, Author of 'So Much Blue.'" *Los Angeles Review of Books* 23 Aug. 2017. Accessed 27 Aug. 2017. https://lareviewofbooks.org/article/coming-home-from-irony-an-interview-with-percival-everett-author-of-so-much-blue/,

"An Interview with Percival Everett." *University Press of New England* Web site. Accessed January 1, 2016. http://www.upne.com/features/EverettQ%26A.html.

Johnson, Pamela J. "The Age of Aquarius." University of Southern California Dornslife College of Letters, Arts and Sciences, December 1, 2007. Accessed January 1, 2016. http://dornsife.usc.edu/news/stories/430/the-age-of-aquarius.

Kirsch, Fred. "On Writing: Visiting Author Brings a Love of Craft to Classroom." *Virginian-Pilot* (Norfolk, Va.), February 26, 1994, B1. Repr. in Weixlmann 3–6.

Markazi, Arash. "USC Department of English Chair Finds Writing a Chore and a Pleasure." *Daily Trojan* (University of Southern California), February 12, 2002. Repr. in Weixlmann 15–17.

Masiki, Trent. "Irony and Ecstasy: A Profile of Percival Everett." *Poets & Writers Magazine* 32 (May/June 2004): 32–39.

Medlin, Andrew, and Trevor Gore. "How We Mean: An Interview with Percival Everett." *The Pinch* (University of Memphis) 29.2 (Fall 2009): 95–100. Repr. in Weixlmann 154–59.

Mernit, Judith Lewis. "What Do You Know? Author Percival Everett Defies Categories and Generalizations." *High Country News* 45.16 (September 16, 2013). Accessed January 1, 2016. http://www.hcn.org/issues/45.16/what-do-you-know.

Mills, Alice, and Jack Lanco. "The South." In Julien and Tissut 229–31. Repr. in Weixlmann 90–92.

Mills, Alice, Claude Julien, and Anne-Laure Tissut. "An Interview: May 3rd, 2005." In Julien and Tissut 217–27. Repr. in Weixlmann 78–89.

Monaghan, Peter. "Satiric Inferno." *Chronicle of Higher Education,* February 11, 2005, A18–20. Repr. in Weixlmann 71–77.

Mulholland, Garry. "Colour Me Blind." *Time Out,* March 5, 2003. Repr. in Weixlmann 29–31.

O'Hagan, Sean. "The Books Interview: Percival Everett." *Observer* (London), March 16, 2003, review pages, 17. Repr. in Weixlmann 32–34.

Rath, Arun. "For Prolific Author Percival Everett, the Wilderness Is a Place of Clarity." *National Public Radio* Web site, September 20, 2015. Accessed January 1, 2016. http://www.npr.org/2015/09/20/441504103/for-prolific-author-percival-everett-the-wilderness-is-a-place-of-clarity.

Reynolds, Susan Salter. "Where's Everett?" *Los Angeles Times Book Review,* July 12, 2009, E5. Repr. in Weixlmann 177–80.

Shavers, Rone. "Percival Everett." *Bomb* 88 (Summer 2004): 46–51.

Spielman, Daniel G., and William W. Starr. "Percival Everett." In *Southern Writers,* 56–57. Columbia: University of South Carolina Press, 1997.

Starr, William W. "Author Everett Prizes Privacy." *The State* (Columbia, S.C.), May 29, 1994, F1. Repr. in Weixlmann 7–9.

———. "I Get Bored Easily." *The State* (Columbia, S.C.), March 31, 2002, E1. Repr. in Weixlmann 18–23.

Stewart, Anthony. "Uncategorizable Is Still a Category: An Interview with Percival Everett." *Canadian Review of American Studies* 37.3 (2007): 293–324.

Taylor, Justin. "The Art of Fiction No. 235: Percival Everett." *Paris Review* 59.221 (Summer 2017): 40–70.

Tissut, Anne-Laure. "An Interview with Percival Everett." In Maniez and Tissut 185–87.

Toal, Drew. "The Tipping Poitier." *Time Out New York,* May 28, 2009. Web. Repr. in Weixlmann 163–64.

"*The Water Cure:* 'In Any Novel, It Is the Reader Who Completes the Tale.'" *l'Humanité* (Saint-Denis, France), November 19, 2009. Repr. in Weixlmann 181–83.

Weixlmann, Joe, ed. *Conversations with Percival Everett.* Jackson: University Press of Mississippi, 2013.

Winther, Tine Maria. "Percival Everett: Whites Want to Read 'Black'." Trans. Evelyn Meyer and Marte Hult. Rpt. in Weixlmann 184–86.

Reviews and News Items

Allen, Jeffrey Renard. "Percival Everett Takes on Strom Thurmond and the Publishing Industry in America." *Chicago Tribune,* June 6, 2004, Books: 4.

Beason, Tyrone. "'Wounded': Race, Sexuality on Modern-Day Frontier." *Seattle Times,* September 18, 2005. Accessed January 1, 2016. http://www.seattletimes.com/entertainment/books/wounded-race-sexuality-on-modern-day-frontier/.

Bell, Christopher. "My Own Private Wyoming." *Gay and Lesbian Review Worldwide* 13.3 (May/June 2006): 45–46.

Bell, Susan. "USC Dornslife Faculty Receive Guggenheim Fellowships." *USC Dornsife College of Letters, Arts and Sciences* Web site, April 30, 2015. Accessed January 1, 2016. https://dornsife.usc.edu/news/stories/2040/usc-dornsife-faculty-receive-guggenheim-fellowships/.

"Big Picture." *Kirkus Reviews* 64 (February 15, 1996): 244–45.

Birkerts, Sven. "The Surreal Thing." *New York Times Book Review,* May 9, 2004, 19.

Bowman, David. "Cowpoke Absurdism." *New York Times Book Review,* June 5, 1994, 43.

Boylan, Roger. "Hostile Territories." *New York Times Book Review,* December 11, 2011, 32.

Briones, Carolyn. Review of *I Am Not Sidney Poitier. Callaloo* 33.2 (Spring 2010): 553–55.

Carroll, Tobias. "'Half an Inch of Water,' by Percival Everett: Stories That Are Surreal and Miraculous." *Minneapolis Star Tribune,* September 9, 2015. Accessed January 1, 2016. http://www.startribune.com/review-half-an-inch-of-water-by-percival-everett-stories-that-are-surreal-and-miraculous/325737791.

Cheuse, Alan. "Lost in Everett's Hall of Metafictional Mirrors." *National Public Radio* Web site, February 13, 2013. Accessed January 1, 2016. http://www.npr.org/2013/02/13/171482592/lost-in-everett-s-hall-of-metafictional-mirrors.

———. "A Satirical Look at Life and Death." *Chicago Tribune,* June 6, 2004, Books: 1.

Ellis, Kelly Norman. Review of *re: f (gesture). Black Issues Book Review* 9.2 (March/April 2007): 20.

Galef, David. "Ralph Walks, Theory Talks." *New York Times Book Review,* November 28, 1999, 20.

Garb, Maggie. *New York Times Book Review,* September 15, 1996, 30.

Garrett, George. "Literary Fiction." *Washington Post Book World,* December 7, 1997, 12.

Gates, Henry Louis, Jr. *The Signifying Monkey: A Theory of African-American Literary Criticism.* Oxford University Press, 1988.

Hunt, Laird. *Believer* (September 2009). Accessed January 1, 2016. http://www.believermag.com/issues/200909/?read=review_everett.

Krusoe, Jim. "Hell in a Handbasket." *Washington Post Book World,* November 14, 2004, 6.

Major, Clarence. "An Alphabet of Future Nightmares." *Washington Post Book World,* May 20, 1990, 4.

Malin, Irving. Review of *Frenzy. Review of Contemporary Fiction* 17.3 (Fall 1997): 237.

Miller, Gregory Leon. "Identity Crisis." *Los Angeles Review of Books,* January 23, 2012. Accessed January 1, 2016. https://lareviewofbooks.org/review/identity-crisis.

Millet, Lydia. "Meet Percival Everett and 'Percival Everett.'" *Los Angeles Times,* February 8, 2013. Accessed January 1, 2016. http://www.latimes.com/features/books/jacketcopy/la-ca-jc-percival-everett-20130210,0,2924977.story.

Muratori, Fred. Review of *Abstraktion und Einfühlung. Library Journal* 133 (November 1, 2008): 70.

Muyumba, Walton. "Insistence." *Los Angeles Review of Books,* January 23, 2012. Accessed January 1, 2016. https://lareviewofbooks.org/review/insistence.

Needham, George. Review of *Glyph. Booklist* 96 (October 15, 1999): 417.

O'Connor, John J. "Troubled Drifter Takes on Small Town." *New York Times,* April 2, 1990, C16.

"The One That Got Away." *Kirkus Reviews* 60 (March 1, 1992): 322.

Ronan, Kelsey. "Stoic Westerners Struggle through Everett's Powerful Short Stories." *St. Louis Post-Dispatch,* September 13, 2015, F10.

Sallis, James. "The Audacious, Uncategorizable Everett." *Boston Globe,* November 28, 2004, D9.

See, Carolyn. Review of *Suder. Los Angeles Times Book Review,* July 31, 1983, 1, 8.

Shavers, Rone. "*Assumption* and *Erasure* by Percival Everett." *Quarterly Conversation* 26 (Winter 2012). Accessed January 1, 2016. http://quarterlyconversation.com/assumption-and-erasure-by-percival-everett.

Simson, Maria. Review of *Frenzy. Publishers Weekly* 243 (November 18, 1996): 67.

Taylor, Justin. "Lucid Dreaming: Two Ways of Looking at Percival Everett." *Harper's* 331.1986 (November 2015): 82–89.

Weixlmann, Joe. Review of *Assumption. African American Review* 44.3 (Fall 2011): 511–12.

"Writer Percival Everett to Receive Longwood's Dos Passos Prize." Longwood University Web site, September 27, 2010. Accessed January 1, 2016. http://www.longwood.edu/2010releases_28282.htm.

Yeh, Jane. "All Unquiet on Everett's Western Front." *Village Voice,* October 19–25, 2005, Books: 75.

Other Cited Sources

Alpers, Paul. *What Is Pastoral?* Chicago: University of Chicago Press, 1997.

Bakhtin, Mikhail. *The Dialogic Imagination: Four Essays.* Ed. Michael Holquist. Trans. Caryl Emerson and Michael Holquist. Austin: University of Texas Press, 1981.

Barthelme, Donald. "Not Knowing." In *Not Knowing: The Essays and Interviews of Donald Barthelme,* ed. Kim Herzinger, 11–24. New York: Random House, 1997.

Beatty, Paul. *The Sellout.* New York: Farrar, Straus, and Giroux, 2015.

Blanchard, W. Scott. *Scholars' Bedlam: Menippean Satire in the Renaissance.* London and Toronto: Bucknell University Press, 1995.

Booker, M. Keith. *Flann O'Brien, Bakhtin, and Menippean Satire.* Syracuse, N.Y.: Syracuse University Press, 1995.

Cassuto, Leonard. *The Inhuman Race: The Racial Grotesque in American Literature and Culture.* New York: Columbia University Press, 1997.

Ellison, Ralph. *Invisible Man.* New York: Random House, 1947.

Frye, Northrop. *Anatomy of Criticism: Four Essays.* Princeton, NJ: Princeton University Press, 1957.

Griffin, Dustin H. *Satire: A Critical Reintroduction.* Lexington: University of Kentucky Press, 1994.

Hutcheon, Linda. *A Poetics of Postmodernism: History, Theory, Fiction.* New York: Routledge, 1988.

Johnson, Michael K. *Black Masculinity and the Frontier Myth in American Literature.* Norman: University of Oklahoma Press, 2002.

———. *Hoo-Doo Cowboys and Bronze Buckaroos: Conceptions of the African American West.* Jackson: University Press of Mississippi, 2014.

Kaplan, Carter. *Critical Synoptics: Menippean Satire and the Analysis of Intellectual Mythology.* Cranbury, N.J.: Fairleigh Dickinson University Press, 2000.

Kharpertian, Theodore D. *A Hand to Turn the Time: The Menippean Satires of Thomas Pynchon.* Cranbury, N.J.: Fairleigh Dickinson University Press, 1990.

Kirk, Eugene P. *Menippean Satire: An Annotated Catalogue of Texts and Criticism.* New York: Garland, 1980.

Kristeva, Julia. "Word, Dialogue, and Novel." In *The Kristeva Reader,* ed. Toril Moi, 34–61. New York: Columbia University Press, 1986.

Mookerjee, Robin. *Transgressive Fiction: The New Satiric Tradition.* Basingstoke and New York: Palgrave Macmillan, 2013.

Musgrave, David. *Grotesque Anatomies: Menippean Satire since the Renaissance.* Newcastle-upon-Tyne: Cambridge Scholars, 2014.

"The Pitch." *Seinfeld: Season Four.* Writ. Larry David. Dir. Tom Cherones. Sony Pictures Home Entertainment, 2005. DVD.

Pynchon, Thomas. *The Crying of Lot 49.* Philadelphia: Lippincott, 1966.

Relihan, Joel C. *Ancient Menippean Satire.* Baltimore: Johns Hopkins University Press, 1993.

Weinbrot, Howard D. *Menippean Satire Reconsidered: Antiquity to the Eighteenth Century.* Baltimore: Johns Hopkins University Press, 2005.

Weisenburger, Steven. *Fables of Subversion: Satire and the American Novel, 1930–1980.* Athens: University of Georgia Press, 1995.

Whitehead, Colson. *Sag Harbor.* New York: Doubleday, 2009.

Willard, Thomas. "Andreae's *ludibrium:* Menippean Satire in the *Chymische Hochzeit.*" In *Laughter in the Middle Ages and Early Modern Times: Epistemology of a Fundamental Human Behavior, Its Meaning, and Consequences,* ed. Albrecht Classen, 767–90. Berlin/New York: Walter De Gruyter, 2010.

Young, Kevin. *The Grey Album: On the Blackness of Blackness.* Minneapolis: Graywolf Press, 2012.

Index

www.ingramcontent.com/pod-product-compliance
Lightning Source LLC
Chambersburg PA
CBHW030307100426
42812CB00002B/600

* 9 7 8 1 6 1 1 1 7 9 6 2 0 *